REFLECTIONS OF A METAPHYSICAL FLÂNEUR
AND OTHER ESSAYS

ALSO BY RAYMOND TALLIS AND PUBLISHED BY ACUMEN

Aping Mankind: Neuromania, Darwinitis and the Misrepresentation of Humanity

Hunger

In Defence of Wonder and Other Philosophical Reflections

Reflections of a Metaphysical Flâneur
and Other Essays

Raymond Tallis

ACUMEN

For la Flâneuse

© Raymond Tallis, 2013

This book is copyright under the Berne Convention.
No reproduction without permission.
All rights reserved.

The right of Raymond Tallis to be identified as the author
of this Work has been asserted by him in accordance with
the Copyright, Designs & Patents Act 1988.

First published in 2013 by Acumen
Reprinted 2013

Acumen Publishing Limited
4 Saddler Street
Durham
DH1 3NP, UK

ISD, 70 Enterprise Drive
Bristol, CT 06010, USA

www.acumenpublishing.com

ISBN: 978-1-84465-666-0

British Library Cataloguing-in-Publication Data
A catalogue record for this book is available from the British Library.

Typeset in Warnock Pro.
Printed and bound in the UK by CPI Group (UK) Ltd, Croydon, CR0 4YY.

If you would know the invisible, look carefully at the visible.
(Auguste Strindberg, *Occult Diary*)

Contents

Preface	ix
Acknowledgements	xv
Overture: Reflections of a Metaphysical Flâneur	1

PART I: BRAINS, PERSONS AND BEASTS

1. Am I My Brain?	29
2. Was Schubert a Musical Brain?	46
3. Wit and Wickedness: Is It All in the Brain?	66
4. Are Conscious Machines Possible?	78
5. David Chalmers's Unsuccessful Search for the Conscious Mind	93
6. A Conversation with My Neighbour	126
7. Silk: Metamorphoses Beyond Biology	132

CONTENTS

PART II: PHILOSOPHY AND PHYSICS

8. Should We Just Shut Up and Calculate? Does Physics Need Philosophy? — 144
9. You Chemical Scum, You — 163
10. Did Time Begin with a Bang? — 169
11. A Hasty Report from a Tearing Hurry — 175

PART III: PHILOSOPHY AND PHYSIC

12. Medical Ethics in the Real Mess of the Real World — 181
13. On Caring and Not Caring — 206
14. Coinages of the Mind: Hallucinations — 229
15. Becoming the Prisoners of Our Free Choices — 238
16. The Right to an Assisted Death — 247

Epilogue: And So to Bed: Notes towards a Philosophy of Sleep from A to Zzzzzzz — 276

Bibliography — 283
Index — 289

Preface

The eighteenth-century German physicist, wit and philosopher Georg Christoph Lichtenberg described his philosophy as "a doctrine of scattered occasions". It would be dishonest – as well as pointless, because no one would be deceived – to pretend that this collection of essays is anything other than the product of scattered occasions. With few exceptions, the pieces were all in some sense commissioned. They began as lectures, reviews and editorials, or as my regular contributions to *Philosophy Now*.

One of the exceptions is the title essay "Reflections of a Metaphysical Flâneur", which I hope will be read as an overture. Some of the themes that appear in subsequent pages are sounded, although sometimes in a different guise. The essay is in part the expression of a lifelong love affair with a story by Robert Walser – *The Walk* – although readers familiar with Jean-Paul Sartre's incomparable philosophical novel *Nausea* will see the ghost of Antoine Roquentin accompanying the Flâneur on parts of his walk. It is an attempt at a mode of philosophical writing that fuses vision and argument, reminiscence and description, and something not far from grumbling. It is a foretaste of a book that has been in progress for over a quarter of a century – *De Luce* – which I promised myself to finish by the end of the millennium. Wisely, I did not specify which millennium.

The remaining essays look backwards and forwards. Those collected in Part I, "Brains, Persons and Beasts" look backwards inasmuch as they are concerned with issues that I have already addressed, most recently in *Aping Mankind: Neuromania, Darwinitis and the Misrepresentation of Humanity*. If I seem unable to let go of Neuromania in particular, it is because I believe that the problems of consciousness will, if they are addressed at the correct depth (a depth no one, least of all the Flâneur, has yet reached), have a revolutionary impact on every aspect of our thought. I cannot resist quoting the philosopher and psychologist Jerry Fodor to this effect:

> we can't, as things stand now, so much as imagine the solution of the hard problem [of consciousness]. The revisions of our concepts and theories that imagining a solution will eventually require are likely to be very deep and very unsettling … There is hardly anything that we may not have to cut loose from before the … problem is through with us.
> (Fodor 2007: 9–10)

Some are unpersuaded by this and believe that it will be possible to find the true nature of consciousness in physical events in matter configured in a particular way. For me, this hardly even begins to explain how matter in some forms (human beings) developed the concept of "matter" and placed it in inverted commas; how some living creatures (human beings) developed the notion of "life" and placed it in inverted commas; and how some conscious beings (human beings) came to be aware that they were conscious, and placed their "consciousness" in inverted commas and were puzzled by it. And the neural theory of consciousness runs into serious trouble well below these elevated heights of human cognition.

The essays in this part provide an introduction to some of the key elements of my critique of materialistic accounts of consciousness in particular, and "biologism" more generally, and they develop several of my arguments further. For the most part they should be accessible and require no knowledge of my, or indeed anyone else's, previous writings on the topic. The toughest of the essays is a critical, but sympathetic, review of the latest book by David Chalmers, whom some regard as the leading figure in the philosophy of mind. This essay is definitely for the aficionados. Those who are already persuaded by other essays in this book that consciousness is not identical with neural activity may wish to skip some of its twists and turns or simply proceed to the next chapter. The unpersuaded may regard this as punishment for their obstinacy, although anyone who follows the arguments of this essay – and the succeeding one, which deals with the question of whether we could ever construct a conscious machine – will be rewarded by the *jeu d'esprit* that follows, in which I take issue with my fellow columnist in *Philosophy Now*, the estimable Joel Marks, about our relationship to the animal kingdom. In the final essay in this section, I take a rather different tack on the uniqueness of human beings. In "Silk: Metamorphosis Beyond Biology" I try to share the joy, pleasure and wonder afforded by contemplating the mystery of *homo faber*.

The essays in Part II, "Philosophy and Physics", look forwards rather than backwards, in the sense of being foretastes of arguments that are developed at length in a work approaching completion, *Of Time and Lamentation: Reflections on Transience*. This is a critical examination of the way time is dealt with in physical science. For some physicists, philosophy has for the most part been rendered redundant by physics. While they are content to leave ethics, meta-ethics, questions of value, politics and so on (mere scraps) to philosophers, they believe that metaphysics – our understanding of space, of time, of the fundamental stuff of the world, and why there is a world anyway – is a matter for scientists, making measurements and using mathematical tools to make sense of what they have observed. It is most certainly not for philosophers, sitting in their proverbial armchairs using that most *passé* of instruments of enquiry, namely unaided human reason examining our everyday understanding and the language in which we express it.

Not all physicists believe this, of course. (Most working physicists probably do not have a view one way or another.) But enough do, and sufficient numbers of people believe them, to make the ambition to rescue our conception of the world from the jaws of physics a worthwhile one, even, or particularly, for a humanist atheist such as myself. At the very least there is a job to be done in connecting our everyday experience of the world with the image of reality constructed by the physical sciences. The essays in this part are the small beginnings of a much larger project.

I was a hospital doctor for thirty-six years; indeed, medicine occupied most of my waking consciousness between 1970 and 2006. Half a dozen years after retirement I am far from being an ex-physician. This will be evident in the essays in Part III, "Philosophy and Physic", which address some of the problems in medicine that still preoccupy me. Readers may be disappointed, given that I am a doctor and philosopher, by the absence of a rigorous discussion of the principles of biomedical ethics. This reflects a lifelong disappointment of my own: that the huge literature generated by bioethicists was so rarely helpful when I was faced with actual ethical decisions, decisions that had to be made by 4pm that day rather than await the resolution of debates that seemed to remain forever at the same distance from conclusion. And the maltreatment of some of the most vulnerable among us (myself, perhaps, in the not-too-distant future) – the theme of a sequence of essays in this section – demands a response that goes beyond either reference to complex ethical principles or the pleasures of moral outrage. This is equally true of our response to the scourge of addiction, the theme of a trio of short pieces in which Tiger Woods makes a surprising cameo appearance, mainly to lighten – and, I hope, lower – the tone. The final essay in this part, on assisted dying, reflects my exasperation at the imposition of unnecessary suffering on those who are dying and have a settled wish to die. If my atheism becomes a little strident in these pages, it is because I resent the power exercised by some who have beliefs I do not share over how I shall end my days.

"Our little life/Is rounded with a sleep", Prospero reminded us. And so, too, is this book. Sleep is at once the greatest enemy of the supreme wakefulness to which philosophy aspires and yet it is, or could be, philosophically fascinating. I hope that the final essay and its predecessors hold the enemy at bay at least for a while and that the reader will feel that the world is more mysterious, or at least more interestingly complex, as a result of reading them.

Acknowledgements

It is a pleasure once again to record my deep gratitude to Steven Gerrard at Acumen for his fantastic support and his enthusiasm for my writing. And my thanks are again due to Kate Williams – eagle-eyed, alert and sympathetic – for her superb editorial work, and to Jonny Pegg, my agent.

I should like to thank the editors and publishers for permission to reproduce the following essays. "Wit and Wickedness: Is It All in the Brain?" – a review of Simon Baron Cohen's *Zero Degrees of Empathy: A New Theory of Human Cruelty* (London: Allen Lane, 2011) and Matthew M. Hurley, Daniel C. Dennett and Reginald B. Adams, Jr., *Inside Jokes: Using Humor to Reverse Engineer the Mind* (Cambridge, MA: MIT Press, 2011) – first appeared online in the neurological journal *Brain* (17 October 2012). "David Chalmers' Unsuccessful Search for the Conscious Mind" was published in *New Atlantis* (Fall 2011) under the title "What Consciousness is Not". An earlier version of "Medical Ethics in the Real Mess of the Real World", which began as a lecture, was first published in the *Medico-Legal Journal* **76**(3) (2008): 95–112. "Coinages of the Mind: Hallucinations" was published as "Oliver Sacks on Drugs" in the *Times Literary Supplement*

(13 February 2013). "A Conversation with My Neighbour", "Should We Just Shut Up and Calculate?", "You Chemical Scum, You", "Did Time Begin with a Bang?", "A Hasty Report from a Tearing Hurry" and "And So To Bed" first appeared in *Philosophy Now*. "On Caring and Not Caring'" and "Becoming the Prisoners of Our Free Choices" are based on articles that first appeared in *The Times*.

"Am I My Brain?" is a modified version of a talk given at a conference on "Persons and their Brains" hosted by the International Ramsay Centre in July 2012 and I am grateful to Dr Andrew Pinsent and Professor Roger Scruton for organizing such a stimulating meeting. "The Right to an Assisted Death" is in part based on the First Ann McPherson memorial lecture, which I gave as Chair of Healthcare Professionals for Assisted Dying in October 2011. "Was Schubert a Musical Brain?" brings together a lecture on music and the brain given at the Natural History Museum, London, and a talk given during BBC Radio 3's Schubert Week in 2012. "Are Conscious Machines Possible?" owes its origin to disagreeing with an inspiring talk given by Professor Murray Shanahan at the Frome Festival of Ideas and our subsequent oral and email exchanges.

OVERTURE

Reflections of a Metaphysical Flâneur

WALKING, LOOKING AND THINKING

In *Twilight of the Idols*, Nietzsche quotes a letter by Gustave Flaubert in which the incomparable author of *Madame Bovary* confesses that he "cannot think and write except when seated". This sets the irascible German off on one. "There I have caught you, nihilist!" he snarls. "Only thoughts reached by walking have value" (maxim 34). "Nihilist" seems something of an overreaction to the preference for sitting still over walking about. Nietzsche, the self-proclaimed "philosopher with a hammer", sometimes uses his chosen instrument to crack a nut.

Nevertheless, while I sympathize with the Frenchman, I do agree with the German that walking is good for thinking. So when I can no longer bear my study and the discipline of sitting still, when thinking has become mere inking, I take to the road, imitating those many thinkers for whom *peripatesis* is a philosophical catalyst, and, in some cases, a necessary condition of thought. Robert Macfarlane (whose invitation in his *The Old Ways* to follow in his mind's footsteps is irresistible) quotes Jean-Jacques Rousseau's *Confessions:* "I can meditate only when I am walking ... when I stop I cease to think; my mind only works with my legs" (2012: 27). And the second most famously melancholy Dane, the philosopher-theologian and father of existentialism, Søren Kierkegaard, echoes this, speculating "that the mind might function optimally at the pedestrian pace of three miles per hour" (*ibid.*).

So the philosopher's walk has much to commend it. Like philosophy itself, it has few infrastructure costs, involving neither getting nor spending, apart from a negligible outgoing on shoe leather. Crucially, it has no external purpose; you end up, after all, precisely where you began and nothing visible is achieved on the way, except perhaps to "arrive where we started/And know the place for the first time" (T. S. Eliot, "Little Gidding", V). At any rate, the number of unticked boxes is undiminished, the to-do list unshortened. The walk does not even have the aim of promoting cardiovascular health. Metaphysical ambles, punctuated by long, thoughtful pauses, will not bring on the tachycardia or the cling film of sweat recommended by the Department of Health to improve the condition of your heart, lungs, muscles and bones, and all those structures that are so crucial to longevity and well-being.

For we are not talking about power-walking but strolling, which sits on the happy midpoint between doing something and doing nothing, between generating and discovering a trickle of Elsewhere that moves so slowly that it does not wash away Here.

At its heart is the primordial recreation of *looking*: the exercise of the fundamental freedom of one who surveys a world from the tor that is his head. You take said head out of the house, along the streets and into the park, for the primary purpose of harvesting qualia, surveying the endless treasure chest of artifacts (each the meeting place of a million ideas shared across a boundless community of innovators) populating the human landscape, as well as appreciating those little arias of nature that the suburbs permit, within limits, to get on with being their relatively wild selves.

With looking comes thinking but not necessarily the thoughts the thinker anticipated when he set out. For, while the aim of the

OVERTURE

peripatetic philosopher may be to untie the seeming insoluble trichobezoars that have grown up in his sedentary mind, the walk may cause him to forget those hairballs, to loosen up into a metaphysical flâneur, distracted by what he sees when he looks purely for the sake of looking. Trees, birds, vehicles, people and houses all offer themselves up to the travelling gaze; and, when the walk is going well, some of these items turn themselves into conversation pieces for one: *bonnes à penser*, "things to think with", as Claude Lévi-Strauss would call them. Thus the connection between "wandering" and what Macfarlane calls its "word-shadow", "wondering". Those who "saunter" – a word that, he reminds us, derives from the French *sans terre*, a contraction of *á sainte terre* – still foster the faint hope of coming upon a "sacred place". For the Flâneur, the sacred place is the profane world seen with the eyes of one whose gaze is unpeeled.

SETTING OUT

And today the *bonnes à penser* seem to be particularly thick on the ground. For example, the birds, no respecters of property, innocent of bye-laws, are an incitement to ignore the boundaries, the enabling and disabling constraints, of categories, themes, well-worn cognitive journeys. Those seemingly purposeful wingbeats taking the skein of geese into distances beyond treetops and roofs hint at other ways of being, suggesting to the voice thinking to itself that there may be other kinds of stories.

And the sentinel poplar, bang in the middle of the middle distance that opens up as the Flâneur leaves his house, invites an even more radical reorientation. Since the breeze is slight, the poplar speaks in only one of its two voices: there is no ground bass, of whole body swishing, to counterpoint the million-tongued leaf-fluttering from which it takes its name. ("Poplar", he reminds himself, comes from *papiller*, whose meaning is "to palpitate" like a butterfly.) Perhaps ten times taller than the Flâneur – its life, as W. H. Auden described it, "one continuous solitary meal" – the poplar today seems like a maypole, an axis around which the suburbs, the houses, gardens and roads, the spaces through which he unwinds the thread of his walk, imprinting the primordial tale of a succession of footsteps, are arranged, dancing to keep up with his walk. Thus arranged, they seem gathered up in his gaze, such that he is able to sense the infinitely varied modes of division of the suburban parterre laid out around him.

It turns what he can see, glimpse, or guess into a vision, uncovering the parcelling of space into roads, houses and gardens; of houses into rooms next to other rooms and separated by corridors and stairs; of rooms into interiors and exteriors (next to and inside the chest of drawers, on top of and between sheets); and of the contents of the small interiors into insides and outsides (inside the jewellery box, outside the jewellery box, the jumper as a heap on the floor and as an inside that encloses). An ever more finely grained division of space that begins as emptiness triangulated by stars and ends in pockets where hands jingle change is encompassed by the multitudinously loculated suburbs. The dialectic between dark interiors and light exteriors comes upon the Flâneur as a critique of the notion of space as mere, and pure, extensity: of the geometer's reduction of space to its own skeleton (three or ten dimensions, it doesn't matter), in turn reduced to pure quantities so that places shrivel to decimal places.

An intuition teases him by remaining just out of reach. Even so, he can see that it is going to be a good walk.

CROSSING THE ROAD

Between the Flâneur and the park is a confluence of busy roads. Their hub is a generous roundabout, a grassy disc slightly plumped like a Frisbee, decorated with two regimented flowerbeds, several clusters of trees and a rock garden. This miniature landscape is spoiled only by an advert for Tiny Toes Nursery: a symptom of a contractual society in which even the commons are hired out to private enterprises in order to narrow the gap between income and outgoings opened up by the increasing demands made upon the council.

There was a phase in his childhood when the Flâneur would have given the roundabout a name, cultivated it as a bonsai country (one of the many variants of the Land of Far Beyond), populated it with a multitude of beings – people and beasts and dwellings – and asserted its status as a country with stamps, flags, a language and an island story of its own. Now, it is a reminder of how the scale of perception, of imagination, and of the canvas on which we paint our lives varies so spectacularly. In October 1946, the limits of his world were mummy (as yet unnamed) and his toes (as yet undiscovered) and now, an eye blink later, he can look back on a multitude of worlds, bubbles in a sea of foam, and say words like "London" or "Cornwall" or "Africa" and not only know what he means but unpack an inexhaustible *cache* of memories and ideas and images corresponding to them.

For the present, the Flâneur's attitude is more focused. There are two modes of crossing the road without being obliterated by the traffic, pursuing intentions broadside to his own. Until recently, he was able to pass over to the other side with the protection of a zebra crossing lightly chaperoned by a pulsing colon of egg-yolk-coloured spheres elevated on zebra-striped posts. But this has now been replaced by a pelican crossing, regulated by lights that mandate rather than advise. The latter, he often reflects, in a mode of thought midway between meditation and grumbling, is a small sign of large changes in the way we interact with the general other that surrounds our singular self.

When he presses the button on the pelican crossing, he has to wait until the lights change in his favour, whereupon the traffic is obliged to stop to permit him to cross. Neither party has any discretion over its behaviour: it is prescribed. And so it is unnecessary for the driver of the car that has stopped to wave him on and it would be odd for him to thank the driver for stopping. The driver and the Flâneur are compelled by invisible laws to which they both conform. By contrast, when the Flâneur used to stand by the zebra crossing to signal his wish to cross, there was no obligation on any particular driver to stop, unless the Flâneur was already embarked. The driver who stopped might wave him on and the Flâneur would most certainly acknowledge the driver's courtesy. Their little dance was choreographed by personal decisions and they exchanged gestures and even smiles.

Since the Flâneur aspires to be a philosopher, the differences – between personal decisions and impersonal regulation, between choice and obligation – orchestrating what happens at a crossing prompt thoughts about related, deeper differences. He sees the replacement of the zebra crossing with the pelican crossing as a small marker of a large trend towards an ever more minutely automated society, of the displacement of informal arrangements by legally binding ones, an example of contract driving out the remnants of covenant. The agreements as to how we should treat strangers are laid down explicitly rather than remaining implicit. Of course, in all literate societies there is always a ubiquitous explicit contractual component in our interactions with one another; what is at issue is how densely it is drawn up and how much space is left for thumbs up, thanks, winking, gratitude and discretionary courtesy.

Just because there are obvious, endlessly discussed themes of this anxiety – progressive bureaucratization of everyday life, the ever more intrusive protective presence of 'elf and safety, the decline of trust in common sense, or in each other (Criminal Record Bureau checks) – doesn't stop the Flâneur from feeling a slight decline in spirits as his gaze at the pelican crossing is unreturned, and the driver who permits him to pass looks at the lights that will shortly give him permission to drive on rather than at the pedestrian in front of him.

In part this is because the Flâneur is – or was – a doctor (with a generous pension, which is why he can afford to be a flâneur). During his medical lifetime, he saw many improvements in the science and practice of medicine and in the treatment and experience of patients. But he also noted that, as doctors became more effective, they were less trusted and ever more closely regulated. Slowly but surely the profession of medicine moved from being a vocation to something else. The open-ended responsibility to care narrowed to a more precisely defined contract. Doctors became increasingly like sessional functionaries, acting in ways that were more minutely prescribed. Evidence-based medicine, guidelines, clinical algorithms, care pathways, throughput targets, mandatory continuous professional development, annual evaluation as a condition of continuing practice, and a less forgiving disciplinary framework all brought huge benefits, of course. But to the Flâneur – at least as he waits for the lights to change in his favour – they seem also to have had the consequence, in part unintended and in part intended, of undermining his profession. Ensuring that ordinary practice is as good – as well-informed, skilful and humane – as the best practice is, of course, entirely laudable. But this has been used to marginalize the role of judgement, to make doctors more self-protective (more preoccupation with work–life balance despite fewer hours, and less willingness to depart from the printed directions), and to reduce the stature of the profession both within their own practice and as a distinct, authoritative voice within society at large.

And there do seem to be other ways in which our relationships – at least those with strangers – are increasingly mediated through authorities defining responsibilities and giving or withholding permissions, regulated by codes of practice and subject to statute. The Flâneur observes a little boy running out of the park to which he is headed. Do you pick up a child who has fallen down in front of you and hurt itself, offer it comfort and even give it a hug? Or, fearing charges of assault on someone who has not invited you to enter his or her personal space, do you wait for a suitably authorized individual to carry out this action? If you are minded to intervene when a group of aggressive youngsters is terrorizing a railway carriage, do you do so? Or do you pause because the others on whose behalf you are intervening will wrap a burqa of inattention around themselves, stare more narrowly and fixedly at their books or newspapers, or retreat more decisively into the "e-lsewhere" accessing every portal of the soul, and leave you high and dry, twitching meat in no-man's-land? Or, more seriously, will you join those who, minding their own statutory business, will ignore the abuse of an elderly person in the care home where you are visiting your mother or where you are, perhaps, a visiting doctor?

The Flâneur reminds himself of the old question: "Is a man relieving himself in a shop doorway in Jermyn Street the end of civilization as we know it or just a man relieving himself in a shop doorway in Jermyn Street?" To which one might reply, along with Homer Simpson, "A little under column A and a little under column B". A Flâneur may be someone who reads the signs of the times but he may also be someone who reads too much about his times (the decline of the professions, the progressive bureaucratization of society) from too few signs (the replacement of a zebra crossing with a pelican crossing); who suffers from "interpretosis". Philosophers should, of course, be alert to what might be unpacked from small items in the world, to the possibility of reconstructing a dinosaur from a wrist bone, but they can go off on one – like Herr Professor Nietzsche, who found evidence of nihilism in M. Flaubert's preference for sitting down over walking – and sometimes not a very original one, either. "'Only connect", he chides himself, "but don't over-connect".

It is time, anyway, for the Flâneur to stop fretting about trends that, on another day, he would regard as unequivocally good: time to stop editorializing, to give himself up to the walk, and lose himself in the world offered to his gaze.

LOOKING

Vision, the Flâneur reflects, at the centre of his field of it, is the richest and the most explicitly free of his five senses. Unlike touch or smell or taste, it permits sensory knowledge without the knower being engulfed or immersed in, or even directly exposed to, that which is known. Unlike hearing, vision has continuity in both space and time: what we see forms a field enclosing us in a 360° solid angle. It gives us the presence of an outside world with which we are connected and from which we are at the same time uncoupled, since what we see is over there, at a distance from ourselves, the seers, who are over here. We are at liberty to redirect our gaze within a visual field or to reposition ourselves in order to open up another visual field. In each case, our viewpoints, unlike "touch points" or "sniff-points", are vantage points. And, what is more, what we see is much greater than we who see it, and greater still than the eyes with which we see. *Opsis* tends to *syn*opsis.

The Flâneur is walking for the sake of walking; and he looks for the sake of seeing. We usually have a particular purpose in looking – in order to see what we are doing or have to do, to see what is coming or has just passed, to navigate, or to guide our interactions with the world. The scene makes demands on us, even if only in order that we shall find our way through it. (The route the Flâneur takes is well worn and unmistakably signposted so little effort is expended in following it. There is still some practical seeing, of course, to negotiate contingent items – mind that dog-dirt! – in the path of his walk.) Visible objects, if they are not merely irrelevant noise, are what psychologists call *affordances*: things to transact business, our business, with. If responses are required of us, our freedom as lookers is compromised; but for us humans, creatures who are not dissolved in the natural, or more broadly the material world, there is always the possibility of looking for its own sake, enjoying the world as a spectacle. Such interested but disinterested looking is a primordial recreation.

It is an extraordinarily profound privilege to be aware of a world laid out before oneself in this way. To the Flâneur's eyes, the Given under such circumstances is most truly a gift. He is not merely a looker but an "onlooker" who gazes at what is before him from a multiplicity of distances that derive from the virtual outside of the human world, the semiosphere that has been built up over hundreds of thousands of years, and is realized in some small part in himself. He looks over there and the "there" is transformed by the "here" from which he is looking. That innocent tree is stained by his personal history, itself a path taken in a shared history, in an n-dimensional space whose coordinates have established the possibility of the path that he has, and is bathed in a light unknown to the sun.

As the Flâneur passes through the ornate park gates, suspended from time-worn sandstone piers, he joins a path that runs parallel to a brook, separated from it by foliage in which Himalayan balsam has started to dominate: a fecund immigrant threatening the local ecology. A little bridge takes him over the brook and then he is next to the lake. Here the path is crowded with Canada geese. They have crossed the Atlantic, measuring their length six million times, to reach this spot. No wonder they are irritated by invaders, although their stewardship of their territory is unimpressive: it is littered with splats of cloacal treasure that look to the Flâneur's cultivated Martian gaze like blobs of puréed badger. The geese protest their ownership of the path with unoiled squawking but nevertheless give way, although with outstretched wings and bad grace.

A circuit around the lake will take the Flâneur by indirection to the Tudor hall and, in front of the hall, to a terrace that affords a grandstand view of the park and its trees instantiating numerous varieties of green. From there he can see the path he had taken by the brook now leading back to the park gate and thence to the outside world where the pelican crossing will regulate his return journey across the road towards the study he has left behind him.

According to Heraclitus, the way up and the way down are one and the same. He might have come to a different conclusion had there been escalators in Presocratic times. Anyway, even on the flat, the way back is not the same as the way out. Leaving aside the question of the direction of travel, and the different experiences that will be had, not the least because the traveller is facing in the opposite direction and harvesting different qualia, the way back is later than the way out. The Flâneur is richer in experience and diminished in time – the possibility of experience – on the return leg.

Of course, the way out and the way back are in themselves one and the same: the path that is taken has both ways, as does any trajectory or line. So what was Heraclitus, whose legs have been still for more than 2,500 years, trying to say? Was he not endeavouring to reveal a truth beneath the transient truths of experience, notwithstanding that he believed that all reality was change and no part of Being was untouched by Becoming. His image of change, however, was the flickering flame of fire, not the damp, uncertain flickering of the second-order being of consciousness. And yet, the path the Flâneur has taken, and the path he will take, are still there and are the same.

The trail of thought goes cold and the Flâneur paces up and down in order to activate the beautiful ballet whereby the items in his visual field adjust their apparent relations to one another as he changes his position. The nearby trees seem to advance towards his advance until he passes them and they become markers of his recent past. The further trees appear to move forwards because their angular displacement is less than those of the nearer trees. Somewhere between the two is the watershed or hinge at which backward movement gives way to forward movement. The bluffs, capes and promontories of the foliage echo the bluffs, capes and promontories of the clouds propelled by inaudible breezes that cause only the tallest trees to bend slightly. Here, up on the terrace, he is reminded of Rilke's reference to space that is great in the sky and small round flowers.

The continuity of the visual field, and the choreography of relative motion that ensures that everything remembers to order itself with respect to everything else as the Flâneur's viewpoint changes, is an immediate expression of the way the world "coheres": the way each part is connected to every other part and changes in one part are coordinated with changes in another. And yet there are discrete events: the history of the park around the Flâneur is dis-tracted, pulled apart, into discrete happenings, each with its own ancestors and its own descendants.

He recalls how, a few minutes earlier, a wood pigeon, alarmed by his footsteps, returned the compliment and made him jump by exploding out of the flank of a tree. A twig broke off and fell on to a smooth side-pool, a silent lay-by, in the brook. A modest train of consequences was set in motion: the falling twig summoned a doppelgänger to the glassy surface of the water; when it landed, ripples spread across the pool, distorting the image of the parent tree, and, when they reached the bank, caused minute tremors in reeds ankle deep in water. Although these consequences had consequences in their turn – there was no end point – they became smaller as they grew more numerous. Eventually they were dissipated beyond the ken of any audit trail into ever more subtle effects of effects, an initial signal dissipated in subsequent noise, as descendent events lost their potency in their multiplication and in the interference arising from other events losing theirs.

His first recognizably metaphysical thought troubles the Flâneur as he looks up at the sky and sees a plane flying overhead.

THE COHERENCE OF THE WORLD

At one (macroscopic) level, the material world is an unfolding continuum. While there are spatial and temporal gaps between distinct objects and successive events, those gaps are crossed, that is to say closed, by causal connections mediated by intervening stuff. Everything is linked with everything else. And yet, as he walks in the park, the Flâneur has observed little arias of causal connectedness standing out from a background in which disconnection seems to be the order of the day. The pigeon's flight, while it may not be a genuine point of origin, is the start of a distinct story, unrelated to the movement of a shadow over the grassy slope in front of the Tudor hall. The remote noise of the traffic has no effect on the dog chasing after a ball. The just-noticeable trembling of the reeds from the fallen twig is seemingly unrelated to the breeze that causes a distant tree to sway. The crumbling of a crumbling wall has nothing to do with the plane flying overhead – the *bonne* that has triggered this *pensée* – and less than nothing to do with the movement of a second glass of white wine requested by the passenger in Seat 3A of BA Flight Number 3016 heading towards the airport. The world is coherent, wired together by causal connections, and yet it is sprung apart, a countless number of seemingly separable stories.

OVERTURE

At first the Flâneur wants to dismiss this. Yes, Event A (say the pigeon's flight) and Event D (the request for a second glass of wine) are not directly connected, are not in a cause-and-effect relationship. They seem to belong to parallel, mutually quarantined, causal sequences. However, those causal sequences must surely have a common ancestor in a materially coherent universe: a single unfolding set of processes gave rise to the separate strands that he follows as he looks about him. This may be the case; after all there is the perfectly respectable (although entirely incomprehensible – do not let anyone pretend otherwise) idea that the universe began as a dimensionless point of infinite density and every event (including all those observed in the park) fanned out from that singularity in accordance with the laws (or, perhaps, law) of the universe. Even if this were so, however – and the Flâneur is not entirely persuaded that mathematical physics has the last word on the truth about everything (perhaps because he is not very good at mathematics and not much better at physics, and does not accept that the vanishing point of the mathematical gaze necessarily coincides with the appearing point of the universe) – it would still leave the puzzle as to how a seamlessly connected global unfolding was teased apart into chains of events that appear to be causally independent of one another.

At this point, the Flâneur entertains the idea that it is the irruption of conscious beings like himself into the continuum of mass-energy that opens it up. As he (and creatures of his ilk, although the scope of his ilk remains uncertain) wakes to the universe, or the universe wakes to itself in him and his like, there is born a multitude of worlds in which events are arranged around self-important centres according to their salience, their importance. The pigeon-burst was not important to his life but did make him jump and so earned its standing as the point of origin of a story unfolding to its anticlimax in the material world. Those worlds cohere to some degree – as does the Flâneur's visual field – and at the same time are teased apart into separate objects and events that may or may not be in a state of interaction. The awakening of viewpoints not only locates items as "here" and "there", "near" and "far", "recent" or "remote", "no longer", "now" or "not yet", but also as significant and insignificant, as connected and disconnected. The primordial viewpoint is the eye of the Flâneur, looking at what is around him. His gaze, which looks back at that which has impinged on him, effectively staring causally upstream to the interactions with light that reveals what he sees, is a little breach in the continuum of the universe. This is the foundation of the human world outside the realm of nature, a space in which freedom can make an entry into material reality.

It is a thought like this, perhaps, that makes the sound of hammering in a workshop at the back of the hall such a source of pleasure for the Flâneur. He imagines into the afternoon that the sound fills and the places where it may be heard – in the trees, behind a hedge, on a seat, within a parked car, on the edge of a bedroom sleep, in the earth – and the human and non-human ears that hear it. The hammering composes, perhaps forges, the moment, underlining a coherence that belongs neither to the material world nor to a viewpoint but to a multitude of viewpoints (or "hearpoints") connected, unknown to itself, into a community.

His recollection that the causal sequence prompted by the pigeon's sudden flight could not include the surprise that he himself felt and the thoughts it prompted completes this egregious if transient metaphysical pleasure. This is what the Flâneur set out to find.

SALVE

He turns a corner and his thoughts at once descend from contemplating the origin of the universe to engaging an item in his path that transforms space itself.

But first a little reprise. The Flâneur's location is not reducible to coordinates, unlike that of his body. "I" is not at the (0,0,0) of spatial coordinates. The very fact that he is aware of being in a particular place – that he is "in the park", "in Bramhall", "in Stockport", "in front of a house a mile or so from home" – means that he is not "in" any of those places in the way that the trees are in the place where they can be found. In the absence of any conscious being, the trees he is looking at are no more "next to" or "far away" than they are "in Stockport" or "in England".

And so to return to the item that has brought the Flâneur down to earth. Like the trees, the item in question is located in his visual field but, unlike the trees, it has a visual field in which he and the Flâneur are located. This is a truism that twentieth-century philosophers of consciousness have mined richly. For the item in question is another human being – a "he", and potentially a "you", and in fact also an "I" – who may have to be acknowledged or ignored, greeted or passed by in silence.

When first spotted, he was forty or fifty yards away, waiting for his arched-back dog to finish easing itself. The Flâneur observes him take out a plastic bag and gather up the evacuated material. He approves of his care for the common spaces: they are brothers, fellow members of civil society, and the Other will therefore be afforded a greeting. The Flâneur remembers only too well the distant decades when his children were small and the first task on returning from a walk was to clean the filth off the wheels of the buggy. What strange glances such memories are, he thinks: the intervening yesterdays are as glass to his involuntary backward glance.

Their paths are set to cross, so the question of the greeting is unavoidable: several questions in fact – (a) if; (b) when; and (c) in what style. As he approaches, the Flâneur's furtive, hermeneutic gaze unpacks – discovers or invents – a life, a world, a personality, stories, from the man walking towards him. He is grey-haired, elderly, wearing a Barbour jacket, has large glasses with 24"-television frames, and looks slightly sad: a widower, perhaps. This thought prompts the Flâneur to increase the planned warmth of what is now a planned greeting. The man's dog, a little ahead of its owner, is somewhat stiff-legged and has a pained look on its face. Gone are the days of running rings around its master's path and chasing after balls, sticks and stones. Its black muzzle is grizzled. As the man gets closer, the Flâneur notices that he has what his late mother would call "a high colour" in his face, grog blossoms and worse, which she always took as a bad sign. A pair of binoculars hangs from his neck.

The ritual exchange of phatic utterances takes place. The possible widower's greeting is as warm as the Flâneur's. The latter is pleased not to have sold himself cheaply in gratuitous ingratiation. Between one good afternoon and another, a kingfisher, which seems to exist entirely in the near-past tense, as something that has just happened, flashes by. This is his fellow-walker's second sighting this week. Behind his head, a heron lands on a rock and folds itself to an ornament. As they part, inserting distance between their point of intersection, the Flâneur goes full Flâneur and reflects on the complexity of his decision to say "Afternoon. What a beautiful day".

Nothing could be more banal, standardized – off the shelf rather than customized – and yet it was the expression of the fully aware human being. The judgement of whether or not to greet (taking into consideration the nature of the recipient, how many people there are in the park – greetings must not be too promiscuous or onerous), what style of greeting to employ, how close a distance to greet from – these are all conscious decisions. The Flâneur is riding one of his hobby horses, correcting the claim, made by so many psychologists and others, presumably themselves engaging in automatic writing, that we are more or less automata. Yes, of course, many of our actions are built out of components that no longer require deliberate thoughts or decisions but we are painfully conscious, self-conscious, even when we are engaging in the trivia of everyday interactions. So much, thinks the Flâneur, for those who claim to believe that we somnambulate through the world, guided by unconscious processes that were honed by mechanisms largely unknown to us.

VALE

The grumpy, lame dog, probably the same age as a boy riding by on his first proper bicycle and perhaps breaking his first bye-law, is a *memento de senectute* that prompts thoughts about the mystery of ageing. The Flâneur's body, stepping out in pursuit of thoughts, has another story that unfolds in a different dimension from the biography it makes possible. The forces that fashioned his body most certainly did not have him in mind; indeed, until living matter started to take control of its own destiny when *Homo* became *sapiens* (and acquired a few other less admirable traits), living matter had nothing at all in mind. It might, however, have seemed as if it did, in view of its remarkable properties, the most striking of which concerns its (temporary) defiance of the most metaphysical of all physical laws, the second law of thermodynamics, in accordance with which localities in the universe, and the universe itself, overwhelmingly tend to increasing disorder.

This tendency can be slowed, even temporarily reversed, by mechanisms of growth and repair operating at the level of the cell, the organ and the whole organism, assisted in the very recent past by physic and surgery and the adoption of a healthy lifestyle, exemplified by the joggers who litter the paths every hour of the day. The miracle of organic order, however, cannot last: the universal forces of disorder soon overcome the most brilliantly designed organism – such as the Flâneur. Probability reasserts itself over this highly improbable item taking himself for granted as he and the equally improbable item whom he has greeted stroll away from each other, one attached to an only slightly less improbable dog.

On cue, reminders of death enter the Flâneur's visual field. By the path around the sunken lawn near the Tudor hall (where no ball games are to be played lest the centuries-old diamond-leaded windows are smashed by a careless shot) are several benches: standing invitations to sit down. Each is dedicated to one of the local dead, their names and the span of their lives carved in wood or engraved on plates. They – the dead – are all much missed. They solicit "the passing tribute of a sigh", but instead they receive the more self-concerned tribute of a calculation. Those who died young awaken a hint of survivor's anxiety in the Flâneur, who is approaching the age when death would not seem tragically premature. Those who died at a great age offer him a dab of reassurance, welcome when each day's awakening reports another involuntary step towards an oblivion that is getting actuarially close.

The Flâneur escapes gloom by thinking of the field above the Camel Estuary outside Padstow, where a necropolis has been constructed out of many such benches. So many – all beloved and much missed – who "loved this town", "loved this spot", "loved this view", have jostled for position in a *cimètiere marin* that all the best spots have gone and some of those "who loved this view" have a view of nothing, which is what all of them, even those who have bagged the best vantage points, have, given that the primordial freedom of the onlooker has been withdrawn from them. This is not such bad luck as it may seem; otherwise the ignominy of being reduced to something less than a hamadryad, supporting the bottoms of strangers eating fish and chips, and overhearing conversations that ignore them, would be insupportable.

THE MAN ON THE PARK BENCH

On one bench, commemorating "Dot" – beloved grandmother, mother, wife, sister and daughter – a man is reading a newspaper in the sunlight. The Flâneur sits down on another bench whence he can observe the newspaper reader without himself being observed.

The sunlight (literally) highlights the reader's face, orientated to his sunlit newspaper. The Flâneur sees his eyes: what it is that he is seeing with; the centre and origin of his visual world. That the eyes are themselves a visible object is a strangeness illuminating the central fact of the condition the two of them share and those commemorated in the benches they sit on once shared: namely that they are embodied subjects, neither mere bodies nor discarnate spirits, but persons who are inseparable from their bodies although not identical with them. These are familiar thoughts: so familiar that the Flâneur finds it almost impossible to think, as opposed merely to recite, them. In search of less familiar truths, he redirects his attention from the man's eyes to what they are looking at.

OVERTURE

The man is reading. The light that falls on his face also falls on the words on the page: black marks like ants drawn up in military ranks on the slightly crumpled surface of the page trembling slightly in a breeze even a poplar would scarcely register. The Flâneur wants to savour the complexity, taking one step at a time.

The first port of mental call is the newspaper itself. It has been derived from a tree, not fundamentally different from the one that is casting its unmoving shadow on the trousers of the reader. The tree once breathed carbon dioxide through its leaves, aspirated water and other essentials through its roots and, with light used not for its brightness but for its energy, made the wherewithal to manufacture the cellulose that is pulped, diluted, rolled out and cut into sheets of paper. On to these less-than-wafer-thin slices of trees are applied dabs of carbon black, also derived from the afterlife of trees, when these children of light have been cremated to darkness. The black squiggles are meaning set out in space and rendered visible in the same sunlight as is shining on the man's face. No tree – such as the ones that are swishing in a momentary breeze that now shakes the newspaper – could whisper as articulately as its posthumous pages. Leaf-talk has been transformed into another kind of discourse.

The blackness of the print reminds the Flâneur of something he wants to find strange: that the metaphorical light of thought, a counter-light to that which awakens his senses, belonging to a kind of underworld that not even Persephone could imagine, can be made visible so that which is most private can be propelled from a distant, invisible source (the minds of writers, the printing presses – what you will) to places where they can be digested via the gaze. So much light and darkness – including the hiddenness of the thoughts of the man holding the paper up for himself to read – are evident before the Flâneur as he examines the man's attention captured by light folded in so many different ways: into wood, to paper, to carbon, to conscious beings, to thought, to printed words.

At different points in the several billion years separating the birth of the sun from this man reading in its light, light has been folded into ligneous plants, ligneous plants have been divided into pages, and paper has been the bearer of print. And thus, finally, did sunlit matter get to know itself as "matter" and as "sunlit"; and carbon (the father of paper and of ink) gets to hear itself uttered and see itself written as "carbon". The *logos* of the world – its order, its sense, its meaning, its necessities that sweep the Flâneur and the man reading the newspaper into and out of being – is recorded, courtesy of the deposit account of logs created out of the current account of leaves.

It is the confluence of lights – literal and metaphorical – that fastens the Flâneur's attention to this man reading his newspaper in the open air: unprocessed sunlight making the page visible; sunlight married to air, water and the earth so that its unimaginable quickness is arrested in tree trunks where the moments are added up to years; the various forms of envisioning and enlightenment that made paper, ink, handwriting; and the machine-writing of the press, rendering what has been written visible to the man sitting on the park bench. So many lenses, confected in brightness and in shades where the roar of the sun is filtered through the atmosphere, through foliage, through curtains, into the unvisited places of cupboards to become focused into an utterly different kind of light: the if-light of possibility, of the world imaged in the black mirror of words!

For the visible darkness of ink is not like the shadow dappling the man's trouser leg, not merely the absence of light. No, it is the light of absences that the man is peering into as he reads a report of a match that took place yesterday or a war being conducted at some distant place beyond any conceivable eyeshot. The words on the page he is holding up to his gaze gather up such absences from a multitude of nears and fars and make them present in the light here and now.

Horatio's objection (as expressed, of course, to the most famous of all melancholy Danes, who pipped Kierkegaard to the top spot) – "'Twere to consider too curiously, to consider so" – is unavailing against the Flâneur's delight. He has a sudden image of the study whence he set out on his walk, a snapshot from a summer evening many yesterdays ago. A gold bar of sunlight fell across the bookshelves, a bright splash of *now* staining the ranks of his books, those corners of forests long felled to pages imprisoned between musty boards, where the only calls are the pickled talk of hearts stopped long ago, the spoors of minds now void of consciousness, the calculated discourse of the dead, and where the tangled tracks of past enlightenment are woven into the shadow-lights of some ghostly *not yet* or *no longer*. Stung by the glory of the *now*, he had stood up from the keyboard and called the Flâneuse to him. Hand in hand, they had walked through the summer evening, between the dripping, fresh-green trees, talking nonsense as they listened to the last of the blackbird's song in the finale of the sun, rejoicing in those treetop and housetop Cs.

Such layered absences, Horatio.

LOOKING AGAINST THINKING

"The Flâneur is walking for the sake of walking; and he looks for the sake of seeing." So he claims, but this is not entirely true. He walks in order to think and he wants to return from his walk enriched, with his satchel full to bursting. The trouble is, while walking unites looking and thinking, they don't necessarily like each other. Indeed, they may compete: the Flâneur looks and what he sees makes him think and, thinking, he ceases to see. Wittgenstein's injunction to those whose thoughts have got knotted – "Don't think, look!" – did not mean "Look around you" but look more closely at the way words and concepts function in everyday life, outside philosophy, where language is "idling".

The Flâneur's view of the things he sees as *bonnes a penser* rather reduces seeing as a means to thought. For much of his thinking life, he has resisted the suggestion that vision can be "deep" in the way that thought is, or may be. Against this, the great French poet and thinker Paul Valéry argued that the artist who paints the visible surface of things is not necessarily less profound than the philosopher who thinks beneath, or at least away from, those visible surfaces. The Flâneur was not convinced.

At the root of his resistance to this thought of Valéry's is the obdurate conviction that looking and seeing are too occasional, too adherent to the particular, too *regional*, to appeal to the truly serious mind wanting to surmount the world in order truly to see it: seeking a synopsis beyond the small synopses of *opsis*. For the ultimate aim of thought, the Flâneur tells himself, is to wake up out of, and hence be liberated from, the particular, including the large, lifelong particular that is himself. Measured against this aim, looking seems less than, even the opposite of, the summarizing effort of thought: a pause in the process by which consciousness detaches itself from merely local occasions in order that it might continue its struggling ascent towards a culminating, summarizing sense.

This must be the moment to address this old conflict and, for the Flâneur, at least to attempt to be *puzzled* by this conflict between sight and sentences, looking and language. What, after all, is the *theatre*, the *plane* of this conflict? It is easy but probably misleading to assume that there is a thing called "attention" that can be distracted or divided: in other words to propose "attention" as the plane upon which sight and thought meet and quarrel over a territory they divide up between them. But what *is* attention separate from acts of attending? What is the plane that can be thus divided? The naive spatial metaphor – here as elsewhere – quenches the thirst for explanation without actually explaining anything.

The profound *connection* between looking and thinking is acknowledged in the word "theory", which is derived from "*thea*", meaning sight, and is connected with "theatre", in which spectacles are presented to the eye – and, of course, to the mind. But no self-respecting thinker would base important conclusions on etymology. More to the point is the Flâneur's recent experience in an exhibition devoted to portraits. He spent a long time looking at a portrait by Walter Sickert: of whom, he cannot remember. It was almost the antithesis of the face, hyperreal in the sunlight, of the man reading the newspaper on a park bench.

For the first time in his life, thinking and seeing seemed inseparable and his consciousness seemed to be unfolding along a plane where ideas and images met. To say that the indistinct face of the dark, bearded man against the dark brown background connoted with precision, but without banal explicitness, a whole world of gas-lit streets, of bar life, of suffering and of happiness – of *being there* in a way that was at once regional and specific and metaphysical and general – would be to simplify the Flâneur's response, although it perhaps indicates the rough direction in which that response lay. The interaction between the painting and his thoughts seemed to illustrate something that Coleridge said: "Painting is an intermediate somewhat between a thought and a thing".

That is why the Flâneur feels prepared, as he takes leave of the man reading in the sunlight, to take seriously the idea that in those visible forms in which reality half articulates itself – landscaped gardens, paintings and (above all) human faces – there are thoughts that lie beneath and beyond thought. He no longer holds it as axiomatic that abstract thought will always take consciousness deeper into itself than the painter's purified attention to the visible appearance of things.

Indeed, there is a parallel between the painter's gaze and the thinker's thought. He seemed to recall that Wittgenstein had suggested this: "How can we make anything clearer to ourselves by thinking about it? – Just in the way that you see something more clearly if you draw it." Both are means of making the explicitness that is consciousness more explicit; and there is no aspect of explicitness – which is itself totally mysterious and utterly irreducible to anything else – that can be dismissed as relatively "shallow" compared with another aspect of explicitness. (This becomes plain to the Flâneur when he thinks of the world formulating itself in the developing consciousness of those young children whose buggies seemed to seek out dog-dirt.) The painter and the thinker, while approaching reality from different angles, do so from the same depth. To think and to paint are different ways of constructing perfected recollections that partake, in different proportions, of the image and of the idea.

So recently the Flâneur has been more prepared to entertain the possibility that thinking and seeing are not in the end so remote from one another. That both the fully imagined thought and the thought-scented view take their rise from, or reach towards, a common root in consciousness where light becomes explicit – as objects that display their own meanings and thought makes articulate sense of it. That what thought and sight have in common – an irreducible *explicitness* that makes things *be there* – is more fundamental than the differences that provide the apparent basis for their conflict. That looking and thinking have a shared origin, even though they stand at opposite poles of consciousness. Thus does the Flâneur license himself to postulate, even dream of, a place where looking and thinking are one, united in some kind of higher *vision*.

At the very least, ordinary vision is innocent enough to unsettle the stale categories of thought and let the freshness of the physical world into the closed universe of sentences. It plays outside that ubiquitous, persistent half-thought that the Flâneur can never fully think nor shake off, and which prevents him from achieving either self-escape or perfected self-presence.

The marriage of thought and vision has, of course, to be at the right depth and on equal terms. The history of conceptual art – the very idea of which makes the Flâneur frown – shows what happens when shallow, third-hand thoughts are attached to items whose construction has required no special capacity for looking and seeing, indeed, no talent at all other than for self-promotion. And now the Flâneur, aware that he is following well-worn paths, thoughts that happen rather than are thought, transfers his frown from the present phase in the history of (some) art to himself. He is aware, also, that he has accumulated rather a large number of ideas that he would like to capture on paper for further development in his study. It is time to turn homewards.

LOOKING BACK ACROSS THE LAKE

It is an hour or more since the Flâneur first reached the lake and now, from the other side, he can see where he was in the near past, when he was threading his way through the geese with their wounded pride and idle threats. "Here" at 4.20pm, he can see "There" at 3.20pm. Or a There that has survived from 3.20pm to 4.20pm, thus preserving the past by resisting some change. What has survived is the material substrate of the Flâneur's journey through the geese: what we might call "objects". The journey itself, or that part of it – "an event" or "a process" or "a phase of a process" – is over.

This, the past seen across the lake, is one of the most elementary ways in which the past is present, out there, in the sense of being visible. There are, of course, many other markers of the past and the Flâneur takes note of them, as something like "a moving present" (but not, in fact, a moving present) that divides the stretch of the walk has become a past he can recall with some degree of accuracy from a future stretch that has as yet no determinate elements. The simplest are footprints he can look back on. They look neither young nor old; he simply knows that they are past because they "lead up" to his present position. Some items, like that rotting log among the balsam next to the brook, scored with deep fissures giving habitation to little platoons of mushrooms, and maculate with brilliant green patches of moss, wear their antiquity on their sleeves. They "are" old, as if their having much past and not much present were itself a present quality; indeed, they are so obviously "old" that the Flâneur is inclined to modify the word to "olde", so that it, too, wears its moss on its sleeve.

Other items bear the presence of the past in a mode that is visible only to the organ of knowledge: we know, but do not see, that they are old. The supreme example is the sun filling the world with undiminished radiance several billion years after its birth. We may "live in an old chaos of the sun" as Wallace Stevens said, but the sun itself is the ultimate renewable; if it is going to age towards darkness, it will be on timescales that are mere numbers whose zeros mark the distance between themselves and the point at which imagination fails, between that which can be thought and that which can be merely recited by the Flâneur finding the limit to which he can think to himself.

Quite unexpectedly, the Flâneur is granted one of those moments when he has a sense of the scope and size of the world whose centre he occupies: his own world. He has the intuition that eluded him on his outward journey and it is born on two words from the hermetic Italian poet Giuseppe Ungaretti: *M'illumino d'immenso*.

It is connected with a memory of a few months before, of a vision afforded him, when he was returning from London on an early train. With the help of a short sleep, a coffee and the sunshine outside, he had woken to intense well-being. Near Stockport station, the train slowed (as it always does) and journeying gave way to approximating (as it always does). It trundled in parallel to the road that leads to the council tip, where, frequently, on a Sunday afternoon, the Flâneur delivered the household waste (dominated by empty wine and beer bottles) and foliage pruned or uprooted by the Flâneuse. From the vantage point of his early Wednesday morning train, he remembered his most recent visit. Sunday afternoons at the tip are always busy and he had – thus he slides from the perfect to the pluperfect because every past has a past – joined a long, slowly moving queue; just as on the train, journeying had given way to approximating. He was able therefore to listen with more attention to an analysis on the radio of Sibelius's Fifth Symphony. Although the day was grey skied and slightly rainy, there was the deliciously evocative hint of spring in a faint hoar-green on a willow tree; all else was brown.

As the Flâneur sat on the Wednesday train, looking at the place where the car had been queuing, and thinking back to the Sunday afternoon, looking and thinking entered into a strangely happy partnership. His eyes seemed to offer him a shortcut to a past by which, his thoughts told him, he was linked by a complex line, wriggling in and out of a multitude of dimensions corresponding to the journeys he had undertaken, the experiences he had had, the intentions he had formulated and in some cases fulfilled, during the intervening sixty or so hours. The journeys connected not only one place with another but the beginning and end of an action, of a thought, of a story, of a meeting. His glance and his thoughts, his eyesight and his mind's eye, joined at the same spot. Doubly illuminated – by thought and by sight – the past occasion was intensely *realized* as the nodal point at the heart of a boundlessly extended web of interconnected things.

OVERTURE

The remembered symphony guided the Flâneur into a wider past: Sibelius had been woven into long years with the Flâneuse and, before this, into his life and solitary walks as an unmarried, childless student. The glimpse lit by the symphony swept round the many hours in which Flâneur and Flâneuse been had been together and the hours before then when they had been apart, unknown to each other. And so his thoughts, alighting here and there on spots of light and time, circled in ever widening gyres. The besuited Wednesday morning of a train showed the tee-shirted Sunday afternoon in the car as it really was: a point of convergence in a nexus of nexuses. The hinterland assumed the foreshore, the penumbra came out of the shade, and out-of-sight came to mind. The Flâneur was a little more mindful of his world: the intricately woven days, co-knitted with fellow occupants of the sunlight, and the collective mindlight of our civic places.

It was, in short, a vision. And not a transcendent vision of an invisible what-might-be but an immanent vision of what was indubitably there; an intuition that turns up the wattage of the mindlight and makes the ordinary fully visible; an unblinding to the blindingly obvious that reveals days as a controlled explosion of a trillion orchestrated events ignited by the remote dispensation of the sun.

RETURN

It stayed with him, the vision, as he walked between the gate piers out of the park, crossed the road between guardians with the striped legs and luminous egg-heads, smiled at the bonsai country pretending to be a roundabout, glanced at the poplar tree simmering with leaf-talk, passed the two sleeping policemen pacifying the traffic in his little road, entered his drive, opened the door ascended the stairs and sat down at his desk.

I have had my vision, thought the Flâneur, the only vision worth having – or pursuing: liberation from the daze of days, to a state of being dazzled by daylight; of a connected as opposed to a disconnected dazzledness. Truly looking about one before one dies. Of course it has passed, as it passed the other month. Someone, after all, had to get off the train, carry his cases, engage with the world rather than marvel at it, and get on with the day's work, and that someone was the Flâneur.

So long as it lasted, it seemed as though, through this sense of interconnectedness, the Flâneur might get a handhold on the glass wall of the obvious and thereby grasp himself and his world. At any rate, just now in the park the universe of his daily life had revealed more of itself: more of its size, its depth, its multiplicity, its unforgetting interlinking, its material and narrative, causal and semantic, coherence. The very complexity that is a burden when translated into busyness and competing preoccupations and necessary gadgets and potentially mislaid possessions had turned from an imprisoning thicket to layered light. The bright sense that any moment was the heart of a limitless universe – *m'illumino/d'immenso* – permitted items that were at other times merely the functional image of themselves to be true presences: relaxed the constricted attention that makes thoughts, facts, words mere paper currency of consciousness.

Such moments, thought the Flâneur, as he waited for his computer to wake up, reopened the possibility of a delight in a life as deep as the suffering that, so his years in medicine had endlessly reminded him, awaits us all: a delight that, if shared, promised to mitigate the pain of the solitude to come.

It is, most of all, out of a wish to honour, and be faithful, to a vision whose fabric is daylight, he thought to himself, that he seeks to be a Flâneur and a metaphysical one at that.

1

Am I My Brain?

Are persons like you and me brains? The short answer is no, but I think I owe you a longer answer. I want to set out some of the reasons why it is wrong to regard people as being identical with their brains and a mistake to talk about brains when we should be talking about people. First, I shall list some of the ways in which persons are identified with their brains. Then I will suggest why so many people are inclined to do this: indeed, see it as plain common sense, validated by neuroscience. After these preliminaries, I shall give some reasons for denying that persons are brains (or *their* brains). This will take up the bulk of this essay. Finally, I shall say something about the challenges that have to be met if we establish that brains and persons are not identical: "Where do we go from here?"

There are many ways of identifying brains with persons, such that personal identity is brain identity and personal history is brain history: persons are all of their brains; persons are parts of their brains; persons are software implemented in the hardware of the brain; and persons are "connectomes" – how their brains are wired up.

The notion that the person is identical with all of the brain was first adumbrated by Hippocrates 2,500 years ago. As he said in his treatise on epilepsy:

> Men ought to know that from the brain, and from the brain only, arise our pleasures, joys, laughter and jests, as well as our sorrows, pains, grief and tears. Through it, in particular, we think, see, hear, and distinguish the ugly from the beautiful, the bad from the good, the pleasant from the unpleasant.

This sounds remarkably similar to Francis Crick a decade or so ago – "Your joys and sorrows, your memories and your ambitions, your sense of personal identity and free will, are in fact no more than the behaviour of a vast assembly of nerve cells and their associated molecules" (1994: 3) – although Crick, in common with many others, thought that the person was located only in part of the brain not the whole of it. His favoured spot was the claustrum deep in the hemispheres where many neural pathways converge.

These, then, are some of the ways personhood is construed as being identical with activity in the brain. Why are we inclined to believe that we shall find personhood in the brain? There are reasons rooted in everyday observation and reasons that seem to come from neuroscience.

First, some homely observations. Most obviously, the "here" of the "I" is located where the brain is. The brain, or the head that contains it, is seen to define the centre of egocentric space: in so far as that space has coordinates, the brain lies at their point of origin. If my brain is in a particular room in Stockport, so am I. My history and the spatiotemporal trajectory of my brain are inseparable. Second, there are the effects of brain damage. Severe brain damage may lead to loss of consciousness and loss of personhood; and less severe brain damage causes impairment or alteration of consciousness and change in personality.

These homely observations have been supplemented by a huge body of knowledge about the impact of injury to, or dysfunction of, different parts of the brain on every aspect of behaviour and awareness. Recordings made from the brains of living subjects using technologies such as electroencephalography (EEG), and various kinds of brain scan such as functional magnetic resonance imaging (fMRI), have demonstrated correlations of neural activity with the levels of consciousness (alert, drowsy, asleep, comatose and so on); with the contents of consciousness – perception, memory, emotion, thought; and less closely, but still impressive to some, with propensity to behave in a certain way. It is reasonable to conclude from this that every aspect of the consciousness of a person, from the most primitive sensation to the most exquisitely constructed sense of self, depends in some sense on, or is caught up with, brain function, and the location, pattern and distribution of brain activity is associated with experiences, moods and so on.

And we are therefore justified in concluding from this that to live a normal life as a person requires a brain in good working order. But are we justified in concluding from this that to live a normal life as a person is *to be* a brain in some kind of working order? And are we justified in concluding that the brain is not only a necessary but also a sufficient condition of personhood – that persons and brains are the same?

In order to answer these questions, I shall look at certain aspects of personhood and see whether they could be identical with what goes on in the brain. The aspects I want to look at are: consciousness, the *sine qua non* of personhood, as that in virtue of which there are phenomenal appearances, and which, from perception upwards has intentionality; first-person being, which underpins having a viewpoint; the unity of consciousness at any particular time; and the temporal depth of consciousness – the sense of "I" extended over time.

First, consciousness. Is brain activity sufficient for consciousness, so that we can identify the one with the other? Before I deal with the arguments, let me set aside an empirical red herring. It is possible by direct brain stimulation to cause individuals to have quite complex experiences. The most famous example is the work of the neurosurgeon Wilder Penfield, who stimulated certain areas in the cerebral cortex of waking subjects. Doing so seems to evoke not only simple sensations, but often quite complex experiences corresponding to previously dormant memories of past events. This would seem to suggest that experiences could be generated in the standalone brain and that, as suggested in the brain-in-a-vat thought experiment, the entire consciousness of a person could be created or constructed by simulation of the neural inputs of a brain sustained in a bath of nutrient.

This conclusion is invalid. After all, Penfield's subjects were already awake; in other words, the background wakefulness required for the experiences to be had and interpreted was provided independently of the stimulation. And the experiences would not have counted as memories of the subject's own past except in relation to a life, prior to the moment of stimulation, in which experiences had been had in the usual way and subsequently qualified as memories.

With red herring set aside, I want to turn to the arguments. Before I consider whether key features of personhood could plausibly be located in brain activity, I want to rephrase the question. The brain is a piece of matter. Could a piece of matter have the consciousness that is necessary to be a person? If not, the brain could not be a person. And by "a piece of matter", I mean a piece of something whose definitive description, or most authoritative portrait, is to be found in the physical sciences. This has been part of the neuroscientist's creed for a long time, as witness this quote from the leading nineteenth-century biologist Emil du Bois Reymond, one of the founders of neurophysiology (in a letter to a friend of 1842): "Brucke and I pledged a solemn oath to put into power this truth: no other forces than the common physical-chemical ones are active within the organism". More recently, this has been spelled out by Daniel Dennett:

> There is only one sort of stuff, namely *matter* – the physical stuff of physics, chemistry, and physiology – and the mind is somehow nothing but a physical phenomenon. In short, the mind is the brain ... [W]e can (in principle!) account for

every mental phenomenon *using the same physical principles, laws and raw materials* that suffice to explain radioactivity, continental drift, photosynthesis, reproduction, nutrition, and growth. (1991: 33)

And Dennett's sworn foe – John Searle – shares his materialism. "[C]onsciousness", he says, "is an ordinary biological phenomenon, comparable with growth, digestion or the secretion of bile" (1998: 6).

Dennett's formulation, which he himself says is the current orthodoxy, should block off the ploy of mobilizing certain terms of rhetoric that are often put in play when materialists are challenged to explain the difference between unconscious matter and conscious people – terms like "emergence", "supervenience" and "complexity" – since, as Dennett says, they believe that *the same physical principles* are conserved when we move from rocks to bacteria to professors of philosophy. I shall touch on these terms briefly at the end.

And so to consciousness, and two features – intentionality and appearance – that I want to focus on. The case for the identity of phenomenal consciousness and neural activity does seem to have been based on a slither. The slither is from (rough) correlation of activity in certain parts of the brain and conscious experience to the belief that the brain activity causes or generates the consciousness and thence to the further belief that brain activity is consciousness. This slither has, of course, been challenged from Victorian times onwards. Here, for example, is the view of the physicist John Tyndall quoted by Alfred Wallace, the co-discoverer with Darwin of the theory of evolution:

The passage from the physics of the brain to the corresponding facts of consciousness is unthinkable ... Were our minds and senses so expanded, strengthened, and illuminated as to enable us to see and feel the very molecules of the brain; were we capable of following all their motions ..., we should be as far as ever from the solution of the problem, "How are these physical processes connected with the facts of consciousness?"

The chasm between the two classes of phenomena would still remain intellectually impassable.
(Quoted in Wallace 1871: 361)

And the reply of the neurophilosophers has usually been: it's a brute fact, get over it. So the question we need to ask is: can you be a sincere or consistent materialist and still believe that conscious persons are brain activity, so you could build a person out of neural activity, "*using the same physical principles, laws and raw materials* that suffice to explain radioactivity, continental drift, and so on"? If we conclude that we cannot in principle then we need to abandon the person–brain identity theory. In addressing this, I am going to go over some very well-trodden territory in full awareness of the philosopher J. L. Austin's observation that one has to be a special kind of fool to rush in where so many angels have trodden already.

But I want to take a slightly different path through this well-trodden territory, as I focus on *intentionality* and *phenomenal appearances*. Let me touch on intentionality, taking a very simple example: the perception of a material object, such as the case of a person looking at a glass; an embodied subject looking at an object that she appreciates as being other than herself. The laws of nature as evident in the material world seem to be in ordinary operation as we follow the causal chain that links the events in the glass – the interference between light and glass – and the events in the retina and visual pathways terminating in the cerebral cortex. The causal sequence passes through the brain and may have a behavioural output. This is not "awareness of the glass". The latter – the gaze looking out, as opposed to the light getting in – is in a sense in the opposite direction. This is not, of course, reverse causation or feedback or some kind of ghostly "reaching" for the glass. It is something quite different. The causal chain, the processes and laws by which the light gets into and passes down the visual pathways do not encompass the gaze looking out.

There is something going on here that is at odds with the laws of material nature as they apply to the things that Dennett listed.

Intentionality is, to use Herbert Feigl's phrase of fifty years ago, a "nomological dangler", which, as he argued, does not fit into the world picture of physical science. We can take hold of this oddness in different ways.

First, intentionality reaches, as it were, causally upstream. If perception of the glass were identical with neural events in the visual cortex, those events would be mysteriously reaching back to their own causal antecedents, interestingly reaching *past* some antecedents (e.g. activity in the retina) and *stopping short* of others: everything from the Big Bang onwards that led up to the light interacting at that moment with the glass. It is important that this is not thought of as *reverse* causation: it does not belong to the causal nexus at all. That is why it is inappropriate to think of the gaze as having effects on the material world, as Rupert Sheldrake does when he thinks of the gaze itself as something that can be felt (as opposed to being seen), as if it were a kind of pressure, so that there is "a sense of being stared at" (2005). To think in this way is to make it too like the inward causal limb and not sufficiently to liberate it from the material world. Second, the objects of our perception (probably unique to humans) exceed that which is revealed to our senses: perception goes beyond sentience. Object perception is the most basic example of the fact that, as Barry Stroud has said, our objects of knowledge are "'underdetermined' by whatever it is that we get through that source of knowledge known as 'the senses' or 'experience'" (2000: 6). This is the level at which experience has reference beyond itself.

In summary, contrary to Dennett's assertion, the law-governed causal pathways seen in the material world do not capture what happens when a person is aware of a glass, never mind when she is aware of another person being aware of her or aware of the pressure to conform to an abstract social norm.

This has prompted some desperate suggestions about how to get rid of intentionality and to deny that consciousness is about anything distinct from itself. These include the assertion that consciousness (or in some cases the mind) is the brain's experience of itself or that consciousness is our perception of some physical processes in the brain: in short, that consciousness and the appearance of that which seems to appear to us are made of the appearance of nerve impulses to themselves. This notion of the manifest world as an idea cooked up by neurons, which telescopes that which is to be perceived and that in virtue of which it is perceived, this view of neural activity mysteriously aware of itself and transforming that awareness into an awareness of a world that causes it, is possibly the unhappiest marriage of materialism and idealism one could imagine.

One or two writers acknowledge this: for example the philosopher of biology Alex Rosenberg in his latest book, *The Atheist's Guide to Reality* (2011). Mind, he argues, is identical with brain. A thought must be an event in the brain. No neural activity can be about anything inside or outside our mind. No thought, therefore, is about anything. What can one say but "speak for yourself, mate"?

So much for intentionality. Now on to appearances. Conscious beings such as you and I are entities in virtue of which items such as material objects have appearances: they appear *to* us. Do material objects in themselves have appearances, corresponding to or forming the basic contents of consciousness? We can approach this in a couple of ways. The first is to note that the concept of matter, or the basic stuff of the world as seen through the eyes of physics, is alien to appearances. The second is that the notion of material objects having an appearance in themselves, independent of any viewpoint, is self-contradictory, and I shall come to that presently.

As materialist accounts of the world advance towards their own idea of completeness there is a gradual *disappearance of appearance*. An aspect of this is the way matter is ultimately seen as purely quantitative rather than qualitative. Let me illustrate the connection between the progress towards a quantitative account of things and the marginalization of appearances with a very simple example. Consider an object such as a table. As I experience it, it may seem large or small, light brown or dark brown, heavy or light. As seen through the lens of physical science, even if we do not drill down to the atomic level, the table boils down to certain quantities. It is 1 m × 1 m; it has such and such a weight; the light reflected from it has a certain mixture of wavelengths. This approach to the table, which bypasses those things that are peculiar to my view or yours, as it becomes progressively more objective and a more appropriate substrate for a law-based understanding, gradually elutes phenomenal appearances: those very items that constitute the world of which we are conscious. The latter are dismissed as being ontologically suspect, as *mere* secondary qualities: the warmth of heat, the opposition of inertia, the brightness of light, are all stripped off. There is a progressive disappearance of phenomenal appearance: of that which fills or (take your pick) constitutes basic consciousness. In short, the world according to physics and the kinds of laws that treat earthquakes and photosynthesis equally – and should treat neural activity likewise – is a world in which appearance has been made wilfully to disappear.

Another way of looking at this is to see that physical science has as its asymptote the most general laws that represent the sum total of things and hence things viewed from no particular perspective. The equations linking patterns of measured change are delocalized: they offer not so much a view from nowhere as a view without a viewpoint. This is another aspect of the fact that the laws of physics are laws of a world in which appearance has disappeared. Although the relationship between measurement and experience is complex, measurement rejects the experiences associated with the process of measurement: all that remains is the number that pops out of the measuring process, a number whose phenomenal appearance is irrelevant. You might think that this argument is based on an elementary confusion between how things are represented and what they are; or between epistemic and constitutive aspects of the material world. But this distinction doesn't alter the fact that if we remove the very viewpoint that generates the notion of matter as something in itself, and material objects as things in themselves, independent of consciousness, appearances, too, would go. We could make this point in a different way by asking how a rock, or a mountain, or the world would appear from no viewpoint. It would have no appearance at all. An item cannot have an appearance that is from neither front nor back, above nor below, within nor without, near nor far, in good light nor poor light. And this would apply to the material world as seen from within the material world construed according to the laws of physical nature: the material world "revealed" by a material object such as the brain.

So a sincere materialist cannot entertain the idea that the brain would be the basis of phenomenal consciousness, conferring appearances on material world. Things are no better if we focus more narrowly on neural impulses – material or, more precisely, biophysical events in the brain. They do not have an appearance in themselves and there is nothing within them to make other items appear so that they are that in virtue of which appearance is possible.

This is connected with one of the many intractable problems facing those who wish to neuralize consciousness: very little of the activity in the central nervous system is associated with consciousness. From this we can infer that there is nothing in nerve impulses *per se* that would make them conscious of themselves or of a world. So the hunt is on to identify those additional characteristics that neural activity would have to have in order to transform it from the background to, or condition of, consciousness into consciousness itself. Location in a particular part of the brain, or in several parts linked together in an ensemble, and the assumption of certain patterns of activity (such as synchrony) and/or rising above a threshold have all been suggested as that in virtue of which neural activity would be conscious. None of these offers any plausible explanation of how biophysical events should take on an entirely different character. We know travel broadens the mind but it is not clear why travel to a particular place in a brain would broaden neural activity into a mind. And it is unclear, what is more, whether consciousness reposes in the travelling or in the arrival, or in the excitation of the circuit that can be seen from the outside to combine the two.

What little plausibility candidates for the criteria for neural activity that will become conscious has is often borrowed from an outside, conscious viewpoint. A pattern, an ensemble or a circuit counts as *one*, able to tot itself up to a conscious entity, only from a viewpoint that synthesizes it. They do not synthesize themselves.

This is connected with an earlier point: since the universe described by the laws of physics has no viewpoint, and persons inescapably have viewpoints, the former cannot capture the latter. Nor can it capture the existential reality of personhood, the perspectival, interest-rooted viewpoint of the person. This has even less place in the material world than does phenomenal appearance. No piece of matter would or could be the centre of egocentric space. The brain *qua* matter could not insert a centre into the intrinsically centre-less and periphery-less material world. There is no near or far, inside or outside, mine or not-mine, no here or there as layers, elaborations or tenses of egocentric space. (And, as we shall discuss, there is no "now" either.) There is, what is more, nothing to provide the basis for my being identical with my brain, for the claim "I am my brain", because first-person being (with the "I", and the possessive, and the "am", as opposed to "is") could not get a foothold in a universe that is not even third-person: it is no person.

This is, of course, connected with the unavailability of intentionality in the material world. The first-person, the "I", the "self", is the subjectively experienced centre of a world opened up by a viewpoint in an intrinsically centreless material world. Human perception, which locates items "out there" with respect to me "in here", locates me at the centre of things because the lines of intentionality have a genuine origin or vanishing point at a me, located in my body. As a first-person being, I *face* or confront a world, rather than merely being causally wired into it like a stone or a bacterium or any unconscious bit of living matter.

Even if we were to shrivel the person in question to mere self-moments, first-person being would still pose another problem for the neuralizers of consciousness. It is this. The many experiences that we have at any one time – sights, sounds, smells and other sensations, as well as memories, thoughts and emotions – are in some sense unified, having a "subject unity" where they are experienced as belonging to the self at the same time. They constitute a sense of *me-here-now*, a consciousness of many things all at once. It is difficult to see how this integration is possible because neurophysiology assigns them to spatially different parts of the brain, so they are kept very tidily apart. The pathways for perception are separate from those for emotion, which are separate from those for memory, which are separate from those for motivation, which are separate from those for judgement, and so on. Within perception, vision, hearing, smell and so on have different pathways and destinations. And within, say, visual perception, different parts of the brain are supposed to be responsible for receiving the colour, shape, distance, classification, purpose and emotional significance of seen objects. Yet they are also required to come together. And however this convergence is envisaged as being accomplished neurophysiologically – say, by merging the pathways between the different parts of the brain – those contents would surely, in the very act of becoming unified, lose their distinctiveness, merging to some unholy soup of undifferentiated awareness.

To take an example at random, when I see my red hat on the table, over there, and see that it is squashed, and feel cross about it, while I hear you laughing and recognize the laughter as yours, and I am upset, and I note that the taxi I have ordered has arrived so I can catch the train that I am aware I must not miss, many things that are kept apart must somehow be brought together. There is no model of such synthesis in the brain.

There have been many attempts to find a solution to this so-called "binding" problem: the mystery of how the field of consciousness, of the momentary self, is at once unified while still retaining the distinctiveness of its contents. These attempts mostly depend on the idea that certain physical properties *common* to large swathes of the brain can *bring together* activity scattered across different regions: all the different regions will be activated at once in the moment of consciousness, but without losing their spatial separateness. Proposed candidates for the special properties have included electromagnetic fields, quantum coherence and synchronous electric oscillations in large sections of the cerebral cortex. But all these candidates fail for the simple reason that they rely on *objective*, or externally observed, unity being translated into *subjective*, or immediately experienced, unity, with no reason offered for why this should happen. If we accept that physical unity *per se* is sufficient to create experiential unity, then the anatomical unity of the brain or, indeed, the body, should be considered of equal power to explain the unity of consciousness. What is more, this assumption would result in conflicting unifications with a loss of distinction between the components of consciousness. Even if they solved the problem of bringing together the multiple components of the conscious field, this would then exacerbate the problem of how they retain their distinct identity so that we can be separately aware of one item or aspect rather than another.

The appeal to synchronous activity to explain how the moment of consciousness is unified is particularly revealing because it illustrates how insincere materialism is. Insincere materialists ascribe to matter properties that are borrowed from mind. The assumption that neural activity can be intrinsically synchronous locates simultaneity in the material world, something that physicists post-Einstein do not allow: for simultaneity is observer-dependent but we cannot presuppose the existence of an observer since the latter requires the unity of consciousness we have been talking about.

And this insincerity is also evident in the attempts to make neural sense of the temporal depth of the person: of the fact that we remember things that are explicitly past and anticipate things that are explicitly future. Let's just focus on the past. The standard story of memory is that it is, to use the great French philosopher Henri Bergson's sardonic phrase, a cerebral deposit. It is most commonly understood as the effect that past events have had on the excitability of parts of the brain, mediated by, for example, changes in synapses. A memory is a reactivated circuit that is prone to being reactivated because it has been excited in the past. Why is this standard story nonsense? There are numerous reasons but let me focus on the two that seem to me to be the most obvious.

The first is that this account of memory requires the present state of the brain (a) to reach up to causes of its present state and (b) to locate those causes at a temporal distance from the present. Ordinary memories (for example so called "episodic" memories of an event or experience) are explicitly of something not present, something explicitly past. Such a memory has a double intentionality, two layers of aboutness: it is *about* an experience that was itself *about* the event that it was an experience of. As discussed before, intentionality is not something that can be found in the causal nexus of the material world; this applies even more clearly to double intentionality.

This leads on to a more fundamental point: that tensed time – the past, the present and the future – does not exist in the material world as described by physicists, at least at the macroscopic level. (It is unclear whether quantum mechanics retains or loses tensed time or indeed whether it retains or loses time period.) For this I have no lesser authority than Herr Professor Einstein himself. "People like us, who believe in physics", he wrote, "know that the distinction between past, present and future, is only a stubbornly persistent illusion". This was in a famous, although to me rather tactless, letter to the recently widowed wife of his oldest friend. There are no tenses without a conscious viewpoint.

There are other characteristics of the person that cannot be captured by an account that sees him or her as a manifestation of the properties of a material object, even one as upmarket as the brain. I have mentioned ownership: our experiences are *our* experiences – in a rather complex sense of possession that needs much teasing out – and we talk about *our* brains. *The* brain is no one's brain. And then there is agency, which I have discussed elsewhere (see Tallis 2010a). But I want to move on to the question of why, if brainhood and personhood are so obviously distinct, the notion that we are our brains should have commanded so much acceptance. There are four reasons or strategies mobilized in persuading us that the obviously untrue is true.

These are the strategies: (a) thinking by transferred epithet; (b) hopeful hand-waving; (c) denying the reality of what neuroscience cannot see; (d) and arguing that There Is No Alternative.

First, thinking by transferred epithets. This results in personifying the brain in order to brainify the person. This includes ascribing to brains or parts of brains attributes appropriately ascribed to persons and much fancy footwork between brains, machines and conscious minds. I am going to say very little about this because I dealt with it at some length elsewhere (see Tallis 2004).

The next consists of hand-waving, using terms that promise much when they are not examined closely and rather less when we ask for clarity. Terrence Deacon's recent massive *Incomplete Nature: How Mind Emerged From Matter* (2012) – which I had the alloyed pleasure of reviewing – is a perfect example of a gradualist approach that progresses from matter to thermodynamic systems, to living thermodynamic systems, to conscious living thermodynamic systems. The fundamental argument, as is so often the case for those who want to find mind in the material world as it is understood by physics, draws very heavily on the notion that systems have (emergent) properties that are not found in their components and that the more "complex" the systems, the more exotic the emergent properties. On this basis, it is argued, mind – consciousness, self-consciousness – could emerge from matter. Maybe, maybe not.

The appeal to "systems" raises the question of how the elements of the system, merely in virtue of interacting causally with one another, add up to a unity that is defined against that other parts of the world with which it causally interacts, which is defined as "its world". The appeal to "complexity" should be challenged even more vigorously and on two fronts: what is meant by complexity – how is it to be measured or diagnosed; and why should it deliver the difference between say a bacterium innocent of its own existence and a person with all the characteristics I have already discussed? The usual response to this challenge is ever more frantic hand-waving. This often includes an appeal to properties that will supervene when things get more complex. "Supervenience" is a term that amuses me. It is usually invoked as a corrective to the self-inflicted intellectual wound of an "infravenient" description of something.

All three terms – systems, complexity and supervenience – are deployed in order to try to derive something fundamentally different (say a self-conscious person from a material world) while pretending that there has been no break with the laws and stuffs of the material world. There is a strategic ambiguity designed to gloss over the question whether or not the laws governing the behaviour of that from which the emerging and so on took place and that which has emerged are the same. In no cases in which "emergence" is appealed to as an attempt to make material sense of conscious persons I have come across has Dennett's promise – to "account for every mental phenomenon *using the same physical principles, laws and raw materials* that suffice to explain radioactivity, continental drift, photosynthesis, reproduction, nutrition, and growth" – been kept.

Another way of dealing with awkward differences between brains and people is to deny the existence of those things that cannot be accommodated in neuroscience. The self and the ego and agency have frequently been dismissed as ontologically dubious; and bolder, or more desperate, spirits have dismissed qualia and propositional attitudes such as beliefs as relics of pre-scientific folk psychology. The hard problems of consciousness are magicked away, as being the result of unreformed, pre-scientific ways of thinking about minds, consciousness and persons.

A not infrequent claim is that agency and the I and the self are illusions cooked up in the brain. This opens some interesting questions. Why should a piece of matter, a mere byway in the causal net, come to the *false* conclusion that it is somewhat superior to other pieces of matter? And by what material means would another piece of matter make the mistake of becoming aware that it is what it is?

In this brief critique of the notion that persons *are* their brains, I have conflated the different challenges that the sentience found widely in the animal kingdom, on the one hand, and human consciousness, on the other – with characteristics such as full-blown sense of the independent objective reality of the world, reasoning, propositional awareness, knowledge, a normative sense and so on – present to materialism. We need, what is more, to look closer at intentionality and to test its ability to carry the weight that I, along with many others, have placed on it. Why do so many otherwise sensible philosophers, such as Searle, fail to see that it cannot be a biological property, because it is not a property of matter?

What is more, I have focused on the troubles of neurophilosophy but I am aware that anti-neurophilosophy is not without its troubles. Those who believe that personhood boils down to brainhood are entitled to point to several serious questions that opponents like me leave unanswered. Why, if the brain is not the basis of consciousness, is it so intimately bound up with our awareness and our behaviour? And what are we to make of the genuine advances of neuroscience? Should we abandon brain science entirely as a source of understanding of personhood? Where would the brain fit into metaphysics, an epistemology, an ontology that denies the brain a place at their centre? How shall we deal with the fact that we are evolved organisms as well as persons? These are some of the questions that I think anti-neurophilosophers like me should be obliged to address. The critique of neural accounts of consciousness is only the first step. It simply clears the path for the truly interesting philosophical work that is to be done.

2

Was Schubert a Musical Brain?

THE MYSTERY

When the Austrian playwright Franz Grillparzer mourned, in his funeral oration for Schubert, that "here we bury great treasure and greater promise", he did not know the half of it. The definitive catalogue of Schubert's compositions lists nearly 1,000 items. Among them are perhaps the greatest song cycles ever written, seven completed symphonies and three incomplete ones, including the magical Unfinished, the incomparable late piano sonatas, and ... well, I could go on. A quarter of Schubert's output would have sufficed to establish him as a major figure in Western classical music. Yet he lived for little more than a decade after he came to musical maturity. His last year, when he was scarcely into his thirties and probably knew he was dying, was, as Benjamin Britten has plausibly claimed, the most miraculous year in the history of music. The great Symphony in C, the *Schwanengesang* Lieder, the last three piano sonatas, and the peerless String Quintet in C were only some of the highlights.

Almost by definition, the art of a genius is underdetermined by the life, but with Schubert the mismatch between life and work seems particularly extreme. The twelfth of fourteen children, of whom only five survived, this quintessentially romantic composer was physically unattractive: a short-sighted and stocky dwarf, "The Little Mushroom" was rejected as "totally unserviceable" by the military selection panel. His love affairs were one sided: not one woman he truly loved returned his feelings and yet he was not a misogynist. He was forced to earn a living in uncongenial ways but he was not embittered by a sense of entitlement. While he was recognized in his immediate circle, and even beyond, this was scarcely proportionate to his achievement. To the very end he could not guarantee that even commissioned work would be accepted, and most of what he wrote was not played in his lifetime. For over half of his magnificent final decade, he was ill with syphilis compounded by the ghastly side effects of treatment with mercury.

Given such an unpromising outer life, those who cannot tolerate the inexplicable have turned to his inner life to explain his torrent of masterpieces. Psychoanalysts have, of course, been on the case; but we may reject their one-size-fits-all explanations that see the same processes, tensions and dynamisms in all of us. They offer nothing to help us understand how a man could complete the Piano Sonata in B flat, with its soul-freezing and at times terrifyingly beautiful twenty-five-minute opening movement, a few weeks from his death, while coping with the unromantic misery of headaches and vomiting and stomach pain, as the spirochetes working their way through his body were joined by typhoid.

But the appeal to unconscious drives dies hard. Doctor and musician Roger Neighbour has offered a more customized psychoanalytical explanation. He notes, in his essay "The Little Mushroom and the Blighted Twin" (2005), that Schubert was much smaller than his siblings, and speculates that he had suffered intrauterine starvation as a result of competition from a twin brother who died in the womb. This early catastrophic bereavement accounted, he argues, for an emotional precocity and a depth of feeling that his rather ordinary and, by the standards of the time, generally cheerful early life would not justify: an abiding sense of loss and incompleteness prompted "a compulsive search for the missing other half" (*ibid.*: 110). Dr Neighbour goes further and connects the death throes of Schubert's womb-mate with the "dactylic" rhythm (long-short-short, long-short-short) heard so often – as in *Death and the Maiden* or the *Wanderer Fantasia* – and the sudden volcanic eruptions that sometimes inexplicably break into the sunny lyricism.

The image of Schubert haunted by months spent sharing his intrauterine bed with a dead twin has a Gothic power. But there are many reasons for dismissing foetal memories as an explanation of his achievements. The most obvious is the conscious care, the attention to detail, that was essential to Schubert's work. (He took lessons in counterpoint a few weeks before he died.) Nothing could be further from a primal scream than the endlessly worked over final sonatas, which reveal the death-haunted man to be a highly self-critical artist. The appeal to deep psychological forces – whose consequences one would expect to be untidy, to say the least – misses the transcendent craftsmanship that is the necessary condition of genius. The search for solutions to problems that only the artist can see, the transformation of seemingly simple melodies that appear from nowhere, the willingness to learn from revered masters (most notably Beethoven) and from his own failures and successes, and that infinite capacity for taking pains that Thomas Carlyle spoke of – these are closer to the essence of Schubert's genius than unresolved emotional conflicts.

Besides, the appeal to early trauma to explain artistic genius does not withstand the observation that childhood trauma is all too common and great artists are all too rare. While the joy of creation may help artists to come to terms with themselves and their world, their works move us only because they transcend any private forces that may drive them. They address, or dress, the universal wound of the human condition that ultimately derives from our having been born for insufficient reason into a sometimes hostile world and are consequently fated to die after a life of incomplete meanings. Psychological disturbance is not of itself much help. Besides, the reliable image we have of Schubert is of a man of striking sanity, generous to his friends and convivial when he was not prostrated by illness.

We get more enlightenment – although nothing that comes anywhere near an explanation – from looking at the culture of the city that Schubert shared with Beethoven, a father who appreciated music, and teachers and friends who early acknowledged his talents: from Schubertiads rather than putative unconscious forces automating creativity. But even attempts to account for Schubert's genius by looking at the world in which he lived his short life have all the vices of a *post hoc* explanation. As we have observed, Schubert's circumstances hardly favoured his sublime creativity. If they were sufficient to explain what he achieved, we would have had hordes of Schuberts, produced by these circumstances.

The truth is that no explanation – appealing to psychodynamic forces, prenatal experiences or historical circumstances – can get close to the utter singularity of the man who produced such a wonderful body of work, in which profound feeling and technical brilliance are effortlessly reconciled, indeed are as inseparable as the *recto* and *verso* of a sheet of paper. All explanations have to appeal to general factors in order to seem persuasive or even to be intelligible and there is nothing "general" about Schubert.

BRAIN SCIENCE TO THE RESCUE?

But the ache for explanation persists. In a world in thrall to neuroscience, those who state (as a friend of mine did many years ago) that Schubert's genius is explained by the fact that he had "a musical brain" are parroting what is now orthodoxy. This is yet another expression of the general expectation that human beings will ultimately be explained in terms of the activity of their evolved brains and that the combination of neuroscience and evolutionary theory will bring us closer to understanding what human beings are, even the extraordinary phenomenon that is art: that brain research will explain the creation and the appreciation of music, how Schubert came to be such a genius and why his music gives us pleasures so profound that they change our lives. It is important to discuss this because we need to think about ways in which the spectacularly successful scientific enterprise and its vision of the world can be reconciled with other, no less important, ways of understanding our lives and our human nature, that come from the humanities and, more importantly, from the arts. This is the great cognitive challenge of the twenty-first century and it is important to head off myths that get in the way of our meeting that challenge.

I am sure that there are places where science and the arts can cast light on each other; they are, after all, both products of human beings at their most awake, their most inspired. But those places lie very deep and we shall not find them if we do not dig deep enough: if we use somewhat crude science to understand greatly simplified arts, in particular music, as we see in contemporary neuro-aesthetics, the theme of this essay.

It would be difficult to exaggerate the importance of music in our lives. When Nietzsche said that "Without music life would be a mistake", he was exaggerating only a little. And its profound mystery casts light on the mystery that is ourselves: it goes to the bottom of our humanity. There is a deeply moving passage in Franz Kafka's *Metamorphosis*, that terrifying story in which a man wakes up one day to find that he has been turned into a giant bug. Towards the end, he overhears some music and, noting how much it moves him, he thinks to himself, "Could [I] still be an animal when music so captivated [me]?" Man, perhaps, is the music-making animal, at least as much as he is the talking animal.

This must be why the music-maker has always had a special place, highlighted by the anthropologist Claude Lévi-Strauss:

> Music is a language by whose means messages are elaborated, that ... can be understood by the many but sent out only by the few ... [It] unites the contradictory character of being at once intelligible and untranslatable – these facts make the creator of

music a being like the gods and make music itself the supreme
mystery of human knowledge. (1969: 18)

So there is the challenge.

NEURO-AESTHETICS AND MUSIC

How does neuroscience, or more particularly the young would-be science of neuro-aesthetics, shape up in meeting this challenge? Very poorly, I will argue; and I am going to spell out why although I emphasize that my purpose in doing so is positive not negative. At the very least, I hope that by exposing the deficiencies of neurobiological approaches to music I shall highlight the extraordinary nature of music and of man, the music-making animal.

Let me begin with neuroscience research into the *appreciation* of music. This has many dimensions but let me start on the ground floor, as it were, with research into the *perception* of musical sounds. Using methods of recording brain activity such as fMRI and positron emission tomography (PET) scans, researchers claim to have identified the different brain areas responsible for detecting and responding to pitch, harmony, melody and other features of music. For example, we are told that "tempo" activates areas in the parietal, insular, frontal and pre-frontal cortex. And the area said to be associated with pitch perception is located in the superior temporal gyrus.

Does this tell us anything about the experience of music? I don't think so; and it is interesting to consider why it does not. At the most basic level, given that we are not in real life served up these elements – pitch, harmony, tempo and so on – independently, we learn little about the perception of real sounds, less about the perception of real sounds in the bubbling chaos of the real world, even less about the experience of music, and less still about the impact of great music in our lives. We experience melodies as a whole; we do not separately experience pitch or tempo or tonality. What's more, we all have brains that function in roughly the same way but we do not all experience the same melodies in the same way; tastes vary from person to person, group to group, age to age. More to the point, we do not always experience the same melody in the same way; my sensitivity varies from time to time, within an hour or a day. Listening and re-listening, tenth listening and a thousandth listening are different experiences and context is all. That context may include knowledge of the composer or of the tradition from which he or she was drawing, whether you are listening intently in a concert hall or overhearing the music as you drive down the motorway, and what memories or associations a familiar piece of music may awaken.

Not all studies have focused on isolated aspects of individual musical sounds. Some have looked at the response to whole melodies. The findings here are conflicting. Aniruddh Patel, leading researcher in the field, asserts that music engages "everything above the neck" (quoted in Mannes 2011). Robert Zatorre, another well-respected figure, however, argues that there are specific effects of music on particular parts of the brain; for example the famous "shiver down the spine" (Blood & Zatorre 2001). Zatorre and his colleagues used PET scanning to look for correlations between the intensity of the pleasure given by the music and the blood flow in different areas of the cerebral cortex as a measure of neural activity. They found that when the shivers were felt down the spine, the following areas lit up: ventral striatum, amygdala, orbitofrontal cortex, and ventral medial prefrontal cortex. The names will mean nothing to non-specialists but they certainly ring a bell with neuroscientists because these same areas or circuits – that involve the neurotransmitter dopamine – are active in response to other euphoria-inducing stimuli such as food, sex and drugs.

Many neuro-aestheticians think that this is a revelation: we have found the secret of music; it is rewarding because it stimulates the "reward" centres, where dopamine pathways are found in abundance. In fact, this banal finding is worse than banal; it is embarrassing because it betrays how little is revealed by looking at the brains of people enjoying music. A science that cannot tell the difference between the response to music, drugs and sex, getting a hit of Bach and getting a hit of cocaine, or between hearing the organ played and having your organs played with, says little about either. Surely scientists should wonder whether they are missing something. The "discovery" that that thrilling master of Renaissance polyphony Palestrina and the punk rocker Sid Vicious are doing the same thing and that, like the purveyor of soft pornography Hugh Hefner and the cocaine baron Pablo E, they are pushers of stimuli that tickle up the dopaminergic or reward pathways, should surely discredit this approach.

We may set aside the excuse that this is merely "early days yet" and that refinement of techniques will bring more consistent and illuminating results. For as we have seen already, neuroscientific approaches to music involve both teasing apart things that belong together – the pitch of individual notes out of the whole experience of music in a real setting – and clumping together things that should be kept separate – Bach and Hugh Hefner and Colombian marching powder. So we are unlikely to gain much in our understanding of music even if the present techniques were refined so that they could precisely pinpoint the locations that light up in response to different components of music. This would cast no light on the singular joy that melodies may bring and the ineffable difference between great music and that which is merely competent; between sublime and cheap music; between music that makes you feel and think differently about the world and a few nice tunes. Or between what music means to us and what part "musical" sounds play in the natural world.

MUSIC AS A BIOLOGICAL PHENOMENON

Behind the neuroscientific investigation of music is the belief or presupposition that music affects us by virtue of exploiting existing biological mechanisms. Others have agreed with this but have then pointed out that, since appreciating it is not biologically useful like feeding or lovemaking, it merely parasitizes or abuses these pathways. It is a useless exploitation of reward pathways that should be busy responding to activities concerned with survival: feeding, sex and so on. The cognitive psychologist Steven Pinker (1997: 50) has compared music to "auditory cheesecake" or auditory pornography, giving pleasure to a brain used to turning sound into meaning. Zatorre's observation that those shivers down the spine stimulate dopaminergic or reward pathways seems to support this idea. Useless music is linked with other biologically relevant, survival-related stimuli, via their common recruitment of brain circuitry involved in pleasure and reward. Singing is auditory masturbation and if music were to vanish from the world, this would have little significance: the St Matthew Passion, it appears, is a long, communal hand job. Thanks to neuroscience, we now know that J. S. Bach was the Hugh Hefner of his time.

For others, however, music is more than a hitch-hiker on biological mechanisms: it has a biological purpose. And this claim is supported by the claim that the love of music is widespread through the animal kingdom and the conclusion that we humans, like other beasts, are "hard-wired" to enjoy it. The hardest wiring is supposed to be found in those oldest parts of the brain – such as the striatum – which we share with other beasts. Evolutionary theorists of music alight on the musical "tastes" of whales, elephants that play drums, cockatoos that dance, songbirds that appreciate a clarinet and – Kafka did not make it up after all in his little story "Josephine, the Singer" – the ultrasound songs of courting mice.

The overwhelming evidence, however, is that our musical tastes are *not* hard-wired and those few universals of musical taste that can be extracted from the huge variety of pieces that people enjoy are remote from the stunning singularities of works in a particular genre. Musical appreciation is dependent on culture, memory, mood and many other factors such as personal taste. Stuart Kelly (2012) reminds us of the obvious when he writes:

> Each of us brings to a work of art our own histories, memories, connotations and partialities. We are not blank canvases onto

which art is flung, or empty vessels into which it is poured ... Responses to culture are not only conditioned by our background but change over time: your favourite artist at 16 is unlikely to be your favourite artist at 46.

And it is not unknown for people to argue vigorously in defence of their taste in music, for reasons that may have little to do with the dopaminergic pathways.

Nevertheless, the biologizers do seem to have a little more going for them when we consider the *creation* as opposed to the *appreciation* of music. After all, there is the striking example of those extraordinary crooners that fly through the air and perch on our rooftops and give us such pleasure in the spring. And doesn't birdsong have an obvious function in sexual selection – a technique by which males signal to the female populace that they are an excellent genetic prospect?

But are birds *really* musicians like us? The differences between birdsong and human music-making are many and fundamental. First, the creation and/or performance of music in birds are universal – at least in males – and not confined to a few. In animals, there is no division of labour between a talented minority of producers and a majority of consumers. How different this is from the situation in humans, set out so brilliantly by Lévi-Strauss in the passage quoted earlier: "Music is a language by whose means messages are elaborated, that ... can be understood by the many but sent out only by the few". If you are a male bird, you sing: it is a biological imperative.

What is more, the behaviour is switched on automatically. There is no difference between creation, rehearsal and performance. There is no laborious practising or acquisition of the craft of the instrument (their instruments are bodily parts that grow rather than being manufactured) or the art of composition: no active, conscious learning. There are no teachers and mentors, although there is evidence of imitation. The modes of cooperation that we see in human music-making – the choir, the quartet, the band, loose elective associations formed to work together – are not seen in bird land. And, of course, singing in birds is diurnal and seasonal – but not so in humans – precisely because it is directly connected with sexual selection.

If musical creation in humans were about sexual selection it is difficult to see why I, a man, worship certain male performers and why I will queue for hours to listen to them and why they played such an important part in my courtship rituals: why my wife-to-be and I went to concerts together. Why would I put a rival songster on a pedestal and shell out for two tickets to hear him at the Southbank Centre? As for the artist, and the role of music in sexual selection, while some performers do indeed seem to be extraordinarily promiscuous, this is more a question of opportunity; what's more, they seem less keen on gene-spreading and child-rearing than on copulation without issue. In most cases, however, the career of a musician makes active anti-biological sense. There is the love of the craft and the medium for its own sake that drives the pursuit of an idea of perfection, which from the evolutionary point of view is a waste of time, effort and breath. Second, there are easier ways for humans to advertise their genetic health in a manner that will attract females and ensure the replication of one's genes; namely by indulging in fist fights or by making lots of money. Besides, although this seems to have been missed by many biologizers of art, many artists are *female*.

Talking of women, when did you last see a blackbird invite a female to sing along with him? And the dawn chorus is a chorus only to the human listeners; and only they *enjoy* it. For the female, if you believe the story, it is a serious business of checking out a partner.

DOES THE NEUROBIOLOGY OF "CREATIVITY" GET CLOSE TO SCHUBERT?

This notwithstanding, the science of the neurobiology of *creativity* – based on the idea that artistic creation is planted in our brains for adaptive purposes – is a growth industry. The results are predictably meagre, based on experiments that have little to say about the creation of music: a process of vision and revision that even in the case of the peerlessly fluent Schubert could sometimes take weeks – a rather long time perhaps to have one's head in a brain scan. Studies of "brain circuits for creativity" usually focus on only minimally creative tasks such as thinking of things one can do with a brick or listing places starting with the letter A. These would have little relevance to the kind of creativity that is in play when the eerily beautiful tune of *Death and the Maiden* is being transformed into the movement of a quartet opening up new kinds of musical space.

The often repeated claim that creativity involves lessening of inhibition on novelty-seeking, and that this is due to the activity of bits of the brain such as the right parietal cortex, tells us nothing. Novelty *per se* is not unique to original art; it is also present in random movements. Artistic innovation takes place against a background of established rules and required a feeling for a genre. The extraordinary sense – the exquisite artistic tact – that enables great composers to choose enriching innovations as opposed to merely distracting ones, creating new harmonies out of seeming dissonance, is not visible to brain-watchers. After all, structures such as the parietal cortex are universal – operating in musically untalented individuals like me as well as in the handful of Schuberts the world has seen – and many of their characteristic patterns of discharge are seen in monkeys whose contribution to (say) the development of Western music is modest. Observation of electrical activity in the anhistoric general brain will tell us nothing about why the twelfth child of seemingly ordinary Viennese parents was able at the beginning of the nineteenth century to compose a profusion of works that have transformed the possibilities of music and the way we feel about the world we live in. And the mystery of musical as opposed to other forms of creativity is particularly striking if only because so few of us are able to get even to first base. Pretty well anyone can write a third-rate poem or draw a passable picture. But only a minority can compose even a tenth-rate string quartet.

Such thoughts might enable us to take a perspective on Jonah Lehrer's characteristic boast that biology is now casting light on creativity and the imagination: "For the first time in human history, it's possible to learn how the imagination actually works. Instead of relying on myth and superstition, we can think about dopamine and dissent, the right hemisphere and social networks" (2012: 251). This is, well, a prime example of the BS that is propagated by those for whom brain science *must be* the key to humanity and where we must seek the meaning and significance of music.

THE UNBIOLOGICAL MEANING OF ART

It is time now, however, to move on from point-missing technology-driven neurobiological approaches to music to look at music itself. This will give us some idea of what will be necessary if science is genuinely going to advance our understanding of music. I want to talk about the meaning and significance of music in particular and the arts in general. Neuro-aesthetics, by getting so much wrong about them, may help us by default to see more clearly the nature of the aesthetic tendency in humankind. Appreciating that we cannot understand art unless we acknowledge that it is an expression of a uniquely human mode of consciousness – so does not correspond to a general biological prescription or to the kinds of functions that are understood in Darwinian terms – is a start. That uniqueness has many aspects and I can touch on them only very briefly. We have a unique degree of freedom, a unique mode of awareness, which we can broadly call knowledge and, arising out of the latter, hungers that only humans feel. It is as a response to these hungers and in celebration of this freedom that art arises and it is here that we must search for its meaning. Let me say a little – ridiculously little – about each.

Art is an expression of, and a response to, our freedom, a freedom that is in part measured by the distance we have opened up from the exigencies of the natural world and the immersion of an organic body in a natural environment. It is the supreme expression of the way we take the biological givens and make them something entirely different, as when we turn breathing into singing or into playing a wind instrument. This is possible because we operate from a space, the human world, that is in many respects apart from nature: a semiosphere, a sphere of signs and complex meanings and norms and institutions, which is quite different from the biosphere that we share with animals. It is a place of acknowledged, collective, evolving explicit meanings.

We are embodied subjects, related to a world of objects that are explicitly other than us, and in that sense we're uncoupled from the world. We can know the world from a distance. It's revealed to us from a distance. Vision is the primordial and most immediately apparent example of that awareness at a distance. So, to develop the idea of art as an expression or celebration of uniquely human freedom, let me switch from music to painting and consider the unique freedom of the human gaze. Our gaze, when we look at the world, is consciously offset from the world: we are not dissolved into, or tethered to, what we see. Like no other creatures, we *face* the world. And so we have the possibility of elective, or recreational looking.

And let's consider, in a very simple-minded way, how that might develop into visual art. Think of a painting. It is an iconic sign of part of, or something in, the visible world. It is not simply a mirror image, of course; few if any representations are mirror images. Most importantly for the present discussion, art widens the separation between the one who sees and that which is seen and hence the margin of freedom granted to the onlooker. When I look at you over there, I am separated from you but still, as it were, spatially connected to you, potentially interacting with you. If, on the other hand, I were to look at a picture of you in an art gallery, the connection would be of a different order: more tenuous, more on my terms. When what is seen is transferred from its primary setting in a visual field to a wall as in rock art, or to a gallery, it is more securely established as an object purely for recreational seeing. When I see a tiger in a picture, I don't feel moved to run away; and the painted clouds in a Monet don't prompt me to check whether I have my umbrella with me. Art is about seeing for the sake of seeing, and realizing to the full the potential freedom of the see-er.

Now that's very superficial, very fast, but I hope it is sufficient to indicate the size and nature of the distance between art and the biology of the organism *H. sapiens*. And this applies *a fortiori* to literary art, given that the relationship between the word and its referent is not a straightforward one of spatial proximity. Words can be used to signify objects independently of the latter's actual or even possible presence. This allows an expansion of freedom that is potentially limitless. Although for the most part we use words instrumentally, they may be detached from use and enjoyed for their own sake and for the referents they may invoke, as in literature. Paul Valéry was once asked to specify the difference between poetry and prose (I would say it's the difference between literary discourse and all other discourse). He said that it's like the difference between walking and dancing. You walk to get somewhere, and you dance to enjoy movement for its own sake. Of course, activity undertaken for its own sake also characterizes sport and other recreations. When people are running around on a rugby pitch, that is clearly enjoyment of movement itself. But what art has to offer is a *connectedness* that these other recreations don't offer. But that is another, more complex, story (see Tallis 1995).

I want now to move on from human freedom to knowledge, which takes a unique form in humans, to the point where we may say that man is the only animal that truly has knowledge. Our knowledge transcends anything that is revealed by experience, although it is subjected, as the American philosopher W. V. Quine said, to the tribunal of experience. And very little of our knowledge is utilized to shape our behaviour at a given time and much of it is never used in this way. There are many consequences of our being "knowing", as opposed to merely experiencing and reacting, animals. The most obvious is that we have enhanced power to act through sharing of experience and expertise. That's the up side. But there is a down side. As knowing animals, in possession of facts, we are aware that we are a small part of something much bigger than us. We are awake to our condition. We know that the world will outlast us: as our sense of history and of space and time grows so our awareness of our insignificance intensifies. Man is the only animal that can see his life as finite and can actively fear death in the abstract as well as when it is facing him in some concrete form. And the other consequence of knowledge is that our experiences are, as it were, eaten away from within; we are distracted from looking, say, by thinking or merely ruminating. We are frequently "elsewhere". One manifestation of this is that we have the *idea* of experiences that actual experiences may not live up to. From knowledge arises our sense of having insufficient reason for our existence and of living a life – even when it is successful and we are fortunate enough to be well above the poverty line – of incomplete meanings. We are, even if intermittently, aware that we are contingent creatures who will die by virtue of the same accidents that brought us into being; that we are accidents waiting to unhappen.

This brings me to the third unique feature of humans relevant to our understanding of the nature and function of art: a distinct mode of hunger. We have basic hungers that are plainly rooted in biological necessity, as in the hunger for food, drink and so on. And then there are more complex hungers for pleasure that may take their rise from biological functions, such as gourmet eating and the infinite varieties of recreational sex; and others, such as stamp-collecting, that express something remote from biology. There is a third kind of (human) hunger for acknowledgement by others, by a consciousness equal to our own, that is expressed most clearly in parental or romantic love. And finally there is a hunger for the completion of meaning, for something that would offset the effects of the knowledge that throws our assumption of our importance into question and eats into our experiences with ideas of a perfected experience.

It is here or hereabouts that we need to look to understand the meaning, the significance and the nature of art in general and music in particular. The freedom that comes from knowledge, and the wound in our consciousness that arises out of knowledge, are both addressed by art: the former is celebrated, the latter is healed. Art is experience enjoyed for its own sake and perfected for its own sake. This has nothing to do with what matters in the natural world:

nothing to do with what is of evolutionary advantage, the kind of thing that would be inscribed in the structure and function of the standalone brain.

Art matters to us, or we need it, because we have woken to a greater or lesser extent out of the state of an organism. Half-awakened, we endeavour to find a unifying, or at least non-local, significance in our lives. Significance often remains tantalizingly incomplete and stubbornly local and insufficient to address what we know about ourselves. And at times this may open up the feeling that we have not fully realized that we exist – not fully realized the scale and scope of what we are and of the world we live in. We ache to shake off *existential numbness* and to be truly awake, alert, alive.

So let us very briefly return to music to see how it might address our sense of being insufficiently there, of our experiences being in some respects unsatisfactory or hollowed from within. I want to focus on two aspects of music that celebrate and exploit our freedom and do something towards repairing the ache at the heart of consciousness that arises out of the knowledge that gave us our freedom: feelings or emotions and form.

Let me begin with emotions. In us, as in animals, emotions are physiological storms and, as in animals, they may be a response to particular stimuli. But in us, not in animals, they are more, much more than this. One way – not entirely satisfactory – of capturing this "more" is to say that human emotions are a way of understanding or being attuned to a world. Indeed some emotions – joy or depression, or fear or hopefulness – may be free-floating and not have a particular trigger; or they may exceed the particular trigger and become the colouration of an outlook. Emotions may deepen our temporal depth, widening the window through which we look at the world. In music, which can be meaningful or significant, without being about anything in particular, we have emotions disconnected from specific stimuli, except the music itself. Liberated in this way from local causes, the emotions in it are purified, transformed. Unlike the raw stuff of everyday feelings, the sadness of a slow movement is not contaminated with tears that make cosmetics run and mucus flow. The music's own exquisite architecture confers a structure, even a narrative structure, on the evolution of feelings, allowing them to unfold while at the same time remaining true to themselves. How music evokes feelings is unknown because, unlike physiological phenomena, they have a non-specific *aboutness*: musical feelings are about the world we are in.

This brings us to form. In a piece of music, each note is fully present as an actual physical event, yet, because the music realizes a *form* that shapes expectation and assists recall – through conformity to the rules of harmony, of contrast and symmetry, of progression and repetition – the individual notes are manifestly and explicitly part of a larger whole. There is no conflict, therefore, between the form or idea of the music and its actual instants. Our moments of listening are imbued with a sense of what is to come and what has passed. The form to which the music conforms – which ties what has gone and what is to come with each other and with what is present – shines through its individual moments. There is both movement and stillness. The unfolding sound realizes form as the "moving unmoved" (or "the unmoving moved"). The large- and small-scale connectedness within a piece of music breaks the tyranny of "and then", the endless skidding of experience on to the next thing. This is scaled up when we link our successive experiences of a piece of music and the memories that come with it, our experience of this piece with other pieces by the same composer or in the same genre, or across genres, with our growing understanding of what has been achieved in the vast archive of transmitted, perfected sound. Truly has it been said that art is a machine for the conquest of time.

This is experience perfected, fully experienced such that the wound in our human consciousness is, if only temporarily, healed. It seems unlikely to make any kind of biological sense. As Yehudi Menuhin once put it: "Music creates order out of chaos; for rhythm imposes unanimity upon the diversity; melody imposes continuity upon the disjointed; and harmony imposes compatibility on the incongruous". "Chaos", "diversity and unity", and "disjointedness" are hardly matters of concern even to our nearest primate cousins the chimps, whom I doubt suffer from a sense of the unsatisfactory nature of their experiences.

This essay is unsatisfactory in many respects but here are the two of which I am most conscious: that I have been very sketchy on the differences between man and the other animals; and that I have been equally sketchy on the nature and purpose of art, in particular music. Regarding the first, I hope I have said enough for you to at least be willing to concede that there is a huge distance between us and beasts, even perhaps as great as the neuroscientist V. S. Ramachandran has suggested: namely that humanity "transcends apehood to the same degree by which life transcends mundane chemistry and physics" (2012: xiii). And regarding the second, that I have at least said enough about the nature of art for you to accept that it is driven by concerns remote from those that preoccupy animals or would be suitable subjects for neurobiology as it is presently constituted.

UNSCIENTIFIC CONCLUSION

From this we may draw two conclusions about neurobiological approaches to music: they bypass its essential character; and they will miss something fundamental about our unique human nature from which music – and the other arts – take their rise. But this is reason to rejoice not grounds for gloom. It suggests the possibility of a new kind of departure, perhaps even a joint enterprise, in which biological sciences, the arts and the humanities could rethink how they might work together on equal terms. This means that they have to communicate in a different way from that indicated by hybrid pseudo-disciplines such as "neuro-aesthetics". We might be stimulated to think harder about the ways we humans are unique and how, given the truth of the theory of evolution, we became so.

In pursuit of this aim we need to avoid two pitfalls: the theological error of exaggerating our differences from the rest of the animal kingdom and denying our similarities; and the biologism that denies our differences and exaggerates our similarities. Only in this way will we be properly embarked on the great intellectual adventure of the twenty-first century: to develop a clearer, more truthful and rounded view of what manner of being we are. Music might not seem a bad place to start.

In the meantime, it seems perfectly reasonable to concur with Lévi-Strauss that "Music is a language by whose means messages are elaborated, that ... can be understood by the many but sent out only by the few" and that it "unites the contradictory character of being at once intelligible and untranslatable" and his conclusion that "these facts make the creator of music a being like the gods" (1969: 18); or closer at least to the gods than to chaffinches. In Schubert's case, we have a God even more deserving of our thanks for overcoming the indignities, disappointments, the endless illnesses and frustrations of his life to give us a multitude of glimpses of heaven fashioned out of the sounds he heard in his head.

3

Wit and Wickedness: Is It All in the Brain?

Simon Baron-Cohen has a justified reputation as one of the world's leading authorities on autistic spectrum disorders (ASDs). He is not only a prodigiously productive and imaginative researcher, but also a brilliant popularizer, who has done as much as anyone to communicate the clinical and scientific understanding of autism to the world at large. This is not, however, without its hazards, the most striking of which is the Freudian slip of seeing the world beyond the clinic through clinical eyes.

In *The Essential Difference: Men, Women and the Extreme Male Brain* (2003), he argued that people with ASD, most of whom are male, were like men only more so. His reasons for suggesting this are tenuous to say the least but the argument goes as follows. One of the most striking features of autism is a "mind-blindness" that is expressed in an inability to see things from another's point of view, and consequently, to tap into, or empathize with their emotions. Many autists, however, will have preserved, or even enhanced, abilities to engage with the physical world, particularly in the sphere of logical reasoning about it. While they feel utterly at sea in social situations, they are at home in the world of facts and logic and material objects. Isn't that just like a man, who may be good at maths and not notice that you are on the verge of tears? And how unlike a woman, who will indeed see the expression on your face but not be particularly interested in your pitilessly detailed account of the spec of the latest car that has taken your fancy.

Thus, on the basis of the observed characteristics of autistic individuals who lacked empathy and yet are often hyper-systemizers, was launched the notion of the fundamental difference between the empathic female (ideal for nursing) and the systemizing male (ideal for engineering). The basis for the leap from the clinic to the entire human race, and for an essentialist account of the difference between the sexes that marginalizes cultural and historical factors, was a cerebral determinism. Men are low-empathy systemizers because they have low-empathy systemizing brains and woman are high-empathy non-systemizers because they have high-empathy brains that are less inclined to systemize. The reasons for this can be traced to prenatal exposure to testosterone expressed in differences of brain function and, more interestingly, brain structure.

Unfortunately, many of these differences remain controversial, with initial exciting findings disappearing when attempts are made to replicate them. Women, for example, were found in one much-publicized study cited by Baron-Cohen (Bishop & Walsten 1997), to have a proportionately larger corpus callosum (the structure that links the left hemisphere with the right) than men; as a result he speculates that they might have superior verbal fluency. Unfortunately, as he then admits, numerous less publicized studies have failed to find this structural difference in adults. What is more, the behavioural and psychological differences between males and females are small compared to the range of performance *within each sex* (see Eliot [2010] for a thorough, scholarly demolition of the tendency to ascribe sex differences to differences in brain structure and function). So much for the "male" and "female" brain.

In *Zero Degrees of Empathy: A New Theory of Human Cruelty* (2011), Baron-Cohen takes his neuralization of human differences much further and argues that brain science can help us to understand why some people are evil, even monstrously so, and others are not. His thesis has three key props: first, that cruelty is due to lack of empathy; second, that empathy exists in a certain quantity and can be measured; and third, that measured empathy not only correlates with, but it is due to, the state of something he calls the "empathy circuit" in the brain. None of these assumptions withstand close scrutiny.

Is cruelty due to lack of empathy? While many individuals are cruel because they do not, or cannot, be bothered imagining what it is like for their victims, empathy or its absence is not the whole story and sometimes may be only a small part of it. The pleasure sadists derive from hurting others is enhanced by imagining what their victims are going through: sadism does not treat the person as an object but rather *needs* the victim's subjectivity. In non-sadists, episodic violent behaviour may be provoked – and regretted – rather than enjoyed. Cruelty may also be prompted by fear or disgust. We may also be vile out of a desire to conform to others, as many social psychologists have demonstrated, and this is in part driven by an *over*developed awareness of what those others think of us. There are strong, sometimes irresistible, social pressures to treat our fellows abominably, as is evident from the behaviour of soldiers in war, lynch mobs and those who were responsible for running concentration camps.

Baron-Cohen himself points out that many of those who made the Holocaust possible were bureaucrats who were still capable of empathy but reserved it for those with whom they identified. He cites the example of the "Nazi guard who shoots a prisoner in the daytime but then goes home at night, kisses his wife and reads a bedtime story to his young child" (2003: 113). British bomber pilots – whom we think of as opposing, rather than being, evil – risked their lives to ignite urban firestorms that would foreseeably incinerate thousands of innocent children. And we don't have to look to such extreme examples to make this point. Tolstoy's famous story of the princess weeping buckets at the sentimental tragedy in the theatre while her coachman is freezing to death outside captures something about all of us. Holidaymakers in India may feel uncomfortable at the spectacle of starving street children but in most cases this doesn't spoil their trip.

The truth is that empathy and a potential for what may be judged evil behaviour are not only culturally dependent but also situationally dependent. And this is not always a bad thing. No one could be a surgeon and empathize with the experience of the patients he or she operates on, or at least not while performing the operation. It is therefore rather odd to think of empathy as a stable characteristic and yet this is what Baron-Cohen seems to believe. We all have empathy levels, he argues. They are normally distributed in a population: each of us has a place on his "empathy Bell curve". This leads to his second prop: a tool for measuring the empathy quotient (EQ). You can determine your own EQ by self-administering a questionnaire, which includes items such as "I can easily tell if someone else wants to join into a conversation" or "I really enjoy caring for other people" with answers ranging from Strongly Agree to Strongly Disagree.

Even if we set aside the distinct possibility that when the questionnaire is self-administered the EQ may simply measure the extent to which we are deceived about how empathic we are, the questions do not get anywhere near the propensity to the horrific cruelty that preoccupies Baron-Cohen. Indeed, those who have a low score on the EQ – and are ascribed "zero degrees of empathy" by this measure – are likely to be individuals with ASD (although I am surprised that they should be sufficiently self-aware to be reliable respondents) rather than violent psychopaths.

Baron-Cohen realizes this; so, by what seems like an *ad hoc* modification, he divides those who have a low-to-zero degree of empathy into "positives" and "negatives". People with autism are "positive", not only because they rarely intend the upset they cause by their blindness to the needs of others but also because they are likely to be systemizers, which in some cases may be expressed in extraordinary talents from which we all benefit. Being something of a systemizer himself, he finds that the systemizing mechanism in the brain has six settings, just like the empathy circuit: an amazing coincidence.

Baron-Cohen's main concern is with those who have zero degrees of empathy and no redeeming features. These are divided into three types: borderline personality disorder (Zero-Negative Type B), psychopaths (Zero-Negative Type P) and narcissists (Zero-Negative Type N). In fact, his EQ doesn't seem to enable him to sort out these terrifying, appallingly damaged and appallingly damaging characters and allocate them to his categories. So he has to supplement the questionnaire with a checklist to tell us "How to Spot" (his words) them. They include "Impulsivity" and "unstable and intense personal relationships" in the case of Type Bs, "performing acts that are arrestable offences" in the case of Type Ps, and "a grandiose sense of self-importance" in the case of Type Ns. Significantly, "unempathic" is only one out of nine characteristics in the case of the Type N. Nevertheless, Baron-Cohen believes that the fundamental defect in all these types is "zero degree of empathy". He hangs on to this simplifying belief in the teeth of the complex features of the individuals that he himself describes – because he wants to map their behaviour on to a putative "empathy circuit" – his third prop.

The empathy circuit (also called the "social brain") is an ensemble of at least ten areas, encompassing not only the usual suspects such as the amygdala and the inferior frontal gyrus, but also areas less traditionally associated with the ability to think about others, such as the anterior insula and the somatosensory cortex. In a book meant for the general public (of which more presently) it is difficult to judge the consistency with which these structures have been observed to be associated with social capacities (such as the anterior insula with ability to sense another person's emotional state). As already noted with the corpus callosum sex differences, studies that are repeated may fail to deliver the same results. What, however, raises one's suspicions that the identification of the "empathy circuit" is an exercise in neo-phrenology is the way the centres divide the labour between them. The allocation of jobs is quite modern, with the portfolio career replacing the single vocation. For example, the temporo-parietal junction on the right side plays a key role, we are told, in judging someone else's intentions and beliefs (so that it is important for that aspect of empathy which involves putting oneself in another's shoes), but it is also responsible for ensuring that you feel that you are in your own body (essential for putting your own shoes on) and for non-social functions such as attention-switching. This is impressive versatility.

And there is another difficulty. The allocation of different bits of empathy to different places in the brain raises the question of how that which is kept neatly apart is then brought together in the living empathic person. This may seem to be a non-issue because we are talking about "a circuit" whose components are all active at once, so that the "coming together" is realized in this co-activity. But this then raises the question of why they are separated in the first place and also from what viewpoint – or centre – in the brain the activity across the circuit is realized as an integrated totality.

These may seem to be questions for another time and for the future development of social neuroscience; but there is one question that cannot be postponed. It relates to the privileging of brain circuitry in the causation of empathy deficiency, and it is highlighted by the case histories where Baron-Cohen talks about people rather than about bits of brains. Consider Carol, who has borderline personality disorder. Her appalling behaviour towards everyone including her own children, her total self-absorption expressed in unstoppable talk about herself and her volcanic anger are easily traced to the hideous treatment she received as a child at the hands of her parents. Little further explanation is required: those to whom evil is done (early enough, intensely enough, long enough) may well do evil in return. More specifically, those from whom empathy has been withheld and who have been subjected to cruel treatment may be entirely without empathy to others and treat them with great cruelty. What would we gain from an alternative narrative that (for example) argues that chronic stress in early childhood may cause "arborization" of the basolateral nucleus of the amygdala and hence damage the empathy circuit, even if it did correspond to repeatable findings? Does it deepen our understanding of what is going on between Carol and the people who abused her and those whom she abuses in turn? Is it closer to the truth about empathy deficiency than psychological explanations not tethered to the micro-anatomy of brain?

Anyone who maintains that it is closer to the truth must at least concede, on the basis of the alternative narrative of interactions between *people*, that the cerebral empathy circuit, if it is an objective reality, is only one component in much larger (and better understood) circuits: namely, the circuits of interaction between oneself, other selves, and the world and society that make sense of them. The fatal error of social neuroscience is to imagine that brain circuitry is somehow an independent, overwhelming determinant of what we are, rather than a component of the complex dynamics of our social life. In short, it falls into the trap of seeing us as predestined enactors of a cerebral destiny or, rather, passive spectators of an organ that mysteriously has the capacity to initiate events in an otherwise causally closed world in which nothing is initiated by anyone. Our brains play their part, of course, but people act on each other's and their own brains. Brain-based explanations, even if they were plausible, would not trump people-based explanations. For example, the horror of the Holocaust is not to be explained by looking to intracranial causes and postulating an outbreak of a mysterious disease affecting, with stereotactic precision, empathy circuits in the brains of Third Reich Germans. If explanations are to be found, social psychologists, sociologists and historians will have more to offer us.

Even if biology were the best explanation of human behaviour, there would be no reason why we should stop at the brain, which is, after all, a product of genes. Baron-Cohen embraces this conclusion with indecent eagerness and devotes an entire chapter to "The Empathy Gene". (He needs anyway to appeal to genetic variation to explain why some people with appalling childhoods do *not* automatically grow up to have damaged empathy circuits.) The climax of this chapter describes the moment when he and his co-workers "waited with bated breath" to see whether there would be a correlation between certain genes and variation on EQ scores. "[I]magine our excitement", he says, when four out of sixty-eight candidate genes tested "showed a *strongly* significant association with the EQ!"

It is difficult to judge the statistics here, but I could equally imagine being disappointed that the other sixty-four failed to show a significant association. In the original paper, Baron-Cohen concedes that "None of our results would survive an experiment-wide Bonferroni correction for the total number of genes tested" (Chakrabarti *et al.* 2009). And although this is followed by a robust defence against the charge that the findings could have occurred entirely by chance, I think it would have been appropriate to put this finding in context before declaring in a book meant for the general public (although in parts its reads like a monograph) that "we had found four genes for empathy" in a chapter entitled (without a question mark) "The Empathy Gene". As Baron-Cohen himself admits, "Genes simply blindly code for the production of proteins, blissfully unaware of their ultimate long-range effects".

What is more, given that the genetics of something as clear-cut as autism (never mind variations in empathy in people not on the autistic spectrum) is getting more and more complex, with three papers in *Nature* published in one week in April 2012 (Neale *et al.* 2012; O'Roak *et al.* 2012; Sanders *et al.* 2012), it seems unlikely that there will be much of a connection between genes and something as ill defined as empathy. Indeed, genes are a long way from the kinds of awareness and respect for norms that separate empathic from psychopathic behaviour. Complex traits are the result of epigenetic and non-genetic influences, not least those that modulate gene expression. The vast majority of these influences are best described in environmental, in particular, sociological, rather than neurological, terms.

Baron-Cohen's brain-centred story of what makes us evil is flawed at many levels, not least because it does not separate individual from collective, or impulsive from organized, wickedness. But it would be remiss of me not to report one abiding impression left by this book: the deep humanity that informs his enquiry, expressed not only in his horror of the evil things we do to each other but also in his ache to do something about it and his wanting to reach out, to redeem, even those who are beyond the reach of sympathy and of whom many would say "Lock 'em up and throw away the key". But scientific claims must stand or fall by the quality of the relevant arguments and data, not by the goodness of the intentions behind them.

In some respects, trying to explain humour is even braver than trying to make neurological sense of evil. This, however, is what Matthew Hurley, Daniel Dennett and Reginald Adams do in *Inside Jokes: Using Humor to Reverse-Engineer the Human Mind* (2012). If it is true, as Nietzsche said in *Human, All Too Human*, that "a witticism is an epigram on the death of a feeling" (vol. 2, pt 1, §202), it is equally true that every explanation of a joke risks being an autopsy. Their book is peppered with hundreds of jokes, some of them excellent, but the smile they put on this reader's face was soon wiped off and replaced with a frown as I tried to concentrate on the complex claims the authors make about what neuroscience and evolution tell us about humour and what humour tells us about evolution and neuroscience.

There is an excellent survey of the front-running theories about what it is that makes us laugh. This is a formidable challenge because an adequate explanation would have to encompass puns and wordplay, wisecracks, funny faces, rude noises, caricatures, situation comedies, slapstick, cartoons and dignitaries falling on their dignified bottoms. Play, assertion of superiority, release from excessive nervous arousal, incongruity resolution, surprise and the observation of mechanical inelasticity in humans capture some aspects of the beast but, the authors argue, these are merely symptoms of a deeper cause and to find this we need to look to biology. Only an evolutionary perspective, they believe, can unify the protean manifestations of humour and answer the total of twenty questions (all listed) they feel need to be addressed when we try to make sense of laughter.

Their answer neatly encompasses "What is humour *for*?" and "How does it work?" They note that humour, most obviously in the case of jokes, is characterized by surprise, as when you are seduced into an agreement with the apparent premises of a story that are then pulled away. They support this with hundreds of instances, for example: "I celebrated Thanksgiving in the old-fashioned way.

I invited everyone in my neighbourhood to my house and we had an enormous feast, and then I killed them and took their land" (Jon Stewart).

Jokes expose our propensity to have presuppositions, precisely those presuppositions that are necessary for us to function at the requisite quick-witted speed if we are to survive. The slow-witted shall inherit the grave. Our brains are therefore "engaged full time in real-time (risky) heuristic search, generating presumptions about what will be experienced in every domain". Inevitably, some of these presumptions will be wrong. There has, therefore, "to be a policy of double-checking these candidate beliefs and surmisings, and the discovery of these at breakneck speed is maintained by a powerful reward system – the feeling of humor, mirth – that must support this activity". Humour is useful, in short, because it trains us to challenge presuppositions; and it is rewarded with pleasure – to the point where it may become addictive – because it is so useful.

My choice of actions from moment to moment must inescapably be underdetermined by the available facts. I have to jump to conclusions – courtesy of just-in-time spreading activation (JITSA) in neural networks – or it will be too late. The authors argue that JITSA is necessary to create "mental spaces" that close down the potentially infinite range of possibilities fanning out from any moment. This is revealed by what has been called the "frame problem" in artificial intelligence (AI), which becomes evident when we consider all the instructions that would have to be built into a robot performing even the simplest functions in an open domain. In deciding what to do at any moment, we have to compromise between considering all possibilities (which would leave us as a paralysed free gift to predators) and intelligently cutting corners in arriving at a best guess as to what is going on, what will happen next, and what, therefore, we have to do now. Hence the need for JITSA; but its confident pruning of the combinatorial explosion that would result from considering all possibilities, and all appropriate responses, thrown up by the infinity of rules implicit in the transition from a situation to an action to amend it, carries risks. Hence humour, which confounds your expectations and brings you up with a jolt, warning how presupposition can be dangerous. It is "always triggered by the detection of a false belief in a mental space". Humour "pays for its expensive reward system by protecting us from epistemic catastrophe".

The authors attempt to deal with the most obvious objection to their theory: namely, that we find many things that surprise (or even shock) us not at all funny – or rather funny-peculiar rather than funny-ha-ha. We find things funny-ha-ha, they say, when the belief that is confounded is *active* and *committed*. When it is not, we simply register an unexpected event as "funny-peculiar" or not funny at all. This doesn't seem terribly convincing, if only because it is not clear what is meant by "active" or "committed". There is also the problem of laughter: an expensive business that interferes temporally with breathing and can render one helpless. Besides, what makes some people laugh leaves others po-faced; or what makes you laugh on one occasion will fail to do so on another. The receipt of useful presupposition-challenging information is not enough.

The authors alight on the theory put forward by many thinkers that "laughter is a tool to facilitate non-aggressive play": an extraordinary suggestion, given that laughter is often extremely cruel and the prelude to much aggression and conflict. They, too, don't entirely buy it and admit that they find other suggestions from primatologists unpersuasive. Even so, they are committed to evolutionary biology as an explanatory framework as a matter of faith: something Darwinian will turn up.

They slither between mind-talk and brain-talk, via computer-talk, which is not surprising if you think, as they do, that the mind is neural activity, and that neural activity can be validly re-described using computerese. This makes the social sphere in which jokes are thought up, told and enjoyed seem something of an afterthought, especially as they opt for brain-talk as the more fundamental mode of discourse. So they discuss a search for "the neural funny bone" but add that it is not a single brain region but "a very complex, and structurally distributed system that requires a coordinated set of responses involved in generating expectations and associations, perceived incongruities, revision and coherence, and of course [!] the affective and expressive responses". Quite so. And their list of twelve or thirteen regions and systems would be enough to wipe the smile off anyone's face, particularly if one does not think of humour a property of the isolated brain.

In the end, *Inside Jokes* fails because the authors' neurobiological mission forces them to look away from the very domain where jokes have their meaning, a place that cannot be found in the standalone brain or translated into reward circuits in bits of the standalone brain: the community of minds, where the culture that leads people to find some things funny and other things definitely unfunny is forged. This is where we should seek an explanation of why we humans, who after all are not alone in facing the epistemic challenge of rapidly responding to situations on the basis of inadequate information, *are* unique in enjoying and cultivating humour. William Hazlitt hit the spot when he said that: "Man is the only animal that laughs ... for he is the only animal that is struck with the difference between what things are, and what they ought to be" (1819). This normative sense is the reason why we humans are the only objects in the universe that giggle at it. Tracing how the infinitely subtle modulation of our sense of "ought" versus "is" is exploited in humour would take us a long way from neural tissues and indeed from evolutionary theory. Notwithstanding value-laden talk of "reward circuits" and so on, brain circuitry, while most certainly not gormless, is normless. This makes the brain an unpromising place to find the explanation for laughter.

Indeed, I would like to place a bet that *Inside Jokes* could be rewritten without brain-talk and not much of substance would be lost. As it is, we have a rather wonderful collection of jokes embedded in a story cooked up by three authors who subscribe to one of the world's fastest growing faiths: biologism.

It seems that the search for the seat of wit in the brain or parts of it is as ill conceived as the search for a cerebral basis of wickedness. While saluting the ingenuity of the neuralizers of fundamental aspects of their humanity, one cannot but regret the energy expended in this futile quest.

4

Are Conscious Machines Possible?

THE BRAIN AS A NATURALLY OCCURRING CONSCIOUS MACHINE

For some people, the question is a no-brainer. Or, more precisely, a brainer. The argument, as expressed by the philosopher John Searle, goes like this: "The brain is a machine. *It is a conscious machine*... So of course some machines can think and be conscious" (1998: 202). The conclusion, however, is only as robust as its premises.

Take the first premise: that the brain is a machine. It is, of course, possible to describe the brain in machine-like terms if machines are defined in a certain way. But we at once run into problems. Machines are semi-autonomous tools. They get on with what they have to do to some extent by themselves. *Semi*-autonomous, *to some extent*. The most sophisticated machine in the world still has to be taken to the place where it is to operate and, more broadly, be plugged into the niche where it can function. It has to be switched on, tended and switched off. It also has a rather narrow function or set of functions, the definition of whose nature requires conscious beings. It is we, not our machines, who have goals; and those goals make sense only as part of a multitude of interlocking goals. If the brain was a machine and it was the kind of thing that neuralizers of consciousness say that it is, then its autonomy would be of an entirely different order from that of any machines we know.

Another, more liberal, way of defining a machine is that of a system whose inputs are turned into outputs by means of intermediate processes that operate on the inputs. This definition, however, is so broad that it can be extended to encompass any physical system with distinct inputs and outputs. Under such circumstances, the entire universe can be described as a gigantic machine composed of countless sub-machines. Indeed, it has been thus described; for many people, the universe is a "computiverse" and it is engaged, end to end, in information processing (see Tallis 2011a: ch. 5). This is expressed by Paul Davies as follows:

> Compare the activity of the computer with a natural physical system – for example, a planet going round the sun. The state of the system at any instant can be specified by giving the position and velocity of the planet. These are the input data. The relevant numbers can be given in binary arithmetic, as a bit string of ones and zeros. At some later time the planet will have a new position and velocity, which can be described by another bit string: these are the output data. The planet has succeeded in converting one bit string into another, and is therefore in a sense a computer. The "program" it has used in this conversion is a set of physical laws (Newton's laws of motion and gravitation). (1993: 118)

Extending the notion of machine in this way deprives it of specific meaning. What has gone wrong? It overlooks the fact that, without a conscious observer to create a frame of reference that circumscribes a system and makes some events "inputs" and others "outputs" and connect the two by "programmes" or "central processes", there is no "machine" as such. So to describe the brain as a machine is not sufficient: it must be a special type of machine.

The trouble is that the usual way of specifying what kind of machine it is does not help us to deal with the "pan-machinism" just discussed. The commonest way of describing the brain-machine, or the vast coalition of machines that the brain comprises, is as some kind of computer: digital, analogue, serial parallel, actual, virtual. But much of the activity that takes place in the brain is not associated with consciousness, including that which is the necessary underpinning of consciousness. The mindless automata observed by neuroscientists in the brains of insects, monkeys and humans have to rely on an outside observer to circumscribe them and to define some events around them as inputs, others as outputs, and yet others as internal processing. Relying on borrowed consciousness to define them puts them in the same boat as all those processes in the extra-cerebral universe that are ascribed machine status by Davies and many other thinkers too numerous to list.

But, it might be argued, the brain *is* conscious in some overall sense. There are two problems with this. The most immediately relevant one is that the brain's consciousness is not of its own processes except in so far as the brain is of a person forming part of a community of minds working on, or reading about, neuroscience. The consciousness of the brain (if we allow this notion) is not such as to pick out the component "machines" that cooperate to enable the brain to do what people say brains do. The brain, if it can be said to be conscious, is conscious not of itself but of its world.

So there is a problem in describing the brain as a machine, except in the banal sense of something that has inputs and outputs, although even that sense relies on a borrowed conscious viewpoint. But there is just as much of a problem with describing brains – as opposed to people – as conscious. I won't discuss this here, because I have addressed this elsewhere in some detail, including in some essays in this book (see Chapter 1, "Am I My Brain?" and Chapter 5, "David Chalmers's Unsuccessful Search for the Conscious Mind"). Let us instead set aside the idea that the brain is a naturally occurring "conscious machine" and deal with what is currently a more popular reason for believing that conscious machines are possible; namely that such machines can be constructed artificially.

ARTIFICIAL CONSCIOUS MACHINES

The fundamental idea is that consciousness originates from, and is guaranteed by, certain configurations of matter. The simplest version of this is that the consciousness of Raymond Tallis (let us call him RT for short) is located in the particular configuration of his brain. Two things follow from this: if RT's brain is destroyed or sufficiently damaged, RT's consciousness will go out; and if RT's brain is reconstructed neuron by neuron and those neurons are wired up in the same way as they are wired up in RT's brain, RT's consciousness will be restored. The story of his waking life will be resumed. A less simple, more abstract, version of this is that what matters is how the neurons are connected, determining the way they fire together and under what circumstances. Neurons of a sufficiently similar type that are wired up into networks that have the activity patterns replicating those in RT's brain will replicate or reawaken RT's consciousness. More abstract still is the notion that the material out of which the replica is made doesn't matter at all; what matters are patterns of neural activity and their propensity to be triggered by external and internal stimuli. This has led to the further idea that immortality can be guaranteed by storing the "information" in RT's brain on some other medium, a notion that is fatally flawed because of the confusion we have just discussed, and the problem of defining what is meant by "information" once we remove the conscious individual who passes on, possesses or receives said information.

Somewhere intermediate between the initial idea that RT's consciousness lies in the actual stuff of RT's brain and will be found in any material replica of it and the idea that RT's consciousness is to be found in certain abstract patterns of activity, howsoever, or in whatsoever, they are realized, is the notion that the essence of RT is in the way his neurons are wired up. He is what has been called, by

Sebastian Seung and others, a certain "connectome": the sum total of every connection made by all the neurons in a brain. (See e.g. Seung, "I Am My Connectome" [2010], an engaging, if conceptually wobbly and empirically aspirational, video). We can, in theory, learn how to specify RT's connectome by imaging his brain using technologies that will be available at some unspecified time in the future. If you reproduce RT's connectome, it is then argued, you will reproduce RT.

Let us call a replica of RT, created on the basis of a specification constructed by non-destructive tissue imaging, RTr. If RT and RTr have identical physical properties (micro- and macro-structure and activity), then, it is argued, RTr will be a conscious machine just as RT is a conscious machine. My argument against this is based on a critique of the assumption that RT and RTr will be cognitively indistinguishable because they are physically indistinguishable.

The most obvious objection is one that may not cut much ice with some philosophers: we do not have a clear sense of the sense in which the replica is identical to RT. The specification of RTr will be based on work carried out over years, on large numbers of slices of the brain, frozen in mid-activity. There will be parts of RTr corresponding to RT at 6.03pm Wednesday 6 May 2000 (Slice 2,000,000,007) and parts corresponding to RT at 6.05pm on Thursday 13 December 2012 (Slice 3,000,000,008). In short, RTr will be a higgledy-piggle of phases of RT, of states of RT's brain over many years. These could turn out to be contradictory. For example, Slice 2,000,000,007 could be taken when RT was in a state of terror and Slice 3,000,000,008 when he was feeling happy. If the areas associated with happiness and terror overlap, then we shall have a given part of RT in two different activity states.

We may not need to appeal to global brain states such as those associated with emotions to find contradictions. What RT is looking at, or hearing, at the moment the slice is taken will be reflected in patterns of activity. So you could have a version of RTr in which Neuron X is both firing and not firing, and both in communication and not in communication with Neuron Y.

This objection exploits an uncertainty regarding what it is that is being replicated. Is it a pure structure (the neural network, the wiring)? Or is it a structure that, on the basis of its history, will have a propensity to fire in a certain way in response to external or internal stimuli (the wiring with its habits)? Or is it a pure function (the firing pattern extracted from an ensemble of neurons, the habitual firing of the wiring)? The lattermost seems to correspond most closely to the idea in play; that what is replicated, common to RT and RTr, amounts to a photograph, as it were, of *an ensemble-of-neurons in characteristic action*. But characteristic action will be difficult to capture: the activity whenever the photograph is taken will be tied to the moment in which the relevant bit of the brain is imaged; in other words, the propensity over time will have to be inferred from a snapshot, from a single datum obtained at a particular time.

It is easy to miss this point, in part because we slide between neuronal micro-structure and neuronal micro-activity. In fact, a connectome *is* what a connectome *does*. Since being and doing are difficult to separate, we always have to envisage the connectome when it is doing something or other – either in State X or in State Y. Half way between being and doing are notions such as "patterns of excitability", putative standing states corresponding to propensities to respond to certain inputs and to produce certain outputs. But it is difficult to think of extracting and replicating those standing states.

The fatal error is to think of the neurons as the hardware/wetware and the patterns of excitability as equivalent to the software. While in a computer the program *is* distinct from that in/on which it operates – it can be brought in from some external source and loaded up – there is no such distinction in the brain. In contrast, the putative program is not inserted separately into the developing brain being loaded from without: as the brain grows, develops and is exposed to things that the person experiences, structure and function co-evolve.

There is another problem. Individual areas of the brain participate in a multitude of cooperative actions, and neurons join up in temporary innumerable coalitions. In short, context is all. What is happening in the area that is being photographed will mean different things depending on what is going on elsewhere. It is a bit like language: the meaning of words, of sentences, of paragraphs is context dependent. The photograph, however, takes the activity in a particular region out of context.

There is also the question of labelling or classifying the functions we photograph. These functions will not be divided into natural kinds; rather, they will be elements of consciousness or other items that we divide *according to our ordinary language*, which captures the way we conceptualize the world and our consciousness of it. (This blocks one important escape route: the idea, which I associate with Paul Churchland, that all elements of consciousness – ranging from the taste of Bordeaux to disgust at the government's approach to dealing with the economic crisis – can be re-described definitively as clusters of points or values in vector or phase spaces captured by neural firing frequencies. See his *Matter and Mind* [1988]).

PROBLEMS AND PARADOXES IN THE LIFE OF THE ARTIFICIAL CONSCIOUS MACHINE

It also opens up more serious, and I believe more profound, objections. If we think of the connectome project as Seung and others imagine it – which aims at a complete characterization of the brain as connected, up and running – brain slices will in fact be taken not only at different times when the brain is differently engaged but also from different people. RTr will actually be a rather generic circuit, whose specifications will be drawn from RT and (say) David Cameron, an anonymous criminal who kindly donated his brain (while living) to science, and various other characters. Each slice will have been lifted up from a different personal history, frozen at a particular moment. This personal history will have some features that are, at one level, common to all humans, but at another level will be unique to each individual. For example, the experience of eating an apple will fit differently into RT's history than into David

Cameron's history. He and I will value it differently and this difference will be reflected in activity over large parts of the brain. This problem will be more evident in the case of other memories and experiences, for example, visiting China (which I haven't done and Cameron may have done).

Let us dig a little deeper. When we think of replicating connectomes, we envisage what they do in general, impersonal and (as I shall discuss later) timeless (or at least tenseless) terms. When we talk about conscious machines, we think of them in terms of rather general functions, some of which will be evidence of their being conscious. But humans are utterly rooted in their singularity: their individual histories. The clearest evidence of this is that we have a very individual sense of who we are and this sense is underlined by episodic, person-specific memory that is quite different from factual (semantic) memory – and, of course, even more different from habit memory seen in animals and expressed in the shaping of discriminative behaviour. In the case of humans, however, even habit memory is personal: we have a private take on our own habits and we can recall some of the singular (and now private) experiences that formed our habits. Our sense of what we are is rooted in an explicit sense of our own past.

Contrast this with the "memory" of a neural network that has been "trained" to differentiate between (i.e. produce a different output to) a rock and a mine (to use the hoary old example). This is entirely reducible to the progressive alteration of synaptic weightings in response to feedback. What the network "detects" is not a particular rock (corresponding to singular memories) but a generic "rock" – which does not have any phenomenal appearances – or the difference between a generic rock and a generic mine, which is not a difference in phenomenal appearances.

Let us put this another way. RTr will be a composite of neural networks or propensities taken from different persons at different times. If conscious, it will have to reconcile the conflicting singular pasts and colourations of consciousness of innumerable different individuals. This problem is hidden away by our tendency to think at a very general level when we envisage artificial consciousness, above that of personal experience and the unique tone of consciousness that comes with personal experience. But an actual person has specific phenomenal experiences and tones of consciousness. Will experiences be settled for on the basis of the relative strength of presence of the nervous systems from which RTr is drawn: how much RTr, how much David Cameron and so on? Will experience be the result of a democratic neural vote? Or will apples and trips to China be allowed to have *no* connotations for fear of setting up a conflict between them?

Can we avoid these problems by taking the thought experiment to the limit and postulating that we are able to create a conscious machine RTr by drawing only on RT's brain and pulling this off in too short a time for his brain to move from one state to another, significantly different from, and hence potentially in conflict with it? Alas, this does not help, for all sorts of reasons, some of which go very deep indeed.

Let us suppose that we replicate RT's entire connectome at time t_1; or, more precisely, we extract all the activity in his brain and dump it into a pre-prepared connectome that precisely matches how RT's brain is wired together at that moment. It is all over in a flash: there is no time for conflicts to arise. What will go into the connectome? Supposing RT is sitting down, looking out of the window at a sunny view outside, as the electronic replication takes place, and supposing everything goes as planned, what will RTr's first moment of consciousness be? It will be of RT sitting down, looking out of the window and waiting for the electronic transfer to take place. Several questions arise. Here are two of the most pressing: what *sense* will RTr make of his present experiences; and what happens next?

First, what will he make of his present experiences? Not much, it would seem, unless he is equipped with the memories that make sense of them. Indeed, without the hinterland of memory they will hardly be full-blown experiences at all. While real RT, looking out of the window, will recognize that this is a window in his house, and those things over there are trees in the sunshine, and will remember with a smile of satisfaction how, when he last looked out of the window, he planned this experiment, RTr will have none of this. The difference between RT and RTr is that RT's brain arrived at its present state, or its excitability, by means of experiences throughout his life that built up his understanding of this moment, as part of the history of his life in the world, while RTr's brain arrived at its present state by means of an electronic transfer. It may be argued that it doesn't matter how the two brains (RT's and RTr's) arrived at their present state or that the journey to it was totally different. What matters is what they are *now* and since they are the same now they will have the same experiences, making sense of them in the same way.

Is this true? The most obvious point is that if RTr's experiences somehow contained the memories that make sense of those experiences in RT, all of RTr's memories would be fake: they would be ascribed to a past, a world, that RTr has not experienced or lived in. The duplicate would not have had the experiences to warrant having the memories of the original.

The question that arises from this is whether RTr could in fact have those fake memories. The assumption that his present state would guarantee not only a future like RT's but also a past that only RT had is based on the idea that the present state of a nervous system contains its past and can access it: in other words, that the nervous system not only has access to the states it has passed through in order to arrive at its present state, but that that state replicated elsewhere would have access to the states that it would have had if it arrived at the present state by the normal route. If the first seems highly unlikely, the second seems even more so.

Let us look at the first problem (which I also address in Chapter 1, "Am I My Brain?"). The neural theory of memory requires that a piece of matter (the brain or part of it) should contain or retain the causes that resulted in its present state; in other words, it should be capable, as it were, of looking causally and temporally upstream from the present to events that took place in (its) past. It is required, what is more, to appreciate that those antecedent causes are antecedent, that is to say in the past, distinct from its own present state, and belonging to a prior world it is trying to make sense of with the help of memory. The question of whether memories are transferable cannot be answered without investigating the extent to which individual memories can be separated from the individual world to which they belong; and the extent to which we can separate the act of remembering from the memory and from that which is remembered.

The second requirement is even more problematic: RTr has to reach causally upstream beyond its (or his) own history to that of the history of another item: namely, RT or RT's brain. The causal audit trail, in other words, has to pass through, or leap over, the processes by which the putative physical bases of memory are transferred from one brain to another.

There is another possibility. RTr does *not* after all immediately make sense of what is around him. He is effectively a rather elderly *tabula rasa* who begins his independent existence as a fully formed adult brain in the "blooming, buzzing confusion" of the neonate. Over time, he gradually acquires knowledge and understanding of the world and a sense of selfhood. This would, however, be rather awkward for several reasons. The most important is that it would be at odds with the notion that "I am my connectome", with the fundamental idea driving the thought experiment that my awareness of what is going on now, my making sense of it in the light of past experiences, and my sense of my very self, is identical with a certain replicable disposition of a particular brain. Perhaps less fundamental, but no less awkward, is the idea of an adult brain travelling up a neonatal and infant learning curve.

This might be a rather unhappy hybrid. Isn't this analogous, however, to the situation of an adult person recovering from a severe head injury? Wouldn't he or she face the same challenge? However, the analogy is not precise. The recovering patient is reacquiring skills he or she once had and retrieving memories he or she had once possessed, all on the basis of previous experience acquired in the usual way, underpinning the skills and the memories. RTr could not have anything like this to retrieve; in particular, there would be no episodic or autobiographical memories to guide his path into the future following his moment of delivery, oven-ready as it were, post duplication. More particularly, he does not have the procedural memories to guide him to the recovery of other memories, although it may be argued that these come along with the connectome.

The only way to get round this would be to imagine RTr being synthesized by a process similar to that which led up to RT. One would have to begin at the beginning, say with a few cells multiplying in a womb like that of RT's mother. In short, the only way that RTr could be a conscious machine like RT would be that he should have the same history as RT. He would have to be grown from scratch rather than synthesized. He would also have to have the same trajectory from conception to adulthood as RT has had. In short, he would have to be RT and not a duplicate. The unique trajectory leading up to RT can have only one occupant: the RT who grew in his mother's womb.

FURTHER THOUGHTS

This essay has been prompted by an inspiring talk ("Could an Artificial Mouse Be Conscious? Artificial Consciousness: How to Build a Conscious Brain") given by Murray Shanahan at the Frome Generation Next Festival of Ideas, in which he made a case for the kind of scenario we have been discussing. His presentation anticipated an objection (that I have not yet raised) that the brain does not work as a stand-alone organ: it is embodied and continuously interacting with organs and limbs that are outside itself. He therefore imagined his artificial conscious organism (in this case the mouse, because most work has been done on the connectome in this species) as being connected up to a mouse body. I did not, however, buy his argument for the reasons given in this essay.

In our subsequent correspondence, Murray felt that he could deal with my objection about conflicting states of the nervous system(s) from which the contents of RTr's brain would be drawn. He pointed out that in open heart surgery and difficult brain surgery, patients undergo deep hypothermic circulatory arrest to reduce the metabolic demands on the brain, so that it has more reserves to resist damage. After surgery is over they recover to normal function. The relevance of this technique, he points out, is that "it demonstrates that the brain's electrical activity can cease entirely (flat EEG), but the patient is resuscitated, without apparent effect on their memories, personality, and so on. In other words, it's structure that counts."

First the empirical observations. The "electro-cerebral silence" recorded at the nadir of cooling in patients undergoing operation cannot be demonstrated to be complete (see e.g. Stecker *et al.* 2001). The EEG does not reach much beyond the cerebral cortex and, although so-called evoked potentials were used to sample activity deeper down (in the thalamus and the uppermost part of the spinal cord), recorded "electro-cerebral silence" would not necessarily correspond to a complete shutdown of the brain.

Nevertheless, the extinction of activity relevant to conscious experience is radical enough to carry Murray's point; it is possible to resume normal consciousness after an interval in which the brain has been effectively silenced. From this it follows that preservation of functional microstructure – how the neurons are wired together, how they interact with one another, and how they are tuned to respond to internal and external stimuli – is all that is required. The snapshot is not of the neural network in a particular state but of the network with its connections and propensities.

This argument, valid so far as it goes, invites us to look deeper, and I would suggest more critically, at the very idea of artificial consciousness created by duplication of some features of a naturally occurring entity – such as RT's brain or RT's brain in his body – if what is replicated is not experiences and memories but the capability of having them. This seems to fit with the standard theory in which the brain is not a set of experiences and so on, but the possibility of having experiences and so on. The trouble is, this does not deal with the difficulties that have been set out already. Any memories that RTr has will be fake because they are not based on experiences had by RTr at the time to which the memories of those experiences refer. And without memory, experience does not make any kind of sense.

Our human lives, unlike material objects, have temporal depth. Our explicit past and explicit future exist side by side or, more exactly, impregnate, permeate and go to the heart of, our present. While the current state of a material object may be the product of past events and be part of the route to its future states, and *we* may be able to read its past and anticipate its future, past and future, they are not present in it.

It might be argued, as Murray did, that this point applies only to the question of creating artificial *human* consciousness and not, for example, to creating an artificial mouse consciousness. A duplicate mouse connectome – appropriately embodied – would likewise have no memories that were not fakes. However, it is arguable that the kinds of memories that cause trouble for the idea of artificial consciousness are not the habit memories necessary for the beast to survive but episodic memories and it seems unlikely that mice have such memories. At the very least, they have no sense of self to attach them to. An artificial mouse consciousness, therefore, could consist simply of present experiences whose "interpretation" would consist solely of translation into discriminative and appropriate, that is to say adaptive, behaviour. The artificial mouse could have an inchoate sense of "what it is like to be" itself to the point where it would, for example, be capable of suffering.

Perhaps this point could be conceded: it is possible to envisage artificial consciousness of this kind. This remains an empirical hypothesis to be tested, although it would be unclear how one might test it. The consciousness that resulted would, however, be desperately impoverished and would be remote from anything that would seem like human consciousness. Those who pay large sums of money to have their brains frozen in order that their connectomes could be reawakened at some future time when the science has caught up with their hopes are unlikely to get their money's worth. It would be better spent on having human experiences now, or helping destitute fellow humans rather than on a thin trickle of animal experiences later.

And they might anyway be disappointed even in this modest hope of deferred experience. There is no simple relationship between a network of neurons connected in a specific way and even such relatively unproblematic functions as eating. A living creature has to eat throughout its life but the structures with which it eats are utterly transformed as it grows up. We may assume that the relevant circuits, too, also change. Even more important is the fact that neural activity, most obviously when it is intense, will be associated with fluctuating electrical fields that will spread through a volume of brain tissue, altering excitability in a way that is not tidily confined to distinct circuits. And finally, functions are maintained throughout changes in neural structure. It is a basic premise of neuroscience that all experiences change the pattern of excitability of the neural circuitry and how the elements are wired together. I mentioned before that "a connectome *is* what a connectome *does*"; and it also *is* what has been done to it and what it has itself done. It is structurally highly fluid, conserving function through quite radical changes. In short, there is no mapping relationship between structure and function of the connectome so that photographing and then replicating the structure will, *in the absence of the relevant history*, result in replicating the function.

It seems very unlikely, therefore, that RTr, even when plugged into a replica of RT's body, will have the kinds of sensations that are afforded a mouse, never mind the ability to worry about the things that RT worries over, such as whether or not there can be conscious machines.

5

David Chalmers's Unsuccessful Search for the Conscious Mind

With the publication of his 1996 book *The Conscious Mind: In Search of a Fundamental Theory*, David Chalmers established himself as one of the most assiduous, honest, imaginative and talented thinkers working in the vast and overpopulated field of the philosophy of mind. In that tome, Chalmers did not avoid the abstruse and the technical where they were unavoidable, and only intermittently lost touch with the mysteries that strike us all when we think about consciousness. And for the most part, despite the difficulties, he also managed to explain his enquiries with admirable clarity; in this respect, he came across like the philosopher John Searle, only less combative, less sure of himself and less liable to brush aside or overlook the true problems of consciousness with dogmatic assertions such as that "consciousness is as much a biological process as digestion or photosynthesis" (which comes, incidentally, from a savage attack on Chalmers's book collected in Searle's *The Mystery of Consciousness* [1998]). If Chalmers's scrupulousness and attention to contrary views made his arguments long – sometimes wearyingly so – this was an indirect tribute to his seriousness of purpose.

The opposite of a sophist, Chalmers – then a professor at the University of California, Santa Cruz, and now a professor at the Australian National University and New York University – seemed in the book that launched him to prominence to be someone who really wanted to advance our understanding and his own, rather than simply to win adherents to a position. Nor was he a mere pedant. He proved more willing than many others in the field to experiment with views that were – indeed, still very much are – radically at odds with philosophical orthodoxies. Those views made Chalmers a target for mockery from that orthodoxy; from hard-line materialists such as Searle and Dennett, who, notwithstanding the heavy trade of insults that has passed between those two bruisers over the years, are both dedicated to the fundamental notion that the mental and the neural are one, and that the conscious mind is a solely biochemical phenomenon.

Chalmers's latest book, *The Character of Consciousness* (2010), at least begins well, and there is much in it to recommend. The early chapters are a significant contribution to clarifying and deepening the fundamental questions of the philosophy of mind:

> What is consciousness? How can it be explained? Can there be a science of consciousness? What is the neural basis of consciousness? What is the place of consciousness in nature? Is consciousness physical or nonphysical? How do we know about consciousness? How do we think about consciousness? What are the contents of consciousness? How does consciousness relate to the external world? What is the unity of consciousness? (*Ibid*.: xi)

The multiplicity of these questions is to be entirely expected, given that consciousness is, as Chalmers puts it:

> an extraordinary and multifaceted phenomenon whose character can be approached from many different directions. It has a phenomenological and a neurobiological character. It has a

metaphysical and an epistemological character. It has a perceptual and a cognitive character. It has a unified and a differentiated character. *(Ibid.)*

And that's just for starters. The mystery of consciousness is a network of mysteries, touching on the mystery of ourselves, the mystery of the intrinsic nature (if any) of the non-conscious world, and the mystery of our *knowledge* of ourselves, and of the natural and the human world. If there is such a thing as a First Philosophy, the philosophy of the conscious mind is it. It is the ground in which every other branch of philosophy is ultimately rooted.

Considering the profound importance of these questions, *The Character of Consciousness* ultimately turns out to be a disappointing sequel to *The Conscious Mind*, especially given Chalmers's track record of taking on the conventional wisdom that the answers to these questions are likely to defy. But it is worth considering this book at some length; for, notwithstanding Chalmers's distinctive sobriety and thoughtfulness, it is striking how much his work still falls prey to the same fundamental errors. The book will thus serve as an instructive case study not only in how befuddling are questions about the mind, but how attached are many prominent thinkers who study it to certain sterile approaches to the topic.

THE "EASY" AND THE "HARD" PROBLEMS OF CONSCIOUSNESS

"What is the answer?" she asked, and when no answer came she laughed and said: "Then, what is the question?"
(Reputedly the last words of Gertrude Stein)

It was as the clarifier of questions that Chalmers made his initial reputation. It was he who first proposed the now-standard distinction between the "easy" and the "hard" problems of consciousness. The easy problems are "those that seem directly susceptible to t^h

standard methods of cognitive science, whereby a phenomenon is explained in terms of computational or neural mechanisms" (Chalmers 1995), while the paradigmatic hard problem is "the problem of *experience*". An organism possesses the trait of experience when we can say that it is *like* something to *be* that organism, as Thomas Nagel famously, if confusingly, put it. This is true most notably and most elaborately of human organisms like you and me; it is also probably true of many vertebrate animals, but probably not true of any plants.

Philosophers of mind call specific kinds of experience *qualia*. These are the most basic elements that underpin the hard problem of consciousness and include, for example, the feeling of warmth, the taste of wine, the way the colour red looks, the sensation of pain, and the sound of birdsong. It is these that fill conscious life. In the case of humans, an experience, moreover, is always had *by* someone (and *only* by that someone): it belongs to first-person being, and so lies beyond the reach of third-person (or no-person) objective science. Anyone can witness and so equally partake in the fact that some physical event occurred; but an experience occurs only for one individual person or animal. (Consider the difference between watching a man stub his toe on a stone and experiencing the resultant pain.)

The distinction between hard and easy problems is useful – even profound. But it has been deeply problematic since Chalmers first proposed it, for the place where he draws the boundary between the two yields too much to those who believe neural and computational science can fully explain consciousness. He is too ready to consider parts of the mind that do not entirely belong to the physical world as being no more than physical way stations in the causal chain between sensory inputs and behavioural outputs.

This is evident from Chalmers's list of "easy" problems. It includes: our ability to describe our mental states, to focus our attention or deliberately to control our behaviour; how cognitive systems acquire and integrate information; and the difference between wakefulness and sleep. This list seems far too generous. One would have thought that information, attention, deliberation about controlling behaviour, and wakefulness are things about which we can answer the question "What is it like to be engaged in this?": so, for that matter, is dream-filled sleep, and so are mental states of just about any kind. Indeed, if these mental features did not *feel like* anything, they would not be what they are supposed to be (and a difficult, indeed paradoxical, set of questions would still remain about why they at least *seem* to feel like something). Chalmers's failure to see this fatally damages the enquiry that follows.

Even the first and seemingly least contentious item in his list – in his words, "the ability to discriminate, categorize, and react to environmental stimuli" – should put us on red alert. Although the notions of "stimuli", "environment" and "categories" can in some sense be used in our description of the behaviour of unconscious organisms such as bacteria, these terms are applied to them by extrapolating from organisms with experiences, and so ultimately owe their distinctive meaning to organisms that are conscious in the "hard" sense. By saying that so much of consciousness is amenable to a solely neural-computational explanation, Chalmers gives too much ground to those philosophers who believe there is no fundamental difference between a conscious organism and a mechanism, because they regard the conscious mind as no more than a machine for linking environmental inputs to behavioural outputs in the most effective way. This concession makes Chalmers's fundamental position that "consciousness is not physical" more vulnerable than it need be. And it exposes him to the accusation of inconsistency from committed physicalists, for whom the idea that there are items such as experiences is an illusion: merely ontological spooks left over from "folk psychology".

It is easy to see what unites the elements of the mind corralled together in the pen of "easy problems": they all have direct behavioural correlates. They are usually associated with events in the physical world, observable by anyone, and so at least some part of them can be described as purely physical. And this, for some, means that these can be entirely reduced and translated into physical events, namely their behavioural correlates. The behaviour associated with, say, waving your hand could be simulated by a zombie: a hypothetical being, often discussed by philosophers of mind, that *acts* like a conscious person but is not conscious. Because the actual *experience* of waving is, in theory, not required for you to wave your hand or (more precisely) for waving to occur, the experience must be regarded an accidental add-on. Even if the experience is something, it does not actually *cause* the behaviour of moving your hand, but is rather a sort of bystander to the event.

Of course, even from the evolutionary perspective adopted by most of those who reduce the mind to a physical way station between sensory inputs and behavioural outputs, there are grave difficulties associated with the idea that experience is, as philosophers of mind call it, "epiphenomenal": how could a trait that is incapable of affecting an organism's behaviour, and so its ability to survive and reproduce, be effective at propagating itself through evolution? Why would the capacity for pain evolve if your body could simply withdraw your hand at the requisite speed automatically without it?

Moreover, even if pain *were* epiphenomenal, the experience would nonetheless still exist, and would need to be accounted for and explained. The supposedly "easy" problems, no matter how one comes at them, still have irreducible, "hard" elements. This makes life difficult for thinkers who are committed to a reductive account of the mind, and Chalmers's work, despite his reputation for pushing back against that trend, falls prey to some of the same mistaken assumptions as them.

CONSCIOUSNESS AND ITS PLACE IN NATURE

From the outset, there has been another strange consequence of Chalmers's extension of the "easy" problems of consciousness to encompass activity that would seem to be inseparable from experience: the idea that consciousness extends in some sense to *the entire universe*, or that all matter is conscious. Known as *panpsychism*, it was this idea that earned Chalmers the scorn of Searle. We can see what this means, and why Chalmers adheres to it, by examining his use of the word "information".

One might be surprised to learn that anything involving "information" could literally be located outside experiential consciousness. (The use of the word to refer to the contents of computers, books and so forth is a matter of proxy: these objects store the *products* of a conscious person, and only become "information" when they are translated back into the mind of another conscious person. But as long as it is being stored in or shuffled between them, the content of computers remains "information" only in this indirect, honorary or metaphorical sense.) Far from being eccentric, however, the view that stuff outside consciousness can be "information" is (alas) entirely orthodox. The use of the terms "information" and "information processing" to refer to events taking place in the brain is the mainstay of much cognitive science; the soundness of this idea is the central assumption of the computational theory of mind that dominated cognitive science for nearly half a century. "Information" is used not in the sense in which you and I use it to mean something that is conveyed to me by someone or something, and of which I am conscious; rather, it is merely about the relationship between inputs and outputs in any system. Once this is accepted, we soon reach the position that Chalmers entertained in *The Conscious Mind*:

> wherever there is a causal interaction, there is information, and wherever there is information, there is experience. One can find information states in a rock – when it expands and contracts, for example – or even in the different states of an electron. So ... there will be experience associated with a rock or an electron ...
>
> It may be better to say that a rock *contains* systems that are conscious. (1996: 297)

In light of this redefining of information, it should come as no surprise that in his new book, Chalmers argues that "we have good reason to suppose that consciousness has a fundamental place in nature" (2010: 139) and that "consciousness and physical reality are deeply intertwined" (*ibid*.: 133). This may be true; but his reasons for holding it are not "good".

Chalmers arrives at this position in part by a process of elimination of other ways of seeing the place of mind in nature. He first points to the problems with various kinds of reductive materialism, which holds that the physical realm and the phenomenal realm (i.e. the realm of sensations, perceptions and appearances) are actually the same things. (Some kinds of reductive materialism at least argue that there is a difference in how we *know* about the physical and the phenomenal, although one variety believes that this difference can be eliminated, so that we could view our own experiences as purely biochemical events.) Chalmers's commitment to acknowledging the hard problem of "what it is like" experience means he cannot hold to any form of reductive materialism. He then turns to dualism. One kind of dualism holds that physical and phenomenal events are distinct kinds of things, and that each affects the other: physical events can cause phenomenal events, and vice versa. This position, known as "interactionism", is roughly the same as Cartesian dualism and inherits all its well-known problems. Then there is a kind of dualism that also holds that physical and phenomenal events are distinct kinds of things but the causation goes only one way, so that phenomenal events are *caused by* physical events but cannot in turn cause or affect physical events. As discussed earlier, this is the idea of "epiphenomenalism", and it, along with interactionism, is beset by insoluble problems concerning how it earns its keep. According to Chalmers, this leaves only the idea that the intrinsic properties of the physical world are all also inherently phenomenal properties.

Surprisingly, Chalmers is not alone in giving serious consideration to this last position, which he calls "type-F monism": monism being the idea that there is only one kind of thing, as opposed to dualism, which asserts two. Indeed, the idea is gaining adherents: leading philosophers of mind, such as Michael Lockwood, Donald Griffin and Galen Strawson, have advanced similar views. Type-F monism (so called because Chalmers dismisses approaches he labels A to E, which it would be tedious to list) has its immediate ancestry in Bertrand Russell's monism in *The Analysis of Matter* (1927), although it was first expounded by Spinoza in the seventeenth century. For Russell, the idea came from his observation that physical theories characterize physical things only in terms of how they relate to other physical things, but do not tell us anything about the intrinsic properties of those things, which leaves open the possibility that some of the properties of physical things might be phenomenal.

There are, however, many problems with type-F monism, which is a form of panpsychism. Most concerningly, it would seem to spread consciousness, or something like it, too far: it would *feel like* something to be an electron, as Chalmers hinted in his earlier book. This was the view mocked by Searle in his review; it reminds us also of the Victorian novelist Samuel Butler's tongue-in-cheek line that "Even a potato in a dark cellar has a certain low cunning about him which serves him in excellent stead". Chalmers's po-faced claim about an experiencing electron seems even more vulnerable than Butler's teasing one about the potato.

Chalmers tries to get round this by suggesting that there may be something more fundamental than consciousness: some "protophenomenal" property, as he calls it, that is necessary for phenomenal experiences but not sufficient. It is *this* property that all matter possesses, and that is universally present in the physical world. Yet this seems a not especially helpful theory – matter itself already qualifies as the mysterious thing that is necessary but not sufficient for consciousness – but this insight is the beginning and not the end of the problems with type-F monism. Since we already well know that matter has the latent potential to become conscious – conscious beings arose in a world of insentient matter – how does the notion of a protophenomenal property make the situation any easier to grasp than trying to understand consciousness in terms of what we already know about matter itself? Unfortunately, Chalmers simply moves the problem on: What is the difference between the protophenomenal properties of a non-sentient pebble and the phenomenal experiences of a frog, or the experiences of a fully sentient and thought-filled human being? What is it that enables the merely *proto*phenomenal properties that supposedly pervade the air around us to become *fully* phenomenal properties when we breathe that air in and it becomes part of our brains?

With characteristic honesty, Chalmers admits the difficulty of answering questions like these:

> Our phenomenology has a rich and specific structure. It is unified, bounded, and differentiated into many different aspects but with an underlying homogeneity to many of the aspects, and it appears to have a single subject of experience. It is not easy to see how a distribution of a large number of individual microphysical systems, each with its own protophenomenal properties, could somehow add up to this subject of experience ... Should one not expect something more like a disunified, jagged collection of phenomenal spikes? (2010: 136)

The answer to this question is surely yes. Indeed, it is just about impossible to see how a distinct self such as "David Chalmers" could have been constructed out of the mere protophenomenal twinkling of the material world. Even less can one understand how that twinkling could in Chalmers distinguish between *itself* – a set of neural discharges, somehow aware of itself – and the rest of the world. His conclusion, therefore, seems to be more than a little optimistic:

> Overall, type-F monism promises a deeply integrated and elegant view of nature ... [It] is likely to provide fertile grounds for further investigation, and it may ultimately provide the best integration of the physical and phenomenal within the natural world. (*Ibid.*: 137)

Fascinating and remarkable as is Chalmers's long chapter on the metaphysics and ontology of consciousness, one feels compelled to draw the opposite conclusion: I wouldn't start from here.

DAVID CHALMERS'S UNSUCCESSFUL SEARCH

NEURAL CORRELATES OF CONSCIOUSNESS

One of the most impressive parts of *The Character of Consciousness* is Chalmers's investigation of the relationship between neuroscience and the philosophy of mind. In recent decades, neuroscience has increasingly focused on identifying so-called "neural correlates of consciousness" and describing their characteristics. Hence the rash in the media of images from brain-scanning devices that show parts of the brain "lighting up" as a purported explanation for various phenomena of the mind.

There have been various theories proposed as to how neural activity might become consciousness. One key fact, embarrassing for mind–brain identity theorists, is that the overwhelming majority of neural activity – in both the brain and the spinal cord – is not correlated with awareness of any sort. For some, this means that the answer is "location, location". Neural activity in, say, parts of the cerebrum is consciousness and neural activity in the spinal cord or cerebellum is not. Yet location hardly seems an adequate explanation of how some nerve impulses get upgraded from mere biophysical events to bits of awareness. *What* is it about the cerebral cortex that is special? What qualities does it, or whatever part of the brain underlies awareness, possess that the others do not? What *physical* qualities could account for the supposed difference between awareness-causing neural activity in the cortex and neural activity elsewhere in the nervous system that even hard-line reductionists agree is not conscious.

Various alternative theories appeal to neurobiological properties that are less anatomically localized. These include "systems", such as the one emphasized most recently by Gerald Edelman, in which consciousness arises from "loops" of activity between the thalamus and the cortex. Similarly, Francis Crick and Christian Koch speculated that consciousness might involve a particular sort of cell throughout the cerebral cortex, which has "a unique combination of molecular, biophysical, pharmacological and anatomical traits" (2001: 194). Other approaches focus more on what the neurons are up to than where they are: their patterns of activity, their intensity, their frequency, the extent to which they are synchronous, and so on.

But none of these characteristics seem likely to deliver the difference between neural activity that is and neural activity that is not associated with consciousness, not least because they all aim to narrow down a phenomenon that is inherently multifaceted. And the approach faces other inherent limitations. For a start, as Chalmers points out, correlation is not causation: even if one identifies some neural feature correlated with consciousness (say, by stimulating a part of the brain and having the subject report being aware of some mental state), it does not follow that this neural feature is solely or mainly dedicated to consciousness. More to the point, even if some of these phenomena do turn out to be truly and uniquely causative of consciousness, none of them would enable us to get a handle on the "hard" questions. As Chalmers candidly points out, "why should [some particular neural feature] give rise to conscious experience? As always, this bridging question is unanswered" (2010: 11).

THE UNITY OF CONSCIOUSNESS

Any theory of mind will have to address the particularly intractable feature of consciousness that Chalmers encountered in advancing his theory of type-F monism: its unity (which was touched on in Chapter 1, "Am I My Brain?"). The many experiences that we have at any one time – sights, sounds, smells and other sensations, as well as memories, thoughts and emotions – are in some sense unified. They belong to the feeling of *me-here-now*, to what we might call *co*-consciousness: consciousness of many distinct things all at once. This poses a radical challenge to any putative neuroscience of consciousness. The different contents of consciousness are supposed to be kept apart by existing in different parts of the brain; yet they are also required to come together somehow. And however this convergence is accomplished – say, by merging the pathways between the different parts of the brain – those contents would always seem, in the act of becoming unified, likely to lose their distinction, boiling down to a mush of undifferentiated awareness. The mystery is that the field of consciousness *is* unified while still retaining the distinctiveness of its contents.

This is the so-called "binding problem", and there have been many attempts to find a solution to it. These attempts mostly depend on the idea that certain physical properties *common* to large swathes of the brain can *bring together* activity scattered across different regions: all the different regions will be activated at once in the moment of consciousness, but without losing their spatial separateness. Proposed candidates for the special properties have included electromagnetic fields, quantum coherence and synchronous electric oscillations in large sections of the cerebral cortex. But as I observed in Chapter 1, all these candidates fail for the simple reason that they rely on *objective*, or externally observed, unity being translated into *subjective*, or immediately experienced, unity, with no reason offered for why this should be enough. If we accept that physical unity creates experiential unity, then the anatomical unity of the brain or, indeed, the body, should be considered of equal power to explain the unity of consciousness. But this suggestion makes clear that the theory would deliver too much, conflicting, unification.

Chalmers devotes an entire chapter (in which he is joined by co-author Tim Bayne, who had been his PhD student) to this mystery. He begins, usefully, by teasing out the different aspects of conscious unity. First, there is the unity of *elements* of consciousness that are all focused on the same object, as when I look at an item and see that it is red, it is a book, it is oblong and so forth. Then there is the unity of two items in my visual field that are seen to belong to the same space, as in a car that is near to a tree. There is also "subject unity", where two elements of consciousness are experienced as both belonging to the self at the same time. These kinds of unity can be further distinguished, as between phenomenal unity, where two conscious states are experienced at once (so that it is *like* something to experience both at once), and "access unity", where the two states can be accessed at once for verbal report, reasoning and deliberate control of behaviour. And at the most fundamental level, there is "subsumptive unity", in which all of the self's experiences are subsumed into a unified conscious field. This unified field is not simply the conjunction of all of the self's conscious states, but *is* a conscious state in and of itself.

Chalmers's main aim in highlighting the inescapable reality of conscious unity is to demonstrate that it is incompatible with some theories of consciousness that he wishes to discard. Among the problems besetting the search for neural correlates of consciousness is the unavailability – indeed, impossibility – of a "consciousness meter" which would allow us to directly detect and record consciousness. Instead, we can only infer the presence of consciousness through behaviour, most obviously the behaviour of someone verbally reporting that he is having a particular experience. This limitation has inspired one of the most ludicrous theories of consciousness: the higher-order thought (HOT) theory, advanced by City University of New York professor David Rosenthal. According to HOT theory, a mental state is conscious if and only if a subject is articulately aware of it. For example, I am phenomenally conscious of seeing red when I am having the thought that I am seeing it. So consciousness arises when thought lights up unconscious sensation.

HOT theory seems to turn everything upside down: surely thoughts *about* something would seem to depend upon *having* the conscious experience of that thing in the first place. Further, the having of thoughts requires at least some linguistic, or pre- or protolinguistic, mode of communicating with oneself. HOT theory is much like the idea that in order to be conscious you have to be self-conscious or conscious of being conscious, but it runs even more quickly into a regress.

Chalmers's critique of HOT theory includes the argument that it provides no way to understand phenomenal unity. While two conscious mental states A and B could be unified by the subject having the thought "I am experiencing A and B", this would be unusual. Just to become conscious of an object would require becoming conscious of all of its characteristics; this would be impossibly burdensome, because the thought corresponding to *what I am seeing* now would be endless. The prospect becomes even more mind-boggling when one attempts to unify the entirety of a conscious field: to have a *thought* about everything at once of which one is conscious (including the thoughts themselves).

Chalmers also uses the evident unity of consciousness to criticize representationalism, the hugely (and absurdly) popular theory that a mental state is conscious when it *represents* some object in the world, and when that representation plays a functional role in how the mind creates "outputs" in the form of behaviours. But if behavioural output is the direct product of consciousness, then the unity of consciousness would require a unified behavioural output. This is clearly not true: our behaviour is not unified in the way our consciousness is. I do not, for example, behave in response to an entire visual field, but only to something in it judged to have salience.

It is difficult to understand why anyone should want to defend either of these theories in the first place. Representationalism seems as vulnerable as HOT theory and for a rather similar reason. A *re*-presentation presupposes a prior, or primary, *presentation*, and it is presentations that are the fundamental stuff of consciousness: things in the world, and in our own bodies, are *presented to* our consciousness, and are *present in* it; and they must be present before they can be reflected upon or re-presented. This is true just as visual objects are the necessary precursors of *images* of objects, of reflections of what is there.

Representationalism and HOT theory both place the cart before the horse: the derived second-order contents of consciousness before the primary, the mediated before the immediate. This inversion is attractive because it is rooted in a longstanding metaphor that says the mind is a place in which the world is mirrored. The fact that one is conscious *of* objects out in the world seems to be explained by the idea that consciousness shares properties with those objects: the object is replicated in the mind in patterns of neural activity that are somehow isomorphic with the object. This notion can be traced back to Aristotle's claim that perception extracts the form of an object without its content, rather as a mirror image extracts the appearance of the object while leaving the object itself intact.

In other sections of the book, Chalmers expresses some sympathy for representationalism, giving it more consideration than it deserves, so we shall return to it in due course. But it is easier to understand why he chooses to attack it, along with HOT theory. For these theories aim to elude the hard problem by moving phenomenal consciousness, the problematic core of the conscious mind, to the territory that Chalmers has conceded to the easy problems. HOT theory reduces consciousness to "access" consciousness: to that which I can describe and report. And representationalism moves phenomenal consciousness even further in that direction: the representation is *caused* by that which it represents, and it is to be characterized in terms of the function it performs. In short, representationalism fits within the materialist notion that consciousness is fully wired into the causally closed material world, and the mind is simply a way station between sensory inputs and behavioural outputs.

COULD PHILOSOPHERS BE ZOMBIES?

Since Robert Kirk first released them in 1974 to roam the dark alleys of the Republic of Philosophical Letters, zombies – beings that are physically identical to us in every way, and that behave exactly as we do, but lack consciousness – have been haunting philosophers of mind. As we shall see, the zombie thought experiment is less interesting in and of itself than for what it reveals about the propensity of philosophers of mind to depart from the actual substantive questions into realms of technical minutiae and hypothetical fancy.

Contemplating these hypothetical beings raises some key questions for the philosophy of mind. Does the fact that you can (in principle) know everything about the physical processes of an organism without being certain that it is conscious mean that consciousness is something real and additional to physical processes? If knowing that a being is conscious means knowing more than the details of its physical composition, does that have metaphysical implications?

If zombies were possible, would we not have to conclude that consciousness plays no role in our behaviour – that it is superfluous, if not outright illusory? And would it not follow from this that, although our actions seem to be the product of the conscious decisions of free minds, they are really just physical processes that were destined to occur anyway in accordance with the laws of nature? A less disturbing consequence of the possibility of zombies would be that consciousness is not reducible to the physical, so it is something over and above the physical.

It is the latter conclusion that Chalmers is particularly interested in. Materialism is the idea that physical theory can account for everything that exists; but if zombies are possible, then something exists that physical theory does *not* account for, so materialism would be false. This may seem a small victory: even in this case, physical theory would still account for everything that *physically* exists, including all our actions and every physical event that occurs – which would leave materialism relatively unscathed and consciousness again reduced to a powerless bystander – but this is nonetheless what Chalmers is after. The key question, then, is whether zombies really *are* possible and, perhaps surprisingly to non-philosophers, this is where things start to get confusing. For Chalmers tries to base his argument that zombies are possible on the fact that they are *conceivable*. This, one might imagine, is no easy challenge. Is it valid to draw ontological conclusions from what we can or cannot entertain as possible?

"Conceivability" is a slippery notion, whose boundaries are determined both logically and psychologically. In order to set aside mere psychological limits to conceivability, Chalmers introduces the notion of "ideal conceivability", in which what is conceived of cannot be ruled out even on ideal rational reflection by a person without psychological limitation. If this gives the impression of circularity, nothing that follows dispels this impression. Nevertheless, his discussion of the relationship between logical, physical and metaphysical possibility, conducted in a whispering gallery of objections and rejoinders from a large cast of thinkers, is worth following. For this sort of discussion is crucially needed but typically missing from those thought experiments of which philosophers of mind are so fond. Even so, it also still ends up becoming a cautionary tale for how prone those experiments are to spiralling away from the realities they are supposed to help us account for or make sense of.

Numerous arguments have been launched against the premise that conceivability implies possibility. Chalmers deals with fourteen of them, the most important of which derive from Saul Kripke's argument that there are many true statements of identity that are both *necessarily* true and true as a matter of empirical discovery (i.e. true *a posteriori*) rather than out of logical necessity. For example, water and H_2O are identical; this is a necessary truth of chemistry, but it was an empirical discovery – there was a point in time at which it was not known. So we do indeed have an example of something that is *conceivable* but is not possible: namely, it is conceivable that water and H_2O are not identical, but it is not possible. Therefore we cannot agree that conceivability, or logical possibility, implies metaphysical possibility.

Chalmers tries to fend off this challenge to the notion that conceivability implies possibility. He invokes a response to Kripke made by Robert Stalnaker, who suggests that the statement in question actually expresses not one but *two* propositions. "Water" refers first of all to the *sensory* thing we experience; and this "watery stuff" could have turned out to have been made of H_3O or XYZ rather than H_2O. (To put it another way, we can imagine some possible world where what we experience as "water" turned out to have been made of something different.) In this sense, the proposition that water and H_2O are identical is only contingently, not necessarily, true. But "water" also refers to whatever the word *actually* picks out in this world – our physical world – and *this* connection is necessary, since the physical stuff known as water is identical to the physical stuff known as H_2O. Based on this distinction,

Chalmers claims that it really is metaphysically possible that the sensory stuff we call "water" could turn out not to be identical with H_2O. And so, it seems, the notion that conceivability entails possibility is safe, and the zombie thought experiment does after all show that consciousness is not reducible to the physical properties of an organism.

The water/H_2O relationship has also been invoked as an analogy by others in explaining certain features of consciousness, such as the relationship between perception and neural activity. Perception and neural activity, this explanation says, are identical, but they may not *seem* identical because they are different aspects of the same thing. An initial problem with this idea is that two different aspects of the same thing are *not* in themselves identical: the front of a house is different from the back of a house, even if they are both views on the same house. This is related to a point I have elaborated in Chapter 1 and elsewhere (in "What Neuroscience Cannot Tell Us About Ourselves" [2010b], and more recently in *Aping Mankind: Neuromania, Darwinitis and the Misrepresentation of Humanity* [2011a]), which is that physical events do not *have* intrinsic appearance, much less something corresponding to the contrast between appearances and what they are appearances of. This rules out the claim that perception and neural activity are two different aspects of the same thing, for "aspects" are a *kind* of appearance. That is, aspects are *already* a content of consciousness, and so cannot be appealed to in order to *explain* consciousness, even less the relationship between consciousness and its supposed physical basis in neural activity. More specifically, it solves nothing to appeal to *different ways of perceiving* as a way of explaining perception.

Although Chalmers does not himself directly invoke the water/H_2O relationship to explain consciousness, it should be clear at this point that he has really gone a long way round to wind up right back at the questions he started with. For as we have seen, the water/H_2O explanation is *already* laden with appearances, yet it is just things like appearances that the example is invoked to explain. And not only is "water" an appearance, but so, too, is "H_2O", albeit a mediated appearance, derived from measurement and theory. Both are ways of understanding and looking at the same physical stuff, so are different appearances of that same physical stuff. Of course, it is always conceivable that two appearances could refer to two different actual things; but in the case of "water" and "H_2O" it is not metaphysically possible, because they both refer to the same thing. So we do, after all, have an example of something that is conceivable but not metaphysically possible, and Chalmers's case for the possibility of zombies remains unjustified, and cannot be used to argue that the mind is irreducible to the physical.

Yet the reason Chalmers's logic fails has to do precisely with the nature of appearances. Specifically, appearances are distinct from the things they are appearances of and different appearances are distinct from each other. Both of these facts mean that an appearance is inherently distinct from the neural firings it is correlated with: the two are not identical. And all of these facts are evidence enough that consciousness is not reducible to the physical, without the need to expend, as Chalmers does, dozens of pages attempting to demonstrate that zombies are possible.

The outcome of the conceivability–possibility discussion would thus seem to be uncertain. The conceivability of zombies proves nothing (not least because a richer conception of consciousness, which acknowledges and accounts for its crucial role in shaping behaviour, would not permit zombies to be ideally conceived of at all). Unless, of course, we notice the obvious: that a world in which we can intuitively understand the difference between zombies and ourselves is probably not ontologically unitary – not made of just one kind of thing. Our ability to conceive of the zombie thought experiment may not indicate that zombies are possible, but it does indicate that, whatever its role, consciousness is something over and above its involvement in our behaviour, and there is a real distance between a conscious being and the material world it inhabits. And on this, at least, we should be at one with Chalmers.

CONCEPTS AND CONTENTS OF CONSCIOUSNESS

Perhaps not surprisingly, it is around about here that Chalmers seems to lose touch with the problems he set out so clearly in his earlier book and in the opening of the present one. The forty pages he devotes (along with co-author Frank Jackson) to the question of whether conceptual analysis is required to justify reducing phenomenal truths about consciousness to physical truths (e.g. about nerve impulses) seem to go round in circles. This is in part due to his continuing to run with the assumption that, even though it seems a matter of empirical fact whether or not consciousness is identical with neural activity, it seems also to be amenable to investigation by purely logical argument. He justifies the appeal to conceptual analysis on the grounds that it is supposed to be of particular relevance as to whether we should be allowed to maintain that the epistemic gap (i.e. the gap in how we get to know them) between the domain of physical processes and the domain of consciousness implies an ontological gap (i.e. a gap in what they really are).

Chalmers's case is not persuasive, and the intellectual effort required to follow a thread that rarely rises above the technical is not rewarded by proportionate enlightenment. Here or hereabouts, the fascinating mystery of consciousness drains away into gray dunes of endless argument and counter-argument, as we progress with all the celerity of a lichen growing over a rock to the opaque conclusion that "if the phenomenal is reductively explainable in terms of the physical, then there is an a priori entailment from physical truths, indexical truths, and a that's-all statement to phenomenal truths" (Chalmers 2010: 247).

It is, therefore, a relief (although only partially) when Chalmers turns to examine consciousness itself. He begins by making a sharp distinction between two sorts of mental states: experiences and beliefs. Experiences are "paradigmatically phenomenal" and beliefs are "paradigmatically intentional, characterized by their propositional content" (*ibid.*: 251). In other words, experiences are characterized by being, well, *experiential*, or qualitative, while beliefs are characterized by being *about* something. (The trait of a mental state being "about" something is what philosophers call *intentionality*.) But this distinction is already muddled. For it is not just beliefs but also perceptual experiences that refer to things: that have intentionality. Chalmers does admit that there is a point where the domains of belief and of perception intersect: namely, in beliefs that are about experiences, as when one believes that one is now having a red experience or that one is experiencing pain. This, however, is another muddle. When I see red or suffer pain this is not a matter of belief. It is not something that is vulnerable to refutation. I cannot mistakenly be in pain.

Chalmers himself recognizes this. He argues that "direct phenomenal beliefs cannot be false"; but in a later chapter he gives reason for thinking that they actually can be. His uncertainty is inevitable given the confusing nature of the phrase "direct phenomenal beliefs". If we take the view that these beliefs are infallible, then they are, of course, not beliefs – not even "direct" ones, whatever that means – for beliefs may be false. These muddles are so elementary (indeed, they are implicitly acknowledged by Chalmers himself) that they must serve some purpose. This purpose is to advance what he now calls "phenomenal realism": the view, for which he has already argued, that phenomenal properties are not conceptually reducible to physical or functional properties.

One way of revealing the autochthonous nature of phenomenal properties is to imagine, as Jackson did in a famous thought experiment known as "Mary's room", the case of a super-scientist named Mary who knows everything about the physical properties and functional relations of colour but is herself completely colour-blind. If, as a result of surgery, she were endowed with colour vision, it is obvious that she would have been introduced to something new, since phenomenal experience is different from the material world as revealed to or described in physics or physiology. This argument, it would seem, is sufficient to show that subjective experience is not reducible to the kind of objective knowledge that describes the physical world.

But Chalmers is not satisfied with this, and has to argue additionally that "pure phenomenal concepts and phenomenal beliefs are conceptually irreducible to the physical and functional because these concepts themselves depend on the constitutive role of experience" (*ibid.*: 274). He also refers to a "class of concepts that have phenomenal concepts as constituents" (*ibid.*). In other words, he asserts that some concepts and beliefs are irreducible by proxy by arguing that some of them depend on experience, and experience itself is irreducible. But this is a narrow and unnecessarily complicated way of asserting that we cannot see how such concepts could arise out of the purely material world. Indeed, how do *any* concepts arise out of the inert matter–energy interchanges of physics? Until we are presented with a plausible account of how the *concept* of "matter" arose out of *matter itself*, we should be prepared to argue that there is nothing in matter as described by physics that would suggest it could rise above itself, and enclose that which it has risen above in quotation marks. (It is this simple insight – and not the confusions, difficulties or incompleteness of quantum physics – that is the great challenge to materialism.)

Once one recognizes the *inherent* irreducibility of concepts, little more needs to be said on the idea of "concepts of consciousness". Certainly that little more need not occupy the nearly ninety closely printed pages that follow. Chalmers could have spared his readers a gruelling trudge, marked from time to time by what he seems to believe are bold assertions: such as that "a wide range of social concepts will turn out to be partly phenomenal" (*ibid.*), as if things could be otherwise. Society could hardly be established in the absence of phenomenal consciousness; and social *concepts* seem to exist about as far into the phenomenal realm as they could relative to the "microphysical" truths that he sees as fundamental to physics. Similarly, it hardly seems that Chalmers should introduce as an "intriguing possibility" the notion that "phenomenology could play a crucial role in a subject's *possessing* a causal or a mathematical concept even though these concepts are conceptually independent of phenomenal concepts" (*ibid.*: 275). The proper response would seem to be: you bet.

That Chalmers has to work at rescuing the contents of consciousness from the physical world is a consequence of what we noted at the outset: his allocating too much to the "easy" problems, ceding to physicalism territory that belongs to irreducible phenomenal consciousness. This is illustrated by his assertion that "many mathematical or philosophical concepts have no obvious tie to phenomenal concepts" (*ibid.*), which may be true, but does not mean that those concepts are not ultimately derived from an irreducibly phenomenal consciousness. Imagining that they could be generated by the physical world is the result of misplacing explicitness, which embeds concepts in the material world that they are *about*.

This tendency can go far into madness. Chalmers explores the idea that microphysical processes are constituted by computational processes: in other words, that reality is actually just one giant computation. (This is sometimes called the "it-from-bit" doctrine.) We should not be surprised at this development: since we have already seen how he believes that "information" can be found in electrons and rocks. Even so, it is interesting to note how the great difficulty Chalmers has in defending the reality of the phenomenal consciousness of features of the mind that clearly exhibit it has as its obverse a considerable willingness to find it in the material world, including the parts of it that are not even alive. If one tries to show how processes that could not occur without consciousness (such as perception and cognition) actually can be explained as purely part of the material world, then one will have to see the physical world as infused with things like "information", which, in normal, non-technical parlance, requires consciousness and first-person awareness. While *narrowing* conscious awareness to encompass only qualia may seem like an opposite move from *expanding* the presence of consciousness to the entire material world, they are actually both consequences of doing away with the gap between the way we talk about physical events and the way we talk about experience. This failure to maintain the ordinary, intuitive distinctions between the physical and the mental undermines Chalmers's project at its very heart.

REPRESENTATIONALISM REVISITED

It will be recalled that Chalmers rejected representationalism: the theory that a mental state is phenomenally conscious if and only if it *represents* some fact about the world and plays a functional role in transforming the organism's perceptual inputs into behavioural outputs. Chalmers resists reduction of experiential consciousness to causal relations manifest in a role in causing behaviour. Yet, in the chapter he dedicates to representationalism, he concedes far too much to the opposition. That chapter begins:

> Consciousness and intentionality are perhaps the two central phenomena in the philosophy of mind. Human beings are conscious beings: there is something it is like to be us. Human beings are intentional beings: we *represent* what is going on in the world. Correspondingly, our specific mental states, such as perceptions and thoughts, often have a phenomenal character: there is something it is like to be in them. These mental states also often have intentional content: they serve to *represent* the world. (2010: 339, emphasis added)

This passage repays close critique, as the wider muddle to which it belongs is pandemic in today's philosophical discussions of the conscious mind. It is guided by the misleading metaphor that we find in the passage above: the notion that an intentional relation is one of representation.

Consider a straightforward example from the field of vision. If I look in the mirror, I see a representation of my face. The relationship between my face and its mirror image is purely physical. The image is an *image* in virtue of having physical characteristics in common with my face: it replicates the surface appearance. It is generated by a causal interaction between the surface of my head and the silver of the mirror, mediated by light that has bounced from one to the other. Now consider myself looking at the image in the mirror. My sensory experience *refers* to the image, but is not a replication of it (at least, not in the sense in which a mirror image is a replication of the surface characteristics of my face). The relationship between my face and its mirror image is a causal relationship, whereas the relationship between the mirror image and my awareness of it is more than a causal relationship. Even if one believes in the neural theory of perception – that neural firings are the cause of perception – there still has to be, in addition to the physical cause, an *intentional* relationship, by which my perception *refers* to the mirror, reaching causally "upstream" from the nerve impulses in the visual cortex to the image that is located in the mirror. But there is no such intentional relationship between my face and its reflection in the mirror: that is, a relationship of representation, or potential representation, to be realized in a conscious being, and no more.

We can further underline the difference between representation and intentionality by noting that, whereas the mirror image is a *re*-presentation of my face, my perception of my face is a *presentation*. (My perception of the mirror image, then, is a presentation of a representation.) There is no representation without presentation (or "making present"). And for presentation, a causal relationship is not enough: it requires intentionality. The representational theory of phenomenal consciousness is actually one that Chalmers should eschew, because it brings him too close to the functionalism that would reduce the contents of consciousness to entities in the causal nexus that passes through the brain, linking inputs with behavioural outputs.

Chalmers is aware of this unwelcome alignment, and tries to wriggle out of it by attempting to preserve the intentionality of representations. This he does first by speaking of "pure" representational properties, which are characterized by "representing a certain intentional content". But it is not clear how an intentional content could be "represented", or why it would be necessary to represent an intentional content anyway if it were already sufficient for referring to something.

He tries even harder to rise above the trap of representationalism by suggesting that representational contents *correspond* to states in the world, and that they have "conditions of satisfaction", meaning that they can either correctly or incorrectly represent those states in the world that they represent. For example, the image of my face in the mirror may display a blemish, but that could be a flaw in the mirror, not in my face; so the image can be verified or falsified as a representation by looking at the thing in the world that it represents. The problem is that mere representations of this sort are simply physical effects of physical causes, and make no claim of satisfaction, unless, of course they lead to expectations *in us* that may or may not be fulfilled. But these expectations are an inferential relationship, and this is what Chalmers implicitly relies on to make his case, when it is just what he needs to be demonstrating.

Chalmers's entire discussion in the chapter on "The Representational Character of Experience" is marred by these confusions. His attempts to distinguish various features of representation – such as "pure" representational properties versus "impure" representational properties, the scope of representationalism versus that of phenomenal consciousness, and Russellian versus Fregean contents of perceptual experience (don't even ask) – end up weaving cognitive hairballs. The complexities of this chapter, and the detailed exegesis of these various distinctions, do not liberate it from its original terminological sin. Nor do they deliver this work from embracing the very reductionism Chalmers is setting himself against, which, as he says, understands representation in purely "causal, informational, and teleological terms". (The aggregation of these three descriptions is notable: "information" is reduced to causal relations, and "teleology" to a sort of causal wiring-in of the organism to the biosphere that ensures its flourishing.)

Ultimately, Chalmers does not persuade that he has made the case for his "nonreductive representationalism", which says that "phenomenal properties are equivalent to representational properties that cannot be fully characterized in nonphenomenal terms" (*ibid.*: 370). This theory is a way of hollowing out the most essential part of experienced consciousness – the experience of it – while acknowledging that it still sticks around as a sort of curious remainder. This, of course, traces back to the fatal first step, of narrowing the scope of phenomenal consciousness in our minds, so that many things are excluded from the scope of the hard problem. If the main tasks he described at the beginning – "the integration of information by a cognitive system; the reportability of mental states; the ability of a system to access its own mental states; the focus of attention; the deliberate control of behaviour; the difference between wakefulness and sleep" (*ibid.*: 4) – do not require awareness or internal experience, then it is easy to see how the barrier between phenomenal consciousness and "representation" could be broken down and the idea of the former could drain into a materialist account of the latter. Most importantly, this allows the causally closed material world to encroach too closely upon consciousness.

The question – which Chalmers poses at the beginning of the chapter – of whether consciousness depends on intentionality or the other way round is empty. Elements of phenomenal consciousness such as perception, conscious beliefs and other propositional attitudes such as fear and hope, are inescapably "about" something or other. The only elements of consciousness that might not be considered intentional are isolated qualia, such as feelings of warmth, tingling or the colour red. Yet even these experiences are dense, layered and multifaceted; more to the point, these sensations are *located* in, and so refer to, intentional objects: warmth refers to, or is *of*, a warm arm; tingling to a numb leg; the colour red to a red ball, or to a memory, or perhaps to some inner state of consciousness itself if one is, say, contemplating a Rothko painting. Although his sympathies lie with those for whom intentionality is grounded in consciousness, Chalmers admits that there is something to be said for the opposing camp. But this ought to lead him to the obvious conclusion that each is actually inseparable from the other, and that the opposing views are simply looking at the undivided pair from different angles.

DAVID CHALMERS'S UNSUCCESSFUL SEARCH

OUT OF THE GARDEN, INTO THE MATRIX

I can look at my perceptions (so to speak) in two ways: in terms of the objects that I perceive; and in terms of the "what it is like" to perceive the objects. Within the flow of everyday life, this is a distinction without a difference. I can, however, stop to reflect, and dissect my perceptions into components, which are likely to be sensations: I can say that I see a chair, *or* I can say that I see a patch of brown or a combination of shapes. The latter seems to be closer to what Chalmers calls "phenomenal consciousness", understood as "what it is like" to have an experience; the former is closer to what he means by the ill-chosen term "representational content". The relationship between these two is of interest to Chalmers. But a more interesting question is opened up by considering what we might call the layeredness of consciousness: the fact that, all at once, we have the experience of sensations; the experience of our body as the bearer of those sensations; the experience of ourselves as bearers of those sensations; the experience of embodiment; the experience of the environment of our bodies; and the experience of what I have called (in *The Knowing Animal* [2005]) "propositional awareness" – our sense *that* certain states of affairs are the case, that encompasses memories, our awareness of things before us in the world, facts, and so on.

Chalmers's starting-point seems to be an attempt to assimilate awareness, phenomenal consciousness, experience and the rest into the single thing that Nagel calls the "*something it is like* to be a conscious organism". This unhelpfully collapses all the many layers of consciousness, gathering up contents as disparate as having a tingling sensation, entertaining a belief and remembering a historical fact, but without carefully preserving their distinctiveness. Experiencing a toothache, seeing a horse, worrying about an exam in a fortnight and remembering the date of the Battle of Hastings are all tinged with phenomenal consciousness, but none of them is fully captured by the "what it is like to be" formula. It is this that prevents Chalmers's conceptual enquiry from getting beyond detailed and circular discussions of, say, "the interface between consciousness and intentionality". And his discussion of the contents of consciousness is equally impoverished. There is a difference between "What it is like to experience an orange", "What it is like to be Raymond Tallis" and "What it is like to be Raymond Tallis experiencing an orange", although it is not clear what "What it is like" signifies in each instance.

The mist clears briefly in the opening to a dense, seventy-page chapter enticingly titled "Perception and the Fall from Eden". In the Garden of Eden, Chalmers says (tongue in cheek), we had unmediated contact with the world. Then there was the Fall. We discovered that the appearance of things varied even when those things in themselves did not change: "we ate from the Tree of Illusion" and realized that there is only a contingent connection between what is in the world and how we experience it. And then "we ate from the Tree of Science" and discovered that our experiences are mediated in a more complex way by physical processes.

But this tale leads back into a discussion of the relationship between the phenomenal character of perceptual experience and its representational content, which seems like an endless circling around something that never comes clearly into view. We are repeatedly told things we probably do not need to be told, such as that "when a certain book appears red to us, there is a quite reasonable sense in which the experience will be satisfied [if and only if] the book in question is red at the relevant location" (*ibid.*: 385). And even if his notion of the "primitive" were clear, Chalmers's conclusion that "consciousness may consist in the phenomenal representation of certain primitive properties" would be a disappointing outcome.

If, as Chalmers seems to be saying, it is "Edenic" content in which we had unmediated contact with the world, then this is extremely puzzling. Even someone as hostile as myself to materialist accounts of consciousness cannot subscribe to the notion that we are "directly acquainted with objects in the world", that objects are "presented to us without causal mediation" or that Edenic content is "the most fundamental sort of content of an experience" (*ibid.*: 386). After all, we always see objects from a point of view that is ours, not theirs; if we manage to escape this limitation it is only by withdrawing from experience to measurement, to a view from nowhere in which the object no longer has a phenomenal appearance (and even this is only appearance at a great remove). In short, the idea of an Edenic appearance is a contradiction in terms.

But in the background of this discussion is the ever-present, crucial question as to whether perceptions really give us access to an outside world. Is it possible we might be systematically deceived as to the seemingly independent existence of the things we are conscious of? Are they in fact internal to consciousness, so that the world of objects out there is an illusion? Chalmers examines this question through the famous thought experiment dramatized in the cult film *The Matrix*. A brain is floating in a vat of nutrients and is stimulated, with the same sort of electrical inputs that a normally embodied brain receives, by a giant computer simulation of the world. The brain is entirely and successfully deceived. How do I know that my situation is any different? Hilary Putnam, who first introduced this thought experiment, argued (decisively, in my opinion) that the hypothesis that I am and always have been a brain in a vat can be ruled out in principle, because "brain" refers to (real) objects in my perceived world, as do "vat", "nutrients" and the "scientist" who set the whole thing up. The thought experiment presupposes the existence of the very things that it is supposed to call into question.

This would seem to leave the thought experiment for dead, but Chalmers squeezes forty pages of argument out of its corpse. He claims that it points to the possibility of a non-sceptical, positive three-part "metaphysical hypothesis". This hypothesis proposes: first, that microphysical processes throughout space–time are constituted by underlying *computational* processes (a daft idea that we have already touched on); second, that physical space–time and its contents were created by beings outside physical space–time (as many religions hold); and third, that our minds are outside physical space–time but interact with it (as Descartes argued). If any or all of these possibilities turn out to be true, then that would undermine the real existence of chairs, tables and bodies, but would mean that their fundamental constituents are bits of information, and originate outside space and time.

Chalmers calls these ideas "a creation myth for the information age" (*ibid*.: 466). Quite so, but he offers neither arguments nor evidence for their truth. And the very use of the word "simulation" to make the case undermines it: if everything is a simulation, then nothing is, not least because there would be no first-order reality to simulate. The philosopher Gilbert Ryle argued against drawing from the fact that perception *often* deceives us the conclusion that it *always* deceives us, by pointing out that "there can be false coins only where there are coins made of the proper materials by the proper authorities" (1954: 94). In other words, we could have no concept of illusion if all our perceptions were illusions. The same rejoinder applies to the metaphysical hypothesis.

More to the point, abstract computation lacks the actual content that is revealed (truly or not) in perception. A computer simulation, which is merely a mathematical shell of the relationship between physical processes, could no more deliver those physical processes than it could, without a subscription to the defunct computational theory of mind, deliver conscious contents. Our simulations of the weather do not create rain inside our computers. Chalmers's toying with what we might call "pansimulationism" brings him close to the panpsychism he entertained in *The Conscious Mind*, and this, when considered in conjunction with his sympathy for dualism, comes close to justifying some of the criticism that earlier volume received.

THE HARD PROBLEM WILL NOT BE EASY

How much further does this new book, of nearly six hundred closely printed, closely argued pages, take us beyond where Chalmers left the story in *The Conscious Mind* nearly fifteen years ago? Alas, it seems, not much further. The work he – and we, his readers – have to do is not justified by the conclusions he reaches, which are often trivial and usually provisional. The endless discussions of responses-to-objections-to-responses-to-responses give one the sense of an interminable in-house and inward-looking philosophical argument, in which the voices often communicate in shorthand. While it is entirely proper that any conclusions should be accompanied by a full presentation of the "working out" that led up to them, *The Character of Consciousness* seems less a work in progress than a work without progress. We reach the end without a clear idea of what has been achieved and what remains to be done. This is in part because the book is essentially a collection of papers Chalmers has published over the past decade. As a result, there is much repetition – admittedly this sometimes gives the reader a much-needed breather – and all of the to-ing and fro-ing undermines any sense of coherent direction. This is all the more reason that Chalmers ought to have offered a final summary setting out what had been gained, and the direction for further enquiries.

Most disappointingly, the excitement at the mystery of consciousness that glowed through Chalmers's first book is virtually extinguished. In part this is due to the fundamental error that we have seen pervade the book: of drawing the distinction between the territory of the "hard" problem and that of the "easy" problem in such a way as to hand over too much of consciousness to functional inputs and outputs handled by "cognitive mechanisms". Consciousness is rather emptied, and the sense of its being reduced to an abstraction is exacerbated by the scores of pages devoted to discussions of technicalities.

This is a great pity, for the seemingly inescapable failure of neural or materialist accounts of consciousness opens up a world of intellectual possibility. Just as rethinking the nature of light transformed our understanding of the physical world, shattering seemingly secure theories of physics to give rise to relativity theory and quantum mechanics, when we are finally able to account for the unfathomable depths of our own minds, it is sure to have profound and transformative consequences for our understanding of what kind of world we live in, and what manner of being we are.

6

A Conversation with My Neighbour

I have always believed that we should do our best to get on with our neighbours. After all you never know when you might need their help at a difficult time. Many of the essays in this book began as pieces for my regular column in the magazine *Philosophy Now*. *Philosophy Now is* a happy street and I particularly like the chap – Professor Joel Marks – who lives next door to me at "Ethical Episodes", *his* regular column. I can tell that he is a good guy because he has a beard like mine and, as is the case with me, the heat of philosophical thought has burnt off the hair that once adorned his cranium. What's more, he usually talks excellent sense.

Unfortunately, a little awkwardness has broken out between us of late. As is so often the case, the trigger has been the behaviour of pets: in this case, his dog. It's nothing serious. The creature hasn't eaten a long-awaited grandchild or chased a cat into permanent exile. It's about the dog cocking its leg. As always with seemingly trivial disputes, there is a bit of hinterland. So get yourself a beer, sit down, and I'll tell you the full story.

In "An Introduction to Incontinental Philosophy" (2012b), I reiterated my argument that our fundamental difference from all other living creatures, including even our closest primate kin, is evident not just in highfalutin' activities such as writing symphonies, debating the finer points of corporate law and fretting over transfinite numbers, but in every aspect of our lives, including the humble project of keeping ourselves dry by emptying our bladders in the right place at the right time. The article was another shot in my long-running battle with those who seem unable to see what is in front of their noses; namely that, while the *organism H. sapiens* is readily understandable in biological terms, *people* are not. Humans have taken the biological givens they have inherited from their animal ancestors and transformed them out of all recognition. They consequently live lives entirely different from those observed in the animal kingdom. One such biological given is urination. Our relationship to this simple and essential biological act is quite different (so I believe) from that of any other living creature.

Pretty unexceptionable stuff you might think. But my neighbour did take exception to it and was moved to write to our editor in defence of the good name of his dog (Marks 2011). He argued that his (the dog's) relationship to urination does *not* illustrate "the great gulf that separates us from the animal kingdom". It is humans, not dogs, who are slow to grasp the rules governing appropriate micturition: "it takes far longer to train a human being than a dog". Dog-walkers know that dogs "exercise a good deal of discrimination about when and where" to relieve themselves. And, finally, in the wild, dogs (and wolves) exercise "a pre-occupation with the niceties of marking".

None of this undermines my argument. The dog's urine-related behaviours are pre-programmed and are driven by present stimuli, quite unlike my decision to go to the loo now in order to bank some space in my bladder because I will not have an opportunity for several hours, or my making an appointment with the doctor to discuss my difficulty controlling my bladder. Humans take longer to be toilet trained than animals because in our case it is about grasping rules rather than the conditioning of behaviour. And it is also about our relationship to those who are trying to train us. Potty-training is in some instances a power struggle. The rule-governed choices of humans are not the same as the programmed responses of animals that prompt them to send messages by p-mail. To put it another way, the toilet-space of humans has no analogy in the *Umwelt* or world of the dog mapped by accidentally encountered scents left by other dogs.

I could bang on about the difference between the world of objective or factual knowledge that is the theatre of our lives, and the randomly encountered sensory world of animals, or about the way we live in a "semiosphere" (a dense realm of often highly abstract symbols) as well as the "biosphere" but I think my point is made. It is more important to look at what lies behind our disagreement. Professor Marks, I suspect, fears that, if we acknowledge the incontrovertible truth that our consciousness is fundamentally different from that of other animals, we might be more inclined to collude in their ill treatment. This does not follow. The fact that animals are profoundly different from us does not mean they do not have the capacity to suffer or that we do not have a duty to minimize this. *Or at least in so far as this is compatible with a due regard to our own welfare.* I presume that my neighbour agrees with this proviso and would have no compunction about swatting flies, stamping on scorpions roaming round the nursery or shooting to kill (without trial) a rampaging lion.

There is still, however, an important area of disagreement between us and I think this explains his resistance to the notion of a fundamental difference between the consciousness of humans and that of other animals. It relates to the exploitation of animals for our own purposes. He thinks that it is wrong and I think it is right.

In an earlier piece ("Veterinarian, Heal Thy Profession!"; 2011b), Marks argues that the Veterinarian's Oath should change its first priority from "the benefit of society" to "respect and concern for non-human animals" and that the relevant "society" includes "*all* sentient beings". This does not seem compatible with concern for our own lives or for those of our fellow citizens. Sentience, after all, is manifested in quite primitive animals. According to Antonio Damasio's latest book,

Self Comes to Mind: Constructing the Conscious Brain (2012), even invertebrates have minds. Marks seems to commit himself to behaving like Jains, who walk barefoot and sweep the ground before them so as not to kill insects, and the Tibetan monks who, according to Wade Davis, "remained indoors in the rainy season for fear of harming the abundant insect life" (2011: 116). This seems scarcely credible. At any rate, an uncontrolled insect population would not be a very healthy environment for humans, particularly in parts of the world less friendly than the ones in which Marks and I live.

If this is Marks's position, it is at least more consistent than that of many who promote animal rights in general but tend to focus on pretty, furry, cuddly, non-aggressive, non-toxic mammals rather than, say, poisonous insects that occur in death-dealing, disease-transmitting or crop-stripping plagues. But it is non-sustainable. His hostility to exploiting animals for our own purposes, what is more, would forbid our using them to lift and carry and transport in places where the relevant machinery is unavailable. It ill behoves those who have cars or tractors, or access to them, to deny others the use of bullock carts or horse-drawn ploughs. The alternative to using beasts to carry burdens is to make humans (at any rate the poorest and least powerful) into beasts of burden.

Marks's position most obviously leads to an anti-vivisectionist stance as he makes clear in a book review (2011c). This is something that my neighbour and I definitely disagree over. "No-one", he says, "has a right to impose significant suffering or premature death on another who is innocent and non-threatening" and "another" includes laboratory animals. Medical research involving animals is therefore "evil".

Time to declare an interest. I have never carried out animal research myself but for nearly forty years I was a doctor. The fact that the remedies I had to offer were more effective than those available over the preceding 10,000 or so years in which humans have sought medical treatment for their woes is entirely due to biomedical research that inescapably involves laboratory animals. Without such research, my treatments would have been as brutal, blind and worse-than-useless as they were in the fifteenth century. (For a glimpse into the horrors of pre-scientific medicine, I would strongly recommend *Orwell's Cough* by John Ross [2012]). Every reader of this book will have benefited both directly and indirectly from animal research, which will have saved or greatly improved their own lives or those of people they love. It is essential not only for testing drugs and other medical technologies but also for the background knowledge that enables us to understand diseases and to know where to begin in developing drugs, surgical procedures and other strategies to prevent premature death and alleviate suffering.

It is, of course, right that we should be constantly endeavouring to improve the welfare of laboratory animals and to reduce the number of animal experiments. (I have been involved with the Reduction, Refinement and Replacement initiatives that attempt to do just that.) But we cannot eliminate them. It is true (as has often been pointed out by anti-vivisectionists) that the findings in animals may not always translate to humans, as is evident in my own area of stroke medicine, but in the overwhelming majority of cases they do and animal research is still a necessary precursor to clinical trials. The alternative – experimentation on human subjects without prior animal testing – would not be possible for lack of volunteers and to proceed without consent is not acceptable outside Dr Mengele's laboratory.

So the case for animal research is clear-cut; or it is, if one subscribes to the view that human suffering and premature death are more important than animal suffering and premature death. And I do subscribe to such a view. It may be "speciesism" to care more for humans than animals and this is a charge to which I plead guilty: I am willing to sacrifice mice in order to cure children, not because we are more rational than animals (as this would lead to valuing infants and mentally impaired humans less) but because humans properly have priority. The world would be a ghastly place if people placed the suffering of frogs or badgers on a par with that of their own children or would be happy to allow their neighbours to starve if this were necessary to keep animals well fed.

A CONVERSATION WITH MY NEIGHBOUR

Opponents of speciesism, who argue, often from a utilitarian standpoint, that we should equate animal with human suffering, do not think of their own suffering or that of people they are close to. A utilitarianism that does not privilege *human* suffering – so that "The greatest happiness of the greatest number" translates into an utterly impartial calculus of pains and pleasures that seeks "The greatest happiness of the greatest quantity of living stuff" – leads to some deeply unattractive conclusions, exposed by the trolley thought experiment. A runaway trolley is at a fork. One limb leads to a human baby on the railway line, the other to ten kittens. Which way should we throw the switch? Should we save ten kittens or just one baby? I don't have any problem answering that question. Should I?

The fundamental solidarity of humans, our acknowledgement of each other as equals, is often frail but it is precious and it is in part based on the assumption that we value our fellows more than we value members of other species. Questioning this assumption takes us to some pretty dodgy places. Am I alone in feeling outraged at Thomas White, professor of ethics at Loyola Marymount University, who asserts that hunting dolphins or capturing them for aquariums is roughly the same thing whites were doing to blacks 200 years ago in the slave trade? *Roughly the same!* I would love to hear Martin Luther King's eloquent response to that equation. But it is a logical consequence of those who are opposed to what they call speciesism, whose very name implies equivalence with sexism and racism.

This doesn't sound at all like the kind of thing my genial, generous, wise and thoughtful neighbour believes, although it is a logical conclusion of his advice to the vets. I think I'll invite him round for a drink to talk things over.

7

Silk:
Metamorphoses Beyond Biology

> Does the silkworm expend her yellow labours
> For thee? For thee does she undo herself?
> (Cyril Tourneur, *The Revenger's Tragedie*)

It is extraordinary how far we humans have travelled in remaking the world in our image and filling it with our artefacts; how we have transformed our needs, and the appetites that correspond to them, into desires that are subject to endless elaboration; how in us alone has organic life become the lives of selves in worlds; how, unlike any other creature, we lead our lives as a multitude of interwoven narratives rather than merely suffer them organically. I have tried to describe this in many different ways in the books I have published over the past several decades. Here is a rather different approach from my usual, rather abstract, talk about "explicitness" and "cognitive handshakes": I want to talk about silk stockings.

Justice demands that I should begin with the creatures themselves, our unwitting beneficiaries, those silkworms who only 4,500 years ago started weaving for us rather than for their own future and became the involuntary servants of the incomparable beauty of the adorned human body.

The silkworm, to be factual and prosaic, even a little didactic for a moment, is the caterpillar phase in the life of the silkworm moth. It may seem odd, perhaps, to refer to the moth as a "worm", to name it according to its immaturity – like calling mankind "childkind" – but this is not merely the product of a human-centred vision. For the moth lives for only two or three days; it does not eat; and it seldom takes to the air. The female lays eggs and the male, so far as I can tell, does nothing.

By contrast, the worm phase is all action. The larva feeds ferociously on an exotic diet of mulberry leaves and grows steadily for forty-five days. The entire life story of this bulimic child is the transformation of very large quantities of plant matter into animal matter, resulting in a 10,000-fold increase in weight. (It does not even pause for breath because it breathes through holes in its body as it eats.) Action did I say? Not quite; for, other than this pauseless consumption, the larva does little and notices even less. It does not appear to be able to distinguish much apart from the difference between light and dark.

Only towards the end of its gargantuan meal of ten thousand merged identical courses of mulberry leaves does action that deserves the name begin: our hero spins a cocoon to protect itself during its transfiguration from a drab grub into a glamorous, barely dirigible, aircraft. The spinner tosses its head in a figure-of-eight and, after three days, during which it will have shaken its head about 300,000 times – the advantage of having a primitive nervous system is that you do not suffer the vertigo that makes the spinning of planet Earth explicit – it is entirely enclosed in a self-secreted bedsit where its makeover will be conducted in secret. (Think of the silence in that capsule as such momentous changes take place!)

Miraculous; but so far not unique. The larvae of many species continually spin adherent silk threads that give them an almost unshakeable grip on the surfaces on which they squat, so that tempests pluck at them in vain. This all-purpose material is also used in the construction of the nests, cases and shelters that protect the larva from the elements and from enemies. But what matters from the point of view of our present reflections are the distinctive properties of the threads that make up the cocoon where the silkworm changes from a grub-in-the-dark into a briefly air-borne creature of light and space and altitude.

The cocoon is composed of a single continuous fibre, nearly 1000 yards long. This is approximately 30,000 times the length of the creature engendering it. The silkworm is like a prodigiously prolific scholar encased in a library made of his own thoughts. The strength of the fibre is as arresting as its length: an elf could abseil quite safely from the highest building in the world equipped with only one cocoon's worth. Its strength is owed to its cunning design. Two filaments, secreted from two separate glands, converge in the so-called spinneret, from which the twinned fibres ooze slimly out. A second pair of glands secretes glue to hold the two filaments together.

Clothed or housed (the darkness of the ambiguity hides much, as we shall see) in a husk woven out of its own substance, the tenant of the cocoon is virtually self-sufficient apart from a bit of respiratory exchange and a little water loss. Not much material for a biographer there. In the darkness, however, there is drama of the most spectacular kind. Most of the worm's cells break down – this is called "histolysis" – as the adult structures are built up from existing rudiments. An ugly barge refits itself into a beautiful galleon that takes to the air.

Well, that was the end of the story of silk for many, many millions of years: until the human race arrived at a level of self-consciousness sufficient for certain ideas to dawn. From then on the silkworm's threads were woven into another tale. Another creature, with a different kind of awareness from the one that wound it, unwound the cocoon, having first steam-killed the solitary occupant to prevent an emerging moth from breaking the filament.

Some general comments about this creature, the one who gives or wears silk cloth, are clearly in order. The key to understanding *H. sapiens* is to grasp that he or she is a creature with a totally different kind of relationship to its own body from that of any other living creature. This relationship – the consequence of many causes (for the full story, see my *The Hand* [2003]) – includes instrumental attitudes to its body. The "ur-tool" of the hand makes the entire body something that operates on and with itself in an explicit way that is not known even to other primates. Uniquely self-used, we are consequently uniquely agents, and embodied subjects facing a world of objects. Man is a living being that "am" what it is. From the hand-tool a sense of material agency permeated the rest of the body. The instrumental relationship to the body widened to include many things the human body interacted with: the world in which you and I live is one of explicit causes linked to explicit effects. The hand-tool bred a world of tools. They were held in common with others, as a consequence of which tools created the basis for community – and, eventually, for language. And so, out of the interaction with the selved body and other selved bodies in the tool-bound community, there grew the complex human world to which human persons were, and are, addressed, and in relation to which they elaborate their self-consciousness.

This may seem dull and irrelevant but it was the wider context that eventually made possible the many steps that led from the spinnerets of the silkworm, denied its couple of days in the sun as the climax of its otherwise glamour-less life, to the glamour of silk.

Or one version of it anyway. Leaving aside just-so (or not-so) stories, one thing is certain. The idea of silk-weaving dawned in China about 4,500 years ago. What a strange idea it was and how many layers of understanding – out of the reach of the brightest visions of our sharpest primate kin – are incorporated in it! There is the prior notion of clothes: things donned and doffed, manufactured, sold and bought, in anticipation of meteorological, spiritual and social circumstances. There is the equally breathtaking notion of fabrication, whose most brilliant expression is weaving, beginning with the idea of unwinding the cocoon, and expropriating the silkworm's "yellow labours" on behalf of human wishes. And there are the large notions in sericulture: of industrial production, of trade, serving vanity and the dream of looking lovely and rich and beautiful.

The first notion is perhaps the most profound: the idea of clothes. While some animals seek shelter from the assaults of a planet that is colder, wetter, windier than is compatible with comfort or even with homoeostasis, their most intimate shelter happens rather than is made. The haberdashery of beasts grows from their own tissues. Human clothes, on the other hand, unite the character of the dwelling – namely that it is found – with that of the hide or fur that is grown; the pelt with the nest. Humans alone sport these portable homes, these moveable burrows, fabricated rather than secreted, capturing the waste heat created by metabolism, so that the body may warm itself at its own fires. The second notion is only slightly less profound: the making of clothes rather than simply finding them on, and ripping them off, the bodies of animals. While hides are halfway between things found and things made – the pelt has been cut and shaped but it is modified rather than manufactured – fabrics, by contrast, are entirely made. No stocking or blouse ever grew. Many distances separate this thing that is made from the secretions it is made out of. The cocoons are unwound to the filaments. The filaments from several cocoons are slightly twisted to make strands. Several strands are twisted together ("throwing") to make yarns. All with the aim of making an unconscious process – the secretion of filaments through spinnerets – serve a conscious one: making pure artefacts. And then the weaving can begin.

Weaving! So many steps, such miraculous transformations, to make the thread unite with itself in such cunning ways that it accrues into sheets. No wonder weaving is a master-metaphor for plots, stories, lifestyles. The creation of a two-dimensional surface out of the one-dimensional yarn is derived from basket-weaving, so we are told, but this makes the act of inspiration no less astonishing. No nest-weaving bird, after all, translated this action to fabric-making. No weaver bird really *wove* anything – or nothing, at least, worth wearing. Lengthwise warp and crosswise weft engage in excited dialogue, like partners speaking the substance of their shared lives. The result is a non-organic, unnatural growth, a pelt reared out of many processes, indefinitely repeated – shedding, picking and beating-up – guided by geometry in the service of beauty.

The marriage of warp and weft, of lengthwise and crosswise, takes place in a loom. The manufacture and care of looms involves yet another set of steps. And all this is only part of the process: a small section of the complex fabric of operations and actions and ideas and inspirations that is sericulture. There is the care of the worms that for hundreds of millions of years had lived and died at random. For a few thousand years, their mortality has been mitigated so that the purposes they unconsciously serve are not frustrated. They no longer merely live: they are farmed. They do not, of course, lead their own lives; but their lives are led. Their demands are anticipated and met. There is the rearing of mulberry leaves and their harvesting. And the culture and science of mulberry leaves. There is the preparation of the yarn; for example, the removal of the sericin – the gummy substance binding the twinned filaments emerging from the spinnerets – to make the silk silkier, soft, lustrous and semi-transparent, more like *soie* (which is the shot separated from the silk), closer to the haptic translucency of soft skin. And there is dyeing – how otherwise did silk stockings become so densely populated with whispers of darkness, when the spinnerets spoke so whitely? – and the theory of dyeing and the transformation of fabrics to make them amenable to dyes and the creation of mordant to make those dyes bite more tenaciously the fabric they adorn.

The fabric is created and then it is cut and stitched. How many implements? How many ideas? There is so much to be said; I must be selective. Let me focus on trade because it is so despised by the chattering classes, who believe they do more useful or elevated things. Besides, the journeys that connect the origin of sericulture in China with the silk dress worn on that special occasion – I cannot help now imagining my finger over the fabric, feeling the softness, the gliding, the slowing, the cushioned stop of the word "silk", listening to the faint contrapuntal scroop – are wonderful, spectacular, heroic.

The legwork from China to silk-stockinged legs extends thousands of miles – sericulture began in China but silk ultimately wrapped itself round many European bodies – and is a story spanning thousands of years and encompassing hundreds of thousands of human lives and yet more (countlessly more) ideas.

Let us look at the miles first. The silk route was at the outset a purely physical journey: wandering, and accidents, and chance encounters. Rumours that hung like the sheen of silk ignited the dreams of explorers – visionaries, madmen, fugitives, the curiosity-ravished – for whom the thirst for knowledge and riches was slaked by distances covered, corners rounded, mountains conquered. Rumours selectively culled by disappointment gave way to facts. Discovery and exploration turned to expeditions and expeditions evolved to trade missions. Wandering, tethered to the lodestar of a goal, created more or less standardized routes just as cries formalize to words. The pathless wastes were inscribed by paths and eventually peregrinations converged to an agreed super-path: the Silk Road.

The Silk Road began (or ended) 4,000 miles away from Rome, the capital of the West, in the capital of the Tang dynasty, Sian, in the Shensi province of China. The caravans followed the Great Wall of China to the northwest, skirting round the Takla Makan Desert, whose 100,000 square miles of waterless dunes are alleviated only by occasional tamarisks, nitre bushes and reeds: its thirst-lands are visited by few beasts and even fewer humans. The route climbed the massive Pamirs and the Kunlun Mountains, where shouts might travel for miles and still be unheard, and entered the high grasslands and peaks (up to 20,000 feet) of the Hindu Kush, which separate China from Central and Western Asia. It traversed Afghanistan, Iran, Iraq and Syria and finally reached the Mediterranean. From here the threads were shipped to Europe and Rome. Between the two ends of the Silk Road, a multitude of terrors visited the caravan: illness, death from cold and hunger and natural disasters, brigands and conmen, thieves and murderers.

The Silk Road was the only link between the two great empires of Rome and China. And so things were for perhaps 500 years. And then, as the Romans withdrew from Asia and the Levant fell under Arab power, the Silk Road became unsafe and (as the encyclopaedia says) "untravelled". And then – those "thens" like distant lighthouses far away and far apart – the Mongols in the thirteenth and fourteenth centuries revived the route, making it comparatively safe for travellers. (A route made safe by Mongols! One can imagine their style of community policing: a stop and disembowel policy.) They came to monopolize the Chinese silk industry. This was the route that Marco Polo followed in his epic journey.

Two legends, like the two wings of a silk moth, enable the history of sericulture to take off.

The manufacture of silk, so the first legend tells, began in China because of a happy moment in the year 2640 BC. (They did not, of course, then appreciate just how BC they were, how deeply buried they were in lucky ignorance of the Word made Flesh.) It happened in the garden of the Emperor Huang Ti, who was concerned that something was eating his mulberry leaves. (He was growing them for their fruit, perhaps to regularize the imperial bowel.) He asked his wife Xi Lingshi to investigate. She discovered that the predators were white worms and they were making shiny cocoons. Huang Ti would have ordered 10,000 malnourished pesticidal peasants to pass their days picking off these delinquents – and that would have been that – had it not been for a remarkable accident. Xi Lingshi dropped a cocoon into warm water and found that she could unspin the silkworm's life-work, draw out a fine filament and wind it on to other reels. And the rest – after, one presumes, pause for thought – is the far-from-silken history of silk.

For 2,000 years, the manufacture of silk was a secret. Imperial law decreed that anybody revealing the secret would be tortured to death. No wonder there were no leaks, at least for about 2,500 years, until the second century AD, when India developed its own sericulture. It still remained a secret that Asia kept to itself until the time of Justinian I, the sixth century (AD – time has passed) Byzantine Emperor. The story of war, diplomacy and trade that forms the background to this next phase of the history of silk is appropriately Byzantine in its complexity. At the heart of it, however, was a second legend, an amazing *coup*: an act of industrial espionage that depended on the courage and ingenuity of two monks.

Silk was the prime commodity of Byzantine trade. Raw silk reached Constantinople through Persian intermediaries and this was highly inconvenient. Justinian persuaded the two monks – described variously as Persian and East Roman (how time puts space out of focus!) – who lived in China to smuggle silkworms to Constantinople in the hollows of their bamboo canes. These illegal immigrants were the ancestors of all the varieties of worm that supplied European sericulture until the nineteenth century.

Whether these legends are true hardly matters. Given that the plain truth is even more extraordinary, they are at best pale symbols of the miraculous ingenuity and astounding tenacity that placed silk on European bodies. The frail chain of the realizations that led to Chinese sericulture is more miraculous than any number of tales of distant emperors and their distant wives. If emperors are invoked, it is only as an inverse tribute to the genius of the mass of humanity anonymized by the amnesia of time, just as we requisition gods to mirror and capture our sense of our own collective wizardry. As for the monks with their canes, they are emblematic of the astonishing fact that, somehow, sericulture was whispered all the way from China without the thread being lost.

First the raw fact of distance. How much greater in scale were these journeys than that of the bodies of those who undertook them. We are impressed by the silkworm spinning a thread that exceeds its one inch body 36,000 times. We should be more impressed by a human trail that, at 4,000 miles, exceeds the 6 foot human body 3,500,000-fold. Those 4,000 miles amount to 7,000,000 steps, not allowing for getting lost, for wandering off, for fleeing from assailants, for visits to whorehouses and cantinas in pursuit of pleasure and relief, for the thousand little digressions for food and washing and all the small change of daily living, and pauses for terror, amazement, illness and despair. It is more impressive for other reasons.

First, no journey of any length is entirely stereotyped, least of all a journey of 4,000 miles, which (in Marco Polo's case) took nearly a year. (Think of this: an action lasting a year!) There is no question of endlessly repeated figure-of-eight movements, a head-tossing like the girl in the advert enjoying the silkiness and glamour of her just-washed hair. Working out which way to go, acting on an answered enquiry, judging the best route up, round or over, the crinkled hazardous surfaces of the trodden, the barely trodden and the untrodden deserts, mountains, planes (avoiding wild animals, wild humans and rumours of both), was the reverse of stereotyped. The only invariant is an idea, an aim, a hope, a project, a duty, a dream, which informs and shapes if not each step, at least the patterns they add up to: as a million dots add up to a picture of a face. These singular journeys are quite different from the equally extended, but stereotyped, passages of migrating birds, who are guided along the path to their destination by forces of which they are unaware and who do not have to "work out" the route on each occasion.

Second, this is no affair of a solitary human being: a madman driven by an *idée fixe*. The thread of the journey is not secreted out of the substance of an individual living body but out of a shared existence in which selves and worlds are interpenetrated, or millions of selves address a world they have woven together. The trail is a story of cooperation and treachery, of assistance and rivalry, of a hundred middlemen, in which raw silk is exchanged again and again for fabrics, furs, leather, jewellery, wine, women, weapons, food, freedom. The continuity of the link between Europe and China is maintained not by a single thread from Sian to Rome but by the overlapping of threads, cross-bridged by exchange of goods, of words, of contracts.

This brings us to the third remarkable feature of those great journeys: the kit and caboodle associated with the caravans; the knowledge, the lore and the myths, the written and unwritten agreements, that held together the group journeying together for mutual protection against natural and human threats; plans, maps, sustenance. The register of items – tools and concepts and agreements – necessary to sustain the journey is endless. What is more, every item is the centre of a complex nexus of meanings and of history. Think of the panniers designed to carry passengers and goods. The ingenuity of slinging two baskets over the back of the burdened beast is too easily taken for granted, as is the wider ingenuity of the basket-weaving that was the first of the crafty arts. Each of the many objects necessary for the journey, embodying the general idea of a need, the standing possibility of a demand – from a cup, to a weapon, to currency, to a map – invokes a whole world of which it is the centre. To focus on one commodity alone: the maps – which superseded the experience of elders and the advice of chance-met strangers – carried a huge deposit of accumulated knowledge, understanding and intuition about the invisible world that lay beyond the horizon and its place in the wider scheme of spaces, hopes, countries and cultures.

The Silk Road, as a conduit for goods between the great civilizations – Rome, Persia, India and China – was also a conduit for ideas. Silk went westwards and versions of Christianity and Buddhism went eastwards. Nestorius' heretical notion that the divine and human natures of Christ were only rather loosely attached took root in India; and Buddha's Middle Way travelled along the Silk Road to China ("Fanatics have their dreams, wherewith they weave/A paradise for a sect" [John Keats, *The Fall of Hyperion*].) Inventions such as the stirrup, paper money and gunpowder climbed up the Hindu Kush while bubonic plague radiated across the globe between tamarisks in the desolation of Takla Makan Desert. The travelling silk merchants helped to weave, out of the warp of understanding and the weft of misunderstanding, the fabric of international relationships. Their paths and hopes informed the negotiations and treaties that permitted and barred free movement. Their weary footsteps threaded the stitches that globalized the globe.

Thus the story of silk: a long yarn woven out of human ingenuity, of lived time; a palimpsestic deposit of collective memory quite unlike the extraordinary threads oozed out of spinnerets that gave the journeys their purpose. All those decisions, all that fatigue, all that sustained tenacity of purpose as one foot is placed in front of another, as the sore thighs rub against the flanks of the swaying camel (2–3 miles an hour for 8–14 hours a day), all that shivering, sweating, weariness, those exercises of wisdom and folly, all those fevers, those inchoate thoughts drowning in seas of bodily humours, those century-long cold nights under the stars ...

The metamorphoses that characterize the natural world are miraculous but the additional steps made possible by the unique sharing of consciousness that characterizes human beings are no less so. For hundreds of millions of years, silkworms uttered thread from their spinnerets and the story ended with those brief hours fluttering in the daylight; and then the threads became "raw material" and a profoundly different kind of story began. When the Empress Xi Lingshi watched the cocoon relax in the warm water into which she dropped it, she could not have foreseen the fantastic fabric of stories that would have been woven out of it: the genius of looms and spinning wheels; the dyers' requisitioning colour from every corner of the earth and the technologies that supported the dyers' hand (from know-how about mordants to the know-that of the molecular chemistry of colour); the great journeys propelled by hope and fear, underpinned by agreements between individuals and treaties between nations; the skirmishes and the wars; the pleased lady and the jealous lady – and courtship rituals that go beyond offers of what lies ready-to-beak; the transmission of disease, gadgets and ideas – even unto ideas about the nature and purpose of human life; the booms and busts, the makings and ruinations.

We humans, fabricators and silk-weavers, have taken the laws of nature and ridden them to our own destination; we have unpicked the matted block of material processes and, as when we first began to unravel cocoons, have woven them into the fabric of our destiny dyed with our human dreams. The story of silk is a story about space (great stretches of it), time (millennia of it) and human consciousness (hundreds of millions of humans' worth of it). It is a story of our distance from nature. To know this story truly is to rejoice and in our delight recapture the lost joy of the silkworm moths, relocated in a special sunlight that only we who are liberated from the darkness of matter can know.

8

Should We Just Shut Up and Calculate? Does Physics Need Philosophy?

> Hans Bethe said that "Oppenheimer worked at physics because he found physics the best way to do philosophy".
> (Ray Monk, *Oppenheimer I*)

NATURAL PHILOSOPHY

Until comparatively recently, the relationship between philosophy and physics was reasonably amicable. As William Simpson has put it: "Physics was part of natural philosophy, and students of physics were trained in philosophical texts and forms of argumentation; they were men of *letters* as well as numbers" (2012).

In the beginning, philosopher and physicist were often one and the same person. It would have seemed odd to ancient Greek philosophers that they should refrain from speculating about the nature of the physical world. Most of the great Presocratic philosophers had their own theories of the character of fundamental stuff of which the world was made. In Aristotle's thought, there was a brisk and fertile trade between his philosophy and his scientific observations. Even Plato, who sought to look past or through the world as revealed to the senses and empirical investigation, and sought the true nature of things in argument guided by reason rather than in sense experience, was persuaded of the importance of mathematics: "Let no one ignorant of geometry enter here" is said to have been inscribed above the entrance to his Academy; and he asserted that "he is unworthy of the name of man who is ignorant of the fact that the diagonal of a square is incommensurable with its side".

Of course, there was a huge disproportion between the quantity of data and the scope of these natural philosophers' theories about the natural world: argument trumped observation. Even so, while we might not entirely subscribe to their theories or approve of the methods by which they were arrived at, their speculations about the natural of the physical world have left an enduring legacy.

This is true even of Parmenides, who argued that the universe was an unchanging, homogeneous, unitary sphere. Despite his dismissal of the deliverance of senses, he is the ultimate godfather of natural science, which has looked for uniformity under variety (matter or mass-energy with fundamental, universal properties) and seen change as concealing an underlying stability (expressed in equations, in the laws of the conservation of matter, and then of mass-energy, and in the invariance of the laws of nature). The most striking manifestation of the Parmenidean fixation of modern physics is the idea of the universe as a frozen space–time manifold. What is more, Parmenides' demonstration that the *appearance* of change was illusory (because the idea of change was contradictory) provoked fifth-century BCE philosophers such as Leucippus and Democritus to propose that the world consisted of unchanging, indivisible atoms, whose different configurations accounted for the change and variety that Parmenides dismissed as being illusions cooked up in our senses. Atomism has a claim to being the most important – fertile and far-reaching – idea in the physical sciences.

The close relationship between philosophy and those we now call "scientists" (a term introduced as recently as the 1830s by William Whewell on analogy with "artists") was maintained long after the scientific revolution in the sixteenth century progressively displaced armchair speculations – often with a theological agenda – in favour of empirical observations and the pursuit of quantitative laws. However, the mutual development of the natural sciences and of the mathematics to interpret, connect and guide scientific enquiry – whose most spectacular early example was the invention of the calculus to allow accelerated movement and continuous change to be captured mathematically – opened a widening gap between physics and philosophy. Galileo's famous assertion that the "book of nature is written in the language of mathematics" and his distinction between discovering "how the heavens go" (the subject of his enquiries) and learning "how to go to heaven" narrowed the scope of not only theology but also of a philosophy that had not yet quite emerged from its status as a servant of religion. Nevertheless, what we might call "active disrespect" for philosophy was a long time coming. Indeed, as Lionel Trilling points out, Michael Faraday refused to be called "a physicist" as being "too special and particular" and "insisted on the old one, *philosopher*, in all its spacious generality" (quoted in S. Ross 1991: 11).

PHILOSOPHERS RETREAT BEFORE PHYSICS

In part this was the result of a change of tack by philosophers, arising out of an uneasy sense that science had progressed while philosophy, trapped in its history, had stood still. While A. N. Whitehead's notorious claim that "the history of Western philosophy was a series of footnotes to Plato" was more than a little unfair, there is no doubt that many of the problems that exercised the ancients were still troubling contemporary philosophers – although they were formulated somewhat differently – and no resolution seemed in sight.

In the continental tradition, Edmund Husserl was only the most prominent of those who argued that philosophy, in the form of phenomenology, should be a rigorous "science", although the claim to science lay in the commitment to "rigour" rather than to empirical investigation. A series of philosophical movements in the English-speaking world (although much of their inspiration came from a tendentious reading of the German Gottlob Frege and the Austrian Ludwig Wittgenstein) saw the most prominent schools of philosophy retreat from a metaphysical enquiry as to the fundamental nature of things – leaving that to the natural sciences – towards a conceptual analysis of the terms we use to understand the world or, in its most unambitious manifestation, of the misuses of language that led us to ask metaphysical questions in the first place. Even those who were still committed to metaphysics often employed formal logic, making the exercise respectably similar to mathematics, sharing with the latter a satisfying opacity.

Another strand in Anglo-American philosophy saw the discipline as a servant of science, helping to synthesize its findings into a unified world picture. This evolved in some cases into a direct capitulation: philosophical enquiry into the nature of things was simply immature science. The philosophy of mind deferred to neuroscience and the philosophy of time looked to physics to answer questions about this fundamental mystery. In the past twenty years, the philosophy of mind has been dominated by *Neurophilosophy* (to take the title of Patricia Churchland's landmark text) which turned uncritically to neuroscience to tell us about the nature of conscious experiences and beliefs, moral sentiments, and even to settle the question of the place of the mental in a material world. And Putnam was speaking for many when he said that there are no longer "any *philosophical* problems about Time; there is only the physical problem of determining the exact physical geometry of the four-dimensional continuum that we inhabit" (1967: 247).

It is difficult to resist quoting Ernest Gellner's acid observation that "When a priest loses his faith, he is unfrocked. When a philosopher loses his, he re-defines his subject". Many philosophers saw themselves as uncritical junior partners of sciences, which they respected without being able to evaluate because they "lacked the mathematics". This trend (which I have called "science cringe") has been encouraged by spectacular advances in the natural sciences that have resulted in theories that not only have extraordinary explanatory (or at least predictive) power and underpin technological developments that are magically effective, but are also utterly remote from the common sense from which much armchair thinking originates.

Science has progressed, at least in part, as a result of ignoring the common-sense assumptions that inform our everyday thinking about how things are "out there". An early example, with profound consequences, was Galileo's demonstration that, in the absence of interference, heavy objects will fall just as fast as light ones. This is the opposite of what Aristotle – and untutored minds – would think. In the succeeding half millennium, the gap between science and the kind of common sense mobilized by armchair philosophers (even when they are *en route* to deeply counter-intuitive conclusions) has widened. An increasingly mathematized physics has gnawed at the very foundations of our ordinary understanding of the world, eating into the ideas of causation, of time and space, of location and identity. The most spectacular instance is, of course, quantum mechanics:

> The introduction of quantum mechanics may be the greatest scientific revolution to date ...; the replacement of classical physics by quantum physics requires a thoroughgoing modification of our world view; or, as philosophers might say, it requires a modification of our fundamental metaphysics.
> (Halvorson 2011: 138)

In short, to use a distinction borrowed from the philosopher Wilfrid Sellars, the manifest image of the world – how it looks to us as we go about our daily lives – and the scientific image have parted company. If it is the latter that tells us how things really are, then there is no place for the philosopher in the armchair: real progress comes from the empirical researches and the mathematical constructions of the physicists. In contrast with would-be revolutions in thought arising from philosophical speculation, those coming from physics have had practical consequences in the technology that permeates our every waking moment.

PHYSICISTS SNUB PHILOSOPHY

Bemoaning the fact that physics and philosophers were once so close that the physicist and the philosopher were one and the same person will cut no ice with many scientists. It invites the rejoinder: that was then (when science was weak and patchy and its methods immature) and this is now, when sophisticated, wall-to-wall science carries all before it. Science has simply outgrown its beginnings in philosophy. Humanity should put away childish things, such as empty, argument-driven speculation. Why, at any rate, waste time with barren philosophy when there is the alternative of a science that is not only practically useful but offers us testable ideas about the fundamental nature of things?

Such views have been expressed with considerable force by some leading physicists, most notably Stephen Hawking. He caused a considerable stir by stating that "philosophy is dead. ... [It] has not kept up with modern developments in science, particularly physics" (Hawking & Mlodniow 2010: 13). The Nobel Prize-winning physicist Steven Weinberg has been even ruder about philosophy: "The insights of the philosophers I studied seemed murky and inconsequential compared with the dazzling successes of physics and mathematics" (1994: 168). Worse still, "The insights of philosophers have occasionally benefited physicists, this generally in a negative fashion – by protecting them from the preconceptions of other philosophers" (*ibid.*: 166).

Many scientists who have little respect for what philosophers have to tell us about the material world do concede that there may be a place for political philosophy or even ethics independent of the enquiries of the natural sciences. I recently debated with Peter Atkins, an apostle of scientism and a leading chemist, on BBC Radio 3's *NightWaves* and he was willing to grant these scraps to the philosophers. There are, however, many who would deny philosophers even this. Those who appeal to neuroscience and evolutionary theory to explain human behaviour are confident that the job of political theory is to devise policies that go with what neuroscience has shown to be "the grain of the brain" and that ethics will uncover the evolutionary principles that should define ethical behaviour as well as explain its origin. So-called experimental philosophy – where philosophers investigate the intuitions of subjects thinking about classic ethical dilemmas, using brain scans, taking the confusion of "is" and "ought" to a higher level – is an example of philosophers giving up even territory that many scientists would be happy to cede to them.

THE PURSUIT OF A THEORY OF EVERYTHING

So has physics rendered philosophy, at least of the metaphysical kind, obsolete? When Sellars wrote that "The aim of philosophy ... is to understand how things in the broadest possible sense of the term hang together in the broadest possible sense of the term" ([1963] 2007: 369) was he not describing a role that has now passed to physics, so that if there is valid intellectual aspiration to arrive at a theory of everything, the place to look for it is not traditional metaphysics but natural science?

I want to argue that, irrespective of whether we shall ever arrive at a theory of everything, our theories will have a greater scope and be less prone to internal inconsistency if we supplement what the physicists have to say with what might be discovered by philosophical enquiry conducted in the time-honoured way: by an analysis and critique of the concepts and of the assumptions upon which any discipline must depend. In particular, philosophy may draw attention to something that the physicist inevitably overlooks – himself. This is an item that some scientists have recognized as a serious embarrassment and a threat to the very truth-claims of physics at its most fundamental level, as we shall see.

It will be resisted, of course. Many physicists will point to the almost miraculous power of their theories at every level: predicting new findings, cohering with or unifying other theories, and, of course, making possible the technology that has transformed every moment of our lives. Don't spend time fretting over the meaning of seemingly incomprehensible quantum mechanics, they say; it cannot be understood (and anyone, as Richard Feynman declared, who thinks they understand quantum mechanics doesn't understand quantum mechanics). No, just concentrate on the fact that it works. Or as the physicist David Mermin said (or didn't say – he attributes it to Feynman), "Shut up and calculate". But I would suggest that we should not shut up and calculate. There are some of us who will say (to take the old joke seriously), "Yes. It works in practice. But does it work in theory?" Or at least, does it make sense? And if it does not, how shall we set about making sense of it? And we want to examine what has been lost when we move to the scientific image of the world from the image manifest in everyday life, such that this huge gap in understanding has opened up.

Let us look at the case for this – essentially philosophical, indeed metaphysical – task by examining five areas in which physics is currently in trouble and will continue to remain so as long as it denies that it has problems: consciousness (in itself, and the consciousness of the observer); time; matter; the observer; and the fact that there is something rather than nothing.

CONSCIOUSNESS

There would be no physics – or indeed the everyday, shared human life from which physics eventually took its rise – without conscious human beings. Physics has grown out of the collective reality conscious humans have created. It cannot reach beneath itself to examine that upon which it is presupposed. Why not, it might be asked? After all, physics has made huge progress in understanding *matter*, notwithstanding that physicists and their instruments are pieces of matter. There is a difference, however. Physics begins with the assumption that the basic stuff of the world is matter – whose most authoritative description is provided by physics – and marginalizes that in virtue of which matter is made explicit: conscious human beings.

Early in the Western European scientific revolution, most of the actual contents of consciousness were excluded from the scientific account of the material world. As Galileo (echoed by many others since) stated, colours, smells, tastes and feelings of warmth and cold are not part of the material world: "If living creatures were removed, all these qualities would be wiped away and annihilated". The material world has only primary qualities such as solidity, extension, motion, number and shape. These are the proper objects of scientific investigation and, when the world is seen through the lens of physical science, are more truly real than experiences such as smells and brightness and warmth, which are regarded as merely "secondary qualities". They belong to the world of appearance, of subjectivity, rather than objective reality. Primary qualities, however, by themselves do not amount to a full-blown appearance. You couldn't imagine, even less experience, an object without a colour (and "colour" here includes black and white). As the physical description of the material world develops, so it becomes ever more purely quantitative and primary qualities are subsumed into mathematical equations.

This creates a problem (although it is rarely recognized) for those who want to find a physical explanation of consciousness by identifying it with (physico-chemical) nerve impulses in parts of the (physical) brain: there is no place for the contents of consciousness in the physical world, because secondary qualities are the fundamental stuff of consciousness and they are not intrinsic to the material world as viewed by post-Galilean science.

These and many other reasons for expecting that physics would have a problem with that which makes physics itself possible, namely the consciousness of human beings, are discussed in Part I (especially in Ch. 1, "Am I My Brain?").

TIME

One of the most striking gaps between the everyday world of the physicist (which is also the world of the rest of us who occupy the same days as physicists) and the physical world (according to physical theory) is to be found in the experience of time. The most obvious source of what should be an embarrassment for physics is tensed time: the difference between past, present and future. This is clear-cut and irreducible in the life of the physicist: he or she will regret, look back on, feel nostalgic for, or simply remember things that happened in the past; and he or she will look forward to, anticipate, hope for, fear, things that may happen in the future. In daily life, he or she will be preoccupied with things that are happening in the present or the near past or the near future, defined with respect to "now". And this lies beyond the reach of physics. Rudolf Carnap discussed this with Einstein:

> He explained that the experience of the Now means something special for man, something essentially different from the past and the future, but that this important difference does not and cannot occur within physics ... that there is something essential about the Now which is just outside of the realm of science. (1963: 37–8)

For some physicists, it is not merely tensed time but time itself that is unreal. The so-called theory of everything, which aims to reconcile the general theory of relativity (which summarizes the behaviour of material objects at a macroscopic level) and quantum mechanics (which summarizes what happens at the subatomic level) will, according to some physicists, do without the parameter "time". Admittedly, this is not universally accepted. For every physicist who celebrates, as does Julian Barbour, "the end of time" and who argues that a fully developed quantum mechanics will "kill time", such that the universe seen aright will be changeless and timeless, there will be one, such as Lawrence Bragg, who suggests that the collapse of the wave–particle duality into wave or particle is the basis of the difference between the past and the present.

In fact, the arguments of both parties seem void of the kind of conceptual clarity that would make it possible to evaluate, and hence adjudicate between, these opposing positions. Those of us who are not dazzled by physics – and reject the assumption that what has no place in physics is not real – might protest that the claim that the difference between past, present and future is unreal is itself unreal; and that the even more radical claim that the difference between "earlier than" and "later than" has no basis in reality should raise questions about what counts as real. In short, we want to send out for a philosopher to look critically at both the arguments and the conclusions and not be too dazzled by the mathematics.

MATTER

So ethics, norms, meaning, intelligibility, mattering, consciousness and tensed or even tenseless time lie beyond the reach of physics. But surely physical science has the last word on the material world and can tell philosophy to back off when it comes to understanding the subatomic world? Even here, however, physics cannot avoid problems that might be regarded as philosophical: problems that go right back to its roots in the marginalization of the conscious observer. One manifestation of this is the so-called measurement problem. Let me present a simplified version of this.

A fundamental notion of quantum mechanics is that there are aspects of reality that are not intrinsically determinate and that they are determined only when they are observed or, more precisely, they are measured. In the unobserved world, there is a quantum *superposition* of two states, such that an electron may be both a wave and a particle or may pass through both of two parallel slits in a screen. This superposition is resolved, so it is claimed, when a measurement is made. Unfortunately, the problem comes back to haunt quantum mechanics itself. This is the result of the fact that superpositions "percolate upwards": what applies to subatomic items may apply equally to large collections of subatomic items, including objects such as the brains of physicists who make observations. While it is true that superposition becomes harder to maintain as we move towards the macroscopic world, there is no fundamental way of defining the upper limit of superposition. It is worse. The phenomenon of "entanglement", such that two objects are so entwined with each other that they do not have any defined characteristics, also percolates upwards. This means that the state of the brain of the observer does not correspond to a particular observation or measurement.

In short, quantum mechanics predicts that those who establish and confirm quantum mechanics on the basis of observations will not have definite states: that is to say, will not have brain states that (according to physics and physicalists) will correspond to definite measurements. As the physicist and mathematician Hans Halvorson summarizes it, "quantum mechanics entails a fact ... that would utterly destroy our ability to test the predictions of quantum mechanics" (2011: 152), or, indeed, to arrive at the theory that would be exposed to testing against predictions. It has provoked David Wallace, a leading philosopher of physics at the University of Oxford to argue that "the measurement problem threatens to make quantum mechanics incoherent" (in Schlosshauer 2011: 55) and, to a cry of despair, "we have no satisfactory physical theory at all – only an ill-defined heuristic which makes unacceptable reference to primitives such as 'measurement', 'observer' and even 'consciousness'" (Wallace 2008). Although this is directed particularly against the Copenhagen interpretation – espoused by the overwhelming majority of physicists – it would apply, it seems to me, just as much to Wallace's own preferred "many worlds" hypothesis. This – in addition to the fact that it is a very expensive way of saving the (mathematical) appearances – has another fundamental problem: distinct worlds cannot communicate or interact, from which it follows that the hypothesis is not susceptible to empirical testing – something of a disability for a scientific hypothesis.

OBSERVATION

This problem is particularly telling because it suggests that if we cannot think clearly about mind ("consciousness", "observer" and "measurement") we are going to have difficulty making sense of the material world. Halvorson argues that it undermines several connected beliefs that underpin the assumption that physicalism – whose claim to authority resides in its conception of matter – can dispense with the notion of mind altogether or should see it as simply a manifestation of particular arrangements of the stuff of the material world. (Or, to put it another way, that the reduction of mind to matter disposes of it as a distinctive problem.) The measurement problem highlights the vulnerability of the assumption that physics will eventually arrive at a theory of everything and will do so without reference to traditional philosophical concerns and the traditional ways of approaching them. The theory of everything, if it is possible, looks, as we have already said, like being *a theory of everything but the theorist*. And a theory of everything that cannot encompass the theorist is fatally deficient; for Wallace, it is a theory of not very much at all.

It may seem surprising that Wallace's concern is not more widely felt or at least expressed. The reason for this is that discussions in fundamental physics often confuse two things: an observer and a measuring device. It is this that gives the false impression that postclassical physics brings the observer to the very centre of the account of the material world. In fact, the observer is a "clock" or "a counter" and not *someone* who "notes what is on the clock" or "takes down that which is displayed on the counter" and then makes sense of it. The observer in physics is not, it seems, an embodied subject like you and me – with a past history, present concerns and future aspirations – and not even a physicist, but a *locus*, best defined mathematically as a frame of reference where a device such as a clock or a counter can be situated. The reduction to absurdity of this view is that the most truthful account of the material world is its sum total seen from nowhere: from a virtual viewpoint outside any possible "where". It is the space–time manifold captured by the timeless field equations of general relativity.

This confusion between an observer and an instrument that an observer might use (such as a clock or a counter) is ubiquitous in scientistic thinking, enabling monstrosities such as the computational theory of mind – which sees the mind as the software implemented in the hardware of the brain and the two as information-processing devices – to have been taken seriously for so long. When minds (and observers, and conscious beings more generally) are described as information processors, they are equated with the instruments used to provide information to people who want, need or value it. This transfer of capacities is possible because the instruments we use to help us acquire information are often described as if they themselves were acquiring, registering and utilizing information. This is as elementary a blunder as thinking that clocks literally "tell the time", as opposed to enabling *us* to tell what time it is. Sloppy or slippery thinking of this sort opens up the belief that anything – any device or even natural object – that has an input transformed into an output is engaged in information processing. The ultimate expression of this is the suggestion that the entire universe is a gigantic computer and that (to use the physicist John Wheeler's formulation) IT (i.e. the universe) = BIT (information).

To extend the notion of information or information processing to encompass all change that affects any entity is to empty the notion of its distinct meaning. And yet the first step – the confusion between an observer who uses a detector to make an observation or a measurement and the detector – leads logically to the final one taken by Wheeler. This confusion is evident in the use made of the idea that information is "the resolution of uncertainty" and that the information content of an event is proportional to the amount of uncertainty it resolves. A frequent conclusion from this is that the collapse of the wave packet into a wave or a particle (when it is observed) is the equivalent of the generation of information. This is true, however, only if uncertainty is *felt (by someone)*. One way of grasping the difference between observers and their instruments or the detectors they use is that the former, and not the latter, entertain (and want to resolve) uncertainty: want to know how things are or will turn out.

The confusion between an observer and a detection device used by an observer may lie at the heart of some of the paradoxes of relativity theory and quantum mechanics. Take, for example, the measurement paradox we have just discussed. Superposition and entanglement percolate upwards from one material object to another: from the observed system to the instruments used to observe it, and finally to the brain of the observer that fields the light signals from the instruments. The measurement paradox arises if we think of the observation that underlies the measurement as the assumption of a particular state in the brain of the observer; or, to put this another way, if we assume that certain brain states corresponds to states of the observer or, more precisely, to observations. We now see that this cannot be the case if quantum mechanics is not going to pull the rug from beneath its own feet. There has to be some way in which measurement itself is quarantined against entanglement and superposition and this means accepting that the consciousness corresponding to an observation is of a different order from the material states of a material object; in short, that there is something in an observer or measurer that lies beyond the reach of the physical world as it is captured in quantum mechanics. That something is what we might call a mental state or consciousness and it is these that mark the difference between a measuring device and a person using it to make a measurement.

WHY THERE IS SOMETHING RATHER THAN NOTHING

The examples so far discussed illustrate how physicists' belief that they can do without philosophy is in part due to their failure to be aware of the philosophical questions raised by their discipline. Most fundamentally, they miss how the consciousness essential for physics is not itself reducible to the properties of the stuff that physics investigates. There is nothing in the material world that corresponds: to the intentionality of conscious experience in virtue of which one object *appears* to another or there is a *field of appearance* that amounts to the world in which conscious beings live; or to tensed time that underpins the difference, say, between memory and anticipation; or to the conditions under which measurement is possible. There is the assumption, where the problem is not overlooked, that somehow physics will develop to explain it.

The boldest physicists, however, acknowledge philosophical problems but assert that physics is already on the way to solving them. Of all the claims made by physicists, the most audacious is that they are able to explain why there is something rather than nothing: how it is that the universe came into being. This goes beyond philosophy, of course, and enters theology. Indeed, as Richard Dawkins claims in his afterword to Lawrence Krauss's *A Universe from Nothing* (2012), "Even the last remaining trump card of the theologian 'Why is there something rather than nothing?' shrivels up before your eyes as you read these pages".

In fact, far from shrivelling up, the question grows before our unpersuaded eyes. The answer that is offered has many variants but the most favoured takes the form of postulating that the universe grew out of a false vacuum: a quantum field or "inflaton", which was temporarily stable but not in the lowest energy state. Random fluctuation (uncaused, as things are in the quantum world) sent the inflaton tumbling into a true vacuum. This generated an equal amount of positive energy (matter) and negative energy (gravity), which adds up to nothing. So the universe could be created from nothing because it adds up to nothing.

Well, one would not have to be much of a philosopher to notice that the unstable quantum vacuum in the starter pack is a bit more than nothing. Even more vulnerable is the idea that we can finesse a Universe from Nothing by a process that generates equal amounts of positive and negative energy, so that the universe has zero total energy. This seems to be somewhat literal-minded, taking the pluses and minuses in an equation for reality. And equally unexplained are the laws that are supposed to be in place to ensure that instabilities in the quantum field unfold into a universe. The physicists' takeover of theology has resulted in the replacement of one question – Why is there something rather than nothing? – by three questions: how did the quantum vacuum arise in the first place? How did it result in generating two universes made of two kinds of something – positive and negative universe? And how come there were already laws of nature to guide it?

This theme is developed by Robert Lawrence Kuhn in his essay "Why Not Nothing?" (2013). He identifies no fewer than nine "levels of nothing" ranging from nothing as space and time that just happens to be totally empty of all visible objects to "no sets, no logic, no general principles, no universals, no possibilities of any kind". No physical account of the emergence of something from nothing even begins to match the sophistication of this kind of analysis.

THE NEED FOR PHILOSOPHY

The philosopher Simon Blackburn has spoken of "the prodigious ranks of those whose claim to have transcended philosophy is just another instance of their doing it badly" (2011). And Halvorson has remarked that "if we put bad metaphysics into our scientific theories, then we can expect to get bad metaphysics out of them" (2011: 163). This essay has provided extensive evidence to back up these remarks. Physicists, I would argue, need to supplement their current methodologies with philosophical approaches to try to make sense of where they are at present – and the impasse in their understanding of the material world described so brilliantly by Lee Smolin in *The Trouble with Physics* (2006) – and to help them deal with such in-house problems as the disappearance of time.

This is acknowledged by some physicists. George Musser has observed that while certain physicists think that being seen talking to a philosopher is "like being caught coming out of a pornographic cinema", others do have different views. Musser quotes Carlo Rovelli, a leading figure in the endeavour to reconcile quantum mechanics with the general theory of relativity, who argues that "the contributions of philosophers to the new understanding of space and time in quantum gravity will be very important" (Musser 2002: 48), although Rovelli himself believes that physics would be better if it did without time. And physics will certainly need to be supplemented by philosophy if it is to aspire to a theory of everything. We have already seen how current approaches, based on a materialist frame of reference that, among other things, confuses instruments such as clocks and other detectors with conscious observers, with living people, cause the theorist to disappear, and remove the very basis for measurement and appearance.

Arguing the need for philosophy is not just about taking sides in a turf war. Physicists and philosophers can work together. Physicists may even do philosophy in-house so long as they have some idea of what they are doing and do not assume that competence in physics automatically makes you a competent metaphysician. It doesn't matter who does the work as long as the work gets done. Nor is the traffic necessarily one way. Halvorson's arguments show how the problems at the heart of physics may generate new metaphysical ideas or even provide new arguments for existing philosophical positions such as mind–body dualism: the existence of mind separate from matter. And just as physicists should not claim to have the last word on metaphysical issues such as the nature of time without knowing what philosophers have thought, philosophers should not imagine that the metaphysics of space, time and causality can be advanced in ignorance of recent developments in science. As William Simpson has said, "*some* of our modern philosophers … often seem determined … to reduce everything to a picture of the world that is a residue of … *antiquated* physics – a picture consisting of pellets set in motion" (2012).

Philosophy and physics are potentially each other's greatest allies in the metaphysical enterprise characterized by F. H. Bradley as "the attempt to comprehend the universe not simply piecemeal or by fragments, but somehow as a whole" (1893: 1). Even those who are sceptical about the role philosophy may have in helping physics to make progress in its own terms should acknowledge that it may help us to interpret the unintelligible picture physics offers of the stuff of the world. More particularly, philosophy needs to take the initiative in examining the relationship between what Sellars called "the scientific" and "the manifest" image of the world: between the physics that throws the very existence of time into question and the physicist who has his breakfast before he has his dinner and hurries to catch a plane to CERN that he is anxious not to miss. This will be a crucial element in any attempt to make sense of the world in which we live and of our place in it. Physics, too, may benefit from a closer dialogue with metaphysics.

It is because this is absolutely fundamental to the intellectual enterprise that is the deepest part of the human story that I, for one, will not be cowed by the command to just "shut up and calculate", and not only because I am not very good at calculations.

9

You Chemical Scum, You

I am sick of being insulted. There seems to be a competition among some contemporary thinkers to dream up the most hostile descriptions of *Homo sapiens*, a species of which I am proud to be an example. Admittedly, badmouthing humanity is not an entirely novel pastime. There is a venerable religious tradition of currying favour with the Almighty by self-abasement, telling him (in case he had forgotten) what third-rate, degraded, fallen, creatures he has created. The female of the species tends to be particularly singled out. Augustine's description of women as "bags of excrement" is a characteristic gallantry. In recent centuries, however, the insults seem to be coming from non-religious sources and inspired by the claim that science has revealed our true standing in the order of things.

Voltaire got things off to a jolly start, quite a while back, by instructing the eponymous hero of his *Zadig* to visualize "men as they really are, insects devouring one another on a little atom of mud". The notion of the earth as "an atom of mud", or at least as a not-very-special address, was prompted by a growing appreciation of the implications of the first scientific revolution. This had begun with Copernicus demoting the Earth to just one among many bits of matter circling in empty space and led – via Kepler, Galileo and Newton and a few other giants of early modern physics – to an image of the universe as a gigantic clockwork machine in which our planet, and consequently its inhabitants, cut a pretty small figure. But the competition to find the most scathing description of humanity seems to have intensified, particularly over the past few decades.

Biology has been the inspiration in some cases. The political philosopher and professional misanthrope John Gray has argued that Darwin has cured us of the delusions we might have had about our place in the order of things: we are beasts, metaphysically on all fours with other beasts. Man, Gray asserts in *Straw Dogs*, "is only one of very many species, and not obviously worth preserving" (2002: 151). And he adds (in case you are still feeling a bit cocky): "human life has no more meaning than the life of slime mould". "Slime mould"? Yikes! Can it get any worse? Yes it can. For physics has again been recruited to the great project of shrinking our stature. Stephen Hawking's declaration in the 1995 television series *Reality on the Rocks* that "the human race is just a chemical scum on a moderate size planet, orbiting round a very average star in the outer suburb of one among a billion galaxies" is much quoted. If we beg to differ, is it only because we are like the mosquito who, according to Nietzsche (in "On Truth and Lie in the Extra-Moral Sense"), "floats through the air ... feeling within himself the flying centre of the universe"?

There is something repugnant about nihilistic grandstanding. For a start, even where it is not merely adolescent, it is insincere. Voltaire did not really consider *himself* merely an insect, any more than Gray considers slime mould *his* peer, or Hawking regards Hawking as a blob of "chemical scum". Behind the desire to shock is the wish to demonstrate that you see deeper and further than others, and thus are able to pierce the layers of self-delusion that support humans' sense of their own importance. This diagnosis of these thinkers, however, is not enough. We need to look harder at these digs at the dignity of man and woman before shrugging our shoulders and moving on.

They originate, after all, from exceptionally intelligent people, although two minutes' thought by persons of average IQ would be sufficient to show that the very act of making such statements proves their untruth. They are examples of something that philosophers call "pragmatic self-refutation". If we really were *insects* we would not have the concept of an insect; nor would we be able to characterize (in order to denigrate) our habitat as an *atom* (technical term) of *mud* (a term used metaphorically). If our lives really had no more meaning than that of a slime mould, it would not have occurred to us that our lives had *any* meaning; even less would we make the mistake of rating their meaning above that of a slime mould, an organism being invoked to stand for a broader category of third-rate stuff. We would not need Professor Gray, therefore, to correct our elevated view of ourselves. And, finally, if we were "chemical scum" on a par with the kind of material we normally call by this term, we would hardly have the concept of the "chemical" or of "scum". It does not dawn on the stuff that remains in the bath after the water has drained out that it is *scum*. Nor does real scum invoke rather abstract reasons for arriving at such an insight into its condition as Hawking does; namely that we are "on a moderate size planet, orbiting round a very average star in the outer suburb of one among a billion galaxies". If scum did entertain such ideas, I would be the first to agitate for scum rights and join the Scum Liberation Front.

Although they are pragmatically self-refuting, these claims do raise some not entirely empty questions about the very knowledge that seems to justify our denigrating ourselves: the Newtonian world picture, the theory of evolution, and the advances in astrophysics that have made us a shrinking part of an expanding universe. We have an interesting, not to say dizzying, situation. The knowledge that reveals us as smaller than we thought is also a testament to our greatness. As Pascal put it so beautifully in his *Pensées*:

> Man is but a reed, the feeblest thing in nature, but he is a thinking reed. The entire universe need not arm itself to crush him .... But if the universe were to crush him, man would still be

nobler than that which killed him, because he knows that he dies and the advantage which the universe has over him, the universe knows nothing of this. All our dignity then consists in thought. By it we must elevate ourselves, and not by space and time which we cannot fill. (§347)

Insects, slime mould and chemical scum do not think; nor do they have knowledge of their own thoughtlessness or entertain the idea of a place – small or otherwise – they might occupy in the greater scheme of things.

So behind the self-refuting claims of the denigrators of humanity is something rather interesting: knowledge itself. This is unique to humans – the consciousness of other sentient creatures being confined to sense experience that plugs them into their immediate surroundings – and deeply mysterious. Karl Popper has characterized knowledge as "the greatest miracle in the universe". Whether or not this is true, knowledge carries within itself a paradox: through it we wake out of our organic selves and the material limitations of our condition to the point where we are able so to distance ourselves from what we are, as understood in material terms, that we can regard ourselves with contempt.

This ability to look down on ourselves, or at least to see how small we are, develops at a quite basic level. It begins with human vision, that mode of our perception that is closest to knowledge. The human gaze discloses a world that is greater than the body that, as a self-conscious human being, I am aware of as *myself*. And, as my gaze extends – when, for example, I climb to the top of a tree or a mountain – I become conscious of myself as a comparatively smaller item in the ever-growing visual field that I command. I see that I am outsized, and outnumbered, by items that will in many cases outlast me.

This simultaneous sense of enlargement and diminution, which presents me as a shrinking thing in a growing world revealed by and to me, acquires dimensions beyond those known to visual sense, when, as is the case with us humans, experience is pooled in the notion of a shared reality sustained in a community of minds, bearing rumours of people, places, and pasts and futures. It is yet more developed when knowledge ceases to be tethered to my individual self or related to a physical horizon that surrounds me; when (to use Bertrand Russell's distinction) "knowledge by (direct) acquaintance" is increasingly supplemented and eventually dwarfed by "knowledge by description"; when the world of experiences becomes a world of facts and includes items – unimaginably large, small or numerous – that can be readily alluded to but not fully imagined, even less existentially filled out; when, in short, we can speak of entities such as "atoms" and "the universe". There is a gigantic mismatch between our cognitive reach and our existence. The gaze of knowledge that makes us cognitive giants presents us to ourselves as existential dwarfs.

This brings us back to Nietzsche's mosquito. In our preoccupied, busy everyday life, we are a bit like that flying mite, unaware of being a minute part of a boundless material world. The dismaying self-image that we are offered in the mirror of objective knowledge is offset by the ineradicable sense that we are at the centre of this great and growing universe that is in part present to us but to a much greater extent hidden from us – extending beyond our actual experience or even possible experience. What Russell called our "egocentric space", in which the material and human world is arranged in concentric circles around our singular irreplaceable selves, for the most part occludes the vast spaces, largely unconscious of us, in which our tiny bubble of awareness is located. This remains true, notwithstanding humanity's cognitive expansion in the centuries since the Sun has ceased to move around the Earth, and we have been displaced from the centre of things to no particular place at all. And so it should: for the microsphere in which we are individually and collectively insulated from the objective truth of our place in the universe is crucially the arena in which we act out our lives and fulfil our mutual responsibilities.

This is why we need to challenge the claim that natural science gives us the final and complete truth on what we truly are. For a start, it cannot explain its own roots, in the insignificant creatures it portrays us as being. Objective knowledge cannot accommodate the subjective reality of those living, thinking, knowing and ethically responsible human beings who made that knowledge possible. Something is missing in a description of us as, say, pieces of matter or living matter lost in a boundless universe: an account of how in us matter came to put itself in inverted commas as "matter"; of how in *H. sapiens* living matter came to utter the word "life"; of how a bit of the universe was able to speak the word "universe".

When, in response to Pascal's famous assertion that "the eternal silence of those infinite spaces terrifies me", Paul Valéry responded with the deflating observation "But the intermittent hubbub in the corner reassures me", he was not only being honest about the limitations of his ability to imagine what knowledge told him about himself, but also gently reminding us that we are not defined by what science reveals, or perhaps more accurately claims, to be the objective truth of our condition.

Reconciling certain objective realities of our nature and the lived truth of our life, and understanding the consciousness that spans them both, is surely the key intellectual challenge of the twenty-first century.

Get thinking, you scum.

10

Did Time Begin with a Bang?

One of the most fascinating puzzles about the nature of time is the question of whether it does or does not have a beginning. It's an issue that has wandered through Western thought for millennia, on the border between philosophy and theology, and no end seems to be in sight.

Possibly the best-known, and certainly the most consequential, intervention in the long conversation is Kant's cunning argument in *The Critique of Pure Reason* (1781). Here he demonstrates to his own satisfaction that time cannot be something in the world out there, a property of things in themselves; on the contrary, he says, it belongs to the perceiving subject. Time is one lens of the pair of spectacles (the other being space) through which that which is "in-itself" is refracted as it enters into the phenomenal world of experience. (For those who don't feel up to reading the original, Robin Le Poidevin's discussion in his brilliant *Travels in Four Dimensions* [2003] is an ideal starting-point.)

Kant's argument revolves around the question of whether or not the world has a beginning in time; or (a slither we must watch) whether or not *time itself* has a beginning. He shows that we can prove both that the world *must* have and that it *can't* have a beginning in time, so there must be something wrong with the very idea of time being something in itself. This is the first of his famous four "antinomies" – philosophical problems with two contradictory but apparently necessary solutions – the others relating to atoms, freedom and God.

The world, Kant says, must have a beginning in time, otherwise an infinite amount of time, an "eternity", as he called it, would have already passed in this world – but no infinite series can be completed. On the other hand, the world can't have had a beginning in time, because this would imply a period of empty time before the world came into being. Nothing (least of all a whole world) can come into being in empty time, as there isn't anything to distinguish one moment in empty time from another. To put this another way: since successive moments of empty time are identical, there would not be a sufficient reason for one moment to give birth to the world while its predecessors were sterile.

The most interesting and illuminating of the current responses to Kant's Antinomy of Time is to say that the world *did* have a beginning – at the Big Bang, 13.75 billion years ago – but that it was not a beginning in already-existing empty time, since the beginning of the world also started time itself. This solution echoes Augustine's assertion that "the world was made, not in time, but simultaneously with time": God brought the world and time into being together, so that the question of (say) what God was doing before the Creation does not arise. Kant's First Antinomy is therefore based on a false premise. Job done. Tick in box. Next question please.

Not so fast. Let us look at the view that time and the world began with the Big Bang 13.75 billion years ago. This is claiming two rather remarkable things: that time began *at a particular time*; and that time and the world began *at the same time*. Let us look at each of these assumptions, starting with the assertion that time began at a particular time.

TIME ZERO

Since the Big Bang can be assigned a date, Something must have come out of Nothing at a particular moment. What was special about a specific moment 13.75 billion years ago? The cosmologists say that there was *nothing* special about it: the universe is a random event that happened for no particular reason. It grew out of a quantum field – the "inflaton" – which found itself in a false vacuum: temporarily stable, but not in the lowest energy state. Random fluctuation sent the inflaton tumbling into a true vacuum, which generated an equal amount of positive energy (matter) and negative energy (gravity). Thus the Big Bang didn't need causes to bring it about because no net stuff was created. Far from solving the problem of creation, this has multiplied the problems (as discussed in Chapter 8, "Should We Just Shut Up and Calculate?"). An energetic quantum vacuum – a fidgety Nothing – looks a little dodgy, for a start. What seems more vulnerable is the idea that we can finesse Something out of Nothing by the generation of equal amounts of positive and negative energy, so that the universe has zero total energy. This seems to be somewhat literal-minded, taking the pluses and minuses in an equation for reality. Worse, it looks as if in pursuit of an explanation we have increased the number of unexplainables; we have to explain two lots of energy. In short, Kant's problem of explaining why one moment of empty time should be privileged to deliver a universe is not solved by appealing to random fluctuations, because fluctuations in Nothing – even if they generate pairs of virtual particles (virtual particle plus virtual antiparticle) – don't seem likely to help us to explain Something.

Some scientists have given up on the idea that the Big Bang is at the beginning of time (and space); rather, it is but a recent event in a much longer history (see e.g. Gefter 2012). Instead of one Big Bang, there is a series of big bangs livening up a cosmos that has been round forever. This, of course, only displaces the problem of the emergence of Something out of Nothing, and Kant's problem of an infinite amount of time having already passed is back.

Meanwhile, there are variants of the Big Bang theory in which it is suggested that time doesn't arrive on the scene at once or, rather, it behaves at first like another dimension of space; in the earliest universe there is a period in which it is too early for time. If so, we have to ask what "too early" could possibly mean in this context. Are we referring to a time *before* time exists – before it makes sense to speak of "before"? In that case we are in the grip of self-contradiction.

There is something dubious about dating the beginning of time in any case. Allocating a time to the beginning of time is like allocating a time to any moment in time. Saying that a time t_1 took place at a particular time t_1 seems like a harmless tautology, but it is actively misleading, because it treats a moment in time as if it were itself a kind of occurrence, and an occurrence in time what's more, as opposed to part of the framework within which things can occur. To say that time began at $t_{beginning}$ is thus to treat the beginning of time more like a kind of event. This impression is confirmed when it is asserted that $t_{beginning}$ occurred 13.75 billion years ago.

Those who want to defend the notion of a moment in time as being like an occurrence might be tempted to say we often think this way when we talk about stretches of time. For example, there is nothing wrong with saying that Wednesday – not in itself an event, but simply a holder for events – began, came into being, at twelve midnight on Tuesday. The analogy is not sound, however. Tuesday and Wednesday are not time in itself, but divisions placed upon time: the same stretches could be labelled as 12 and 13 December and specified not as two days but as 48 hours, and so on.

The Big Bang is supposed to be both timeless and at a particular time: at the beginning of, and yet not part of, the series that it begins. The problem with saying that time began at a particular time is highlighted by this obvious question: if it is perfectly valid to speak of 13.2, 13.3 and 13.75 billion years ago, why is it not valid to talk about 13.8, 13.76 or even 13.755 billion years ago? Stephen Hawking addresses this question by arguing that to talk of time before the Big Bang is like talking about points north of the North Pole. Once you have reached the North Pole, it makes no sense to imagine you can go any further north. This analogy does not work. As mathematical philosopher J. R. Lucas has pointed out, there is a deeper, astronomical sense of north that allows a line pointing in that direction to be extended indefinitely. North is a direction that has no terminus: you *can* be north of the North Pole. So the question still stands.

What about the second assumption: the supposed *simultaneity* of the beginning of the universe and the origin of time? How can we think of the start of time itself (as opposed to the time *of* something) being at the same time as an event (the creation of the universe)? There is no "at the same time as" until the universe has differentiated to the point where one event can be temporally related to other events via an observer. What's more, once the universe *has* come into being, and more than one event has occurred, the notion of simultaneity as absolute and observer-independent is invalidated by the special theory of relativity. Finally, there is a mismatch between a universe, whose coming-into-being is extended over time, and time itself, whose coming-into-being is presumably instantaneous, or at least not extended through time. While we may imagine the transition from Nothing to Something as being instantaneous, the Big Bang, leading to something that could be described as a universe occupying space and in some sense temporalized, itself has several temporally distinct and ordered stages.

HAUNTED BY KANT

So Kant's First Antinomy still haunts us. But we have good reason not to jump from its problems to Kant's conclusion that time is somehow internal to the human mind. If time were only a property of human minds, we would not be able to make sense of what, in *After Finitude* (2008), the French philosopher Quentin Meillassoux called "ancestrals". Ancestrals are those realities that pre-date human beings and hence human consciousness and yet have a clear temporal order. For example, Earth came into being 4.56 billion years ago, before life on Earth originated (3.5 billion years ago) and before conscious humans began emerging (several million years ago). So if we believe what evolutionary science tells us, we cannot reduce time to one of Kant's two "forms of sensible intuition" (roughly, modes of human perception), the other form being space, internalizing it to the human mind.

However, this conclusion, too, can be challenged by arguing that the allocation of events to past dates is itself internal to the calendar time that humans have invented; that we project the framework we have established to structure our time beyond the situation within which it arose. The very idea of "ago" is established with respect to a system that has been built up by humans and extrapolated from ways of seeing that serve us well but do not necessarily reveal truths about how the universe is in itself, beyond our manner of perceiving it. On this matter, the jury remains out.

As we noted in Chapter 8, many physicists despise the kinds of arguments that I have presented and the philosophers who want to make other than mathematical sense of what physics tells us about the fundamental nature of things. It is important not to lose one's nerve, and to note that physicists who dismiss philosophy are often doing philosophy themselves, but very badly.

The question of whether time has a beginning is far from resolution. Equally vexing is the opposite question, as to whether it has an end. Another time, perhaps.

11

A Hasty Report from a Tearing Hurry

And strangers were as brothers to his clocks.
(W. H. Auden, *In Time of War*)

Readers of these essays will by now have formed the impression that I am committed to rescuing metaphysics from the jaws of physics. One manifestation of this mission is my opposition to reducing time to a quasi-spatial dimension and its further reduction to numbers. Thus reduced, time becomes a mere variable – t – that has no qualities, only numerical values, and none of the features that make it central to human life. For example, little t, unlike time as we experience it, has no tenses. The difference between, say, a regretted past and an anticipated future is lost.

I could go on about the poverty of t but I won't because I am also aware that in taking t for granted I am overlooking something rather extraordinary: the mysterious verb "to time". While all beings (pebbles, trees, monkeys) are in some (very difficult to characterize) sense "in" time – immersed or dissolved in it – we humans are alone in *timing* what happens, including (or especially) what happens to ourselves and our very lives. We portion time into days and number days – and parts of them – and know that our days are numbered. Of all the occupants of the solar system – rocks, trees, lemurs and so on – we alone use the relative movements of its components to organize our own affairs. What a delicious piece of cheek to appropriate the rotation of the Earth around the Sun to instruct us when to do what: when, for example to have our Christmas dinner. To vary a saying of Douglas Adams: "time is mysterious; tea-time doubly so".

So we should not allow objections to the reduction of time to little *t* to allow us to overlook the mysterious activity of "timing" or the extraordinary truth that, despite the gap between lived and measured time, measuring has enabled us (via science and technology) to extend, protect, enrich and enhance our existence; indeed, to have the time of our lives. "Measurement began our might", as the poet W. B. Yeats said: it extended our powers beyond anything that could be imagined by our pre-numerate ancestors.

Timing has not only enabled us to see more of how the material world "worked", so that we could work on it, or with it, more effectively, but also greatly extended our temporal gaze. In recent centuries, we have come to situate ourselves in "deep time": the time revealed by archaeologists, evolutionary biologists, geologists and astrophysicists. We locate ourselves in a span of time that exceeds the duration of our lives by billions of years and the duration of the species to which we belong by not much less. Of course, the very measurements that have made us collectively mighty have also created a mirror in which we are individually, existentially small, something I discussed in Chapter 9, "You Chemical Scum, You".

The sense, implicit in the verb "to time", of accessing time directly is, of course, confusing and seduces us into thinking that clocks measure "the passage of time" – a topic for another occasion. For the present, I want to examine another aspect of timing – also easily overlooked – that is more apparent as timepieces become more sophisticated. It is that we note "the time" *at* a time. So I note that it is 4.30 *at* 4.30: "I looked at the clock at 4.30 and saw that it was 4.30". This is stranger than it might seem at first sight; at any rate, it highlights the extent to which, as (old or young) timers, we both stand outside time and are immersed in it. To know that it is 4.30 is to be *at* 4.30 and to be looking on 4.30 as if from a temporal outside. In subjecting time to timing, we seem to have succeeded in some respect to have stepped to one side of time, while, of course, remaining in it.

So, while we are pulling time out of the jaws of physics, we must not forget what an amazing, and deeply puzzling, activity "timing" is. And its consequences are immeasurable. It transforms our social life into a multitude of intermeshing ensembles harmonized by timepieces. Even inside the ever more tightly drawn temporal meshes, the clock rules our every moment: we watch time and time watches us; and the portability of the wristwatch compared with, say, the obelisk, makes the watching and the watched more intimately locked together. The living rhythms spelt out in our breathing, our walking and our beating hearts are overridden by something totally different, symbolized by the way the watch we consult with fast-beating heart clasps our wrist, seeming to strangle our pulse. We dance to the rhythm of the shared day, of the common world, of the universe, that is imposed and embraced, is ours and not ours.

This is not all bad, of course. As already noted, our lives are vastly enriched, and we are collectively and individually empowered, by coordination: dancing to the music of clock time, we can work together more effectively to meet and anticipate our basic needs, to generate ever more complex ways of exploiting nature, and to erect defences against a universe that has no particular care for us. And we must not underestimate what an extraordinary achievement this is. Take a salient example: the operating theatre. There is the surface orchestration of the lives of all the experts – surgeons, nurses, technicians, anaesthetists, cleaners and engineers – necessary to make the procedure happen and happen safely. But beneath this, there is an almost bottomless infrastructure of temporally coordinated life.

Think of the engineer responsible for making sure the complex machinery in the theatre works, and works to time. He has to arrive on time and his journey will have involved a multitude of conductors of his private orchestra of activities, ranging from the alarm clock he set to wake him up to the traffic lights whose efficient working (regulated from some central place) made sure he was not held up forever in jammed traffic. His assumption of his present post as hospital engineer will be the end stage of a long journey that has depended on meeting with others at pre-set times. His skills, for example, will have involved a multitude of people whose tabled time – set out in the curriculum – will have meshed with his, so that he was able to benefit from their wisdom and technical expertise. The equipment on which he learned his skills – either directly or as illustrations of general principles – had to be manufactured, tested, delivered, maintained and demonstrated by an endless army of individuals turning up on time and timing their activities (including the activity of timing the performance of the machinery) to fit in with those of others. The equipment itself will have a multitude of components based on clocks – visible and hidden – created by other clock-watchers and on physical principles whose discovery and application and commercialization involved yet more armies of clock-drilled people. At every point in his life, our engineer will have been borne up by myriads of clock-conducted fellows.

This is a beneficent example. There are other less heart-warming instances of the consequences of orchestration. The gigantic torture chamber that is North Korea is an extreme instance of how the imposed brotherhood of clocks can subordinate individual life entirely to a collective existence, where each is reduced to an atom in a pattern of power servicing the needs of a small elite. The scale of the catastrophic wars of recent centuries would not have been possible without clocks to bring men and materiel together on a giant scale, permitting destruction to be both precise and ubiquitous. The synchronies that enhance our ability to realize our collective power and knowledge, and to enhance that collective power with our ever-increasing collective knowledge, unifying greater numbers of us with ever closer and denser connections, make it possible to hurt each other with appallingly enhanced efficiency. As time gets further from subjective experience, drifts further from our beating hearts, heartlessness may install itself in the heart of our world.

There are lesser woes that may follow from this than the kind of global horror humanity may self-inflict through totalitarian politics and total war. The kitchen clock, my watch, the peeps from the radio, preside over my hurry, your hurry, the hurry of widening rings of friends and strangers who are the soft inflectors of the infinite hard clockwork of the universe, endlessly extending possibility. But our orchestrated lives may be emptied even as they are enriched. The ever greater efficiency of an ever more intimately clocked world adds to our opportunities but also drives a positive feedback cycle in which we demand more of the world and the world demands more of us.

As we seem to get a grip on time, via those numbers, time gets an ever tighter grip on us. We are like Gulliver in Lilliput, pinned to the ground by a multitude of threads, notwithstanding that our hastes become more manic and our passage from one thing to the next is a more fluent slide. The quickening of pace is evident in every aspect of our lives. We supplement the treadmill of work with a treadmill of pleasure. Hurry may seem to be a constant condition, even if the hurry is to catch a plane to go on holiday, to arrive at a concert on time, to honour an engagement whose sole purpose is for a casual get-together. We are forever on the edge of being late and any dereliction in this respect causes us anguish: we are mortified and others are impatient.

The tyranny of the clock extends to our future. The calendar on the wall prescribes what is going to happen or ought to happen. Our days are mortgaged weeks, months, and years ahead. A phone call on the morning of 12 November 2010 commits the afternoon of 14 July 2012. The future we may not even live to see is populated with constraining possibilities, with shared intentions that are mutual obligations.

The newer, faster forms of communication not only permit an instantaneity of response but seem to demand this. Others expect immediate or continuous availability and we expect this of others. We are electronically skewered by emails, texts, phone calls. Our lives are coordinated, shaped, even filled, not by the stars but by satellites that orbit round the nearer heavens. As we "communicate" more electronically, we seem to communicate less. We are attenuated – or, as I have characterized it, "e-ttenuated" – a paradox that symptomatizes what is happening more generally: that, as we travel faster and our journeys are increasingly effortless, so we seem to travel lighter, indeed to *become* lighter. The inability fully to experience our experiences, except when those experiences are unpleasant (hunger, cold, pain, terror, grief), which is something that we are particularly aware of when we seek experiences for their own sake, becomes ever more evident. We look to boredom to restore to time its weight, so that it hangs heavily.

So while we are rescuing time from the jaws of physics, we might spare a little time to think how we might rescue ourselves from the machinery of clocks while still, of course, honouring our responsibilities in an increasingly closely clocked human world, and being duly respectful of what we "timers" have achieved. Thinking about the mystery of time, of timing, and, yes, of the body of knowledge that is physics, seemingly transilluminating the material world, may be a place to start.

I can't start now because – *"My God, is that the time!!"* – I have to finish this essay. I hope you will find time to read it.

12

Medical Ethics in the Real Mess of the Real World

MEDICAL ETHICS TO THE FORE

In this essay, I want to share my perplexity with you about issues in medicine that are usually referred to as "ethical". I was just as perplexed when I left medicine in March 2006 as when I entered medicine in 1970. I am going to tell you why I am perplexed about ethical issues and why I think everybody else should be and then suggest how we might live with or within our perplexity.

Everybody knows why ethical issues are hot, and indeed getting hotter. First, there is survival against the odds. Many people now, as a result of medical advances, live on in states that none of us would wish upon our worst enemies. There is also the issue of consumerism. Once there were patients, then there were clients, now there are users and then ultimately there are litigants: that is roughly the evolution of a patient. One of the aspects of consumerism is the feeling that "Basically, I am no longer going to listen to these doctors, these women or men who are telling me what is good for me, I am going to challenge everything they say, just as I would challenge everything that I am told by the chap who services my car."

Behind this, there is a culture of suspicion: the default assumption that we should always be suspicious of those who pretend they have any kind of authority when they are talking to us. The postmodern challenge to authority, and indeed even to that form of authority that has pretensions to superior knowledge, seems to have trickled down to people who have never read any postmodernism but feel generally – courtesy of journalists and others – hostile to people who claim to be experts. Finally, there are particular areas that have been highlighted as important ethical issues. We used to call them DNR ("do not resuscitate") orders; we now call them DNAR orders, "do not attempt resuscitation", which is not the same as "do not resuscitate" because most of us recognize that resuscitation is something often attempted, and is usually futile, as I shall discuss in due course.

But there has been great concern about DNAR orders. A little while back, the UK charity Age Concern, for which I have huge respect, did older people a power of no good by raising the suspicion that people were not being considered for resuscitation because they were old and that not to consider everybody for resuscitation was a manifestation of ageism. Actually, the right decision about whether or not to resuscitate someone is the decision as to whether they might benefit from it, and that depends not on age but on the presence or absence of serious disease. But certainly there is a suspicion abroad that if you are not at least having your share of cardiopulmonary resuscitation in hospital you really ought to ask for your money back.

AN IDEAL ETHICAL DECISION

What is an ideal ethical decision? It exemplifies the clear application of one ethical principle that everybody subscribes to, and it is consistent with all other fundamental ethical principles and/or (preferably and) is fireproof against criticism from people with strong beliefs about the sovereignty of one principle over another. Such decisions are the things of dreams. And, in fact, the sure sign that you have made an ethical decision is that it leaves you feeling uncomfortable until you forget about it, or you are worried about another ethical decision. You can cope with the ethical decision you felt queasy about, say over Mrs Jones, because you have moved two beds along and now you are on to the next decision that you are feeling queasy about, relating to Mrs Smith.

CONCERNING MRS A

I want to talk about my own perplexities by focusing on an exemplary (because ordinary) case. Of course, there are no ordinary cases, but it seems to me that too much of the discussion about medical ethics has tended to revolve on manifestly extraordinary cases: dividing Siamese twins and that sort of thing. I can't remember the last time I took a knife to separate two Siamese twins and had to decide who should live and who should die, but we are always faced with ethical decisions concerning patients with extremely common problems.

So I am going to talk about Mrs A, who was found comatose on the floor after the police, alerted by neighbours, had broken into her flat. She had had a massive stroke, at the relatively early age of sixty-six.

She had been living alone, the widow of a very violent husband who had physically abused her and physically and sexually abused her children. (She had a lot of children, as we shall see in due course.) The children felt very angry with her, I think; at any rate she had not seen them for a long time. I suspect they felt that they hadn't been protected by her against her abusive husband. Several of the children were receiving counselling and some were under psychiatric treatment.

She was admitted under my care and she didn't make much progress. Three weeks after her admission, she still had impaired consciousness, which is a very poor prognostic sign in stroke; it implies that you are either likely to die or, if you survive, you are going to have severe disability. She was tolerating a nasogastric tube, which was how she was being fed, and she was having subcutaneous fluids. She appeared to be in some distress at times. She had become rather chesty. At that point, some decisions about her management needed to be made. If she had a cardiac arrest, should somebody jump on her chest? If her chestiness turned into pneumonia, should she have intravenous antibiotics? Should feeding through her nasogastric tube, which she was clearly not enjoying, be continued, and what about hydration?

These present themselves as "ethical" issues because, if aggressive treatment were "successful", this might merely protract the dying process. If the patient were to survive a little longer, she would most likely do so in a state of overwhelming, intolerable, disability. The question of withdrawing or denying treatment felt more like an "ethical" issue because the patient herself did not have the mental capacity to participate in the decision.

ALL MEDICAL DECISIONS ARE ETHICAL AS WELL AS CLINICAL DECISIONS

At this stage, I want to highlight what I believe to be a common mistake in our thinking about medicine and ethics; namely, that we consider some decisions to be "ethical" as well as clinical and others to be purely clinical. In reality, all clinical decisions are based on ethical decisions, although in many cases the ethical issues are offstage or merely implicit. Once this is appreciated, we shall want to challenge the notion that there is some kind of ethical asymmetry between, on the one hand, giving treatment and, on the other hand, withholding it; or between withholding treatment and discontinuing it: in other words, the assumption that there is an ethical asymmetry between commission and omission. It has certainly become clear both in some aspects of medical law and in ethical debate that this asymmetry is really quite false. It is just as much an ethical decision to continue with treatment, or indeed to start it in the first place, as it is to withhold it or to discontinue it.

We had already made some implicit ethical decisions when this lady came under my care and she was subjected to all the panoply of modern medicine: drips, nasogastric tube feeding, and so on. Even so, withdrawing any part of this treatment, or deciding not actively to treat some new event, did feel much more like a matter for ethical discussion than our response to the initial situation. But it is false to think that withdrawing life-sustaining treatment (withdrawing life) is an ethical issue while continuing life-sustaining treatment (which may result in inflicting hideous life) is not. The failure to grasp the moral equivalence of our behaviour in each of these situations can lead to absurdity.

Let me illustrate this with a particularly challenging example. There are circumstances in which it may be appropriate to switch off a ventilator even though it is essential for life support. Because stopping ventilation may result in immediate death, it is forbidden in some religions; indeed, it is regarded as homicide. This is clearly problematic where the patient (not to speak of their relatives) has nothing to gain from continuing ventilation indefinitely. In order to avoid the situation where a patient has to be maintained on a ventilator forever, however futile this proves to be, ventilation is treated like a prescription, which is time-limited: "Ventilation for one week". When the week is up, a new prescription may or may not be written, depending on the patient's circumstances. If the decision is made not to rewrite the prescription, stopping ventilation can be seen not as a case of an existing treatment being withdrawn but as a new treatment not being started. This is mere casuistry, of course. It is, however, a consequence of denying the moral equivalence between withholding a treatment in the first place, on the grounds that it is likely to be unwise, futile, or not in the patient's best interest, and subsequently withdrawing it on the same grounds.

A (HOPEFULLY) USEFUL DIGRESSION ON FUTILITY

Let us suppose, then, that withdrawal of treatment *per se* does not present particular ethical problems, or none, at least, that are fundamentally different from those associated with starting treatment. What are the conditions under which you might withdraw treatment? You may withdraw it if it is futile. What are the grounds for judging futility?

Here is a little fossil from the recent past, an article in *The Lancet* published in 1990: "Futility is a professional judgement that takes precedence over patient autonomy and permits physicians to withhold or withdraw care deemed to be inappropriate without subjecting such a decision to patient approval". The paternalistic tone seems to belong to another world. The trouble is that moving on from that world means that physicians are increasingly obliged to do things they are unhappy about. One of the things that I, as a doctor, have often felt very unhappy about is the implicit or explicit authorization of cardiopulmonary resuscitation (CPR) in my patients. The reason for this unhappiness is captured by some observations made by the physician John Saunders:

> Cardiopulmonary resuscitation is attempted on too many patients. At its best, it is the gift of life: chest compression; ventilation, intravenous medication and defibrillation followed by years of productive and fulfilled being …
>
> At its worst [and I have to tell you I have seen it usually at its worst] it offers a scenario of vomit, blood and urine, then a confused, brain damaged twilight, breathlessness from a failing ventricle, pain from rib fractures, until expiring in thrall to the full panoply of intensive care or forgotten in the long darkness of persistent vegetative state. (2001: 457)

Any doctor reading this will recognize that picture.

> No humane doctor would consider this a Good Death, nor would any poet, priest, painter, musician or novelist use images of CPR to represent the Good Death. Rather, the images are more likely to be those of the factory: death in the industrial age. (*Ibid.*)

And this is a consequence, in part at least, of the discrediting of the concept of futility in medical care as defined to some extent by professional judgement. I am going to come back to that.

There have been many high-profile examples of the resistance to the idea that aggressive medical intervention may be futile. Here is one, chosen at random, reported in *The Lancet* a few years ago. It concerned an eighty-seven-year-old man. His age doesn't impress me at all; I was, after all, a specialist in old-age medicine. What is at issue is the ability to benefit from medical interventions. He had multiple organ failure and was on life support. The NHS Trust within which he was being treated sought permission to discontinue dialysis and forgo resuscitation in the event of respiratory failure. The family were opposed to this.

Lord Justice Waller, who was presiding over the case, came to this judgement: "It is only lawful to treat an unconscious patient, who cannot consent, if to do so is in their best interests." It must surely be difficult to quarrel with this. And Deborah Powell, who was representing the NHS Trust, argued that Mr A's interests would be best served if he were allowed to "die a natural pain-free and dignified death". The legal process caused enormous grief to the family, so much so that they couldn't stay in court to hear the judge's pronouncement. "I do not wish to hear the death sentence pronounced on my father", the son said. It demonstrates a faith in the power of contemporary medicine to maintain worthwhile life forever. The idea that withdrawing this medical treatment would be pronouncing a death sentence was misplaced: medicine was unlikely to change the course of events except for prolonging the process of dying in a most unpleasant and undignified way.

THE GENERAL MEDICAL COUNCIL TO THE RESCUE

Futility is a difficult concept. It is an important one, however, and one we should always bear in mind. It would be reassuring to think that the doctors' regulatory body, the General Medical Council (GMC), would help the profession to find a safe path through some very tricky territory surrounding the decision that treatment is futile. In this respect – and relevant to Mrs A – a document had recently been produced for me to consult: *Withholding and Withdrawing Life-Prolonging Treatments*. This guidance has since been revised and greatly improved, but important ambiguities and even contradictions remain. In the 2002 document, all bases – including the GMC's own back – were covered. "There's the bit where you say it and the bit where you take it back", as the philosopher J. L. Austin once said of some philosophers who appeared to be making extraordinarily radical statements but actually left nothing changed.

Here are some of the passages from this document:

> Doctors must take account of the patient's preferences when providing treatment; however, where a patient wishes to have a treatment that – in the doctor's considered view – is not clinically indicated, there is no ethical or legal obligation on the doctor to provide it.
> (General Medical Council 2002: para. 16)

That is almost coherent. Unfortunately, it is contradicted elsewhere:

> You should usually comply with patients' requests to provide CPR, although there is no obligation to provide treatment that you consider futile. (*Ibid.*: para. 89)

> A patient's own views, about whether the level of burden or risk outweighs the likely benefits from successful CPR, would be central in deciding whether CPR should be attempted.
> (*Ibid.*: para. 86)

Let us suppose the patient has formed her views of CPR from what she has seen in medical soap operas, where the frequency of success depends on the whims of scriptwriters. Should her views be central?

Thank you GMC. We shall return to this source of wisdom in due course.

NUTRITION AND HYDRATION

The issue of whether or not to resuscitate, or to institute aggressive life-sustaining treatment, is difficult enough. But there is another aspect of Mrs A's treatment that required our ethical consideration. She was being fed through a nasogastric tube and receiving fluid via a drip. The continuation or discontinuation of nutrition and hydration is a particularly sensitive issue for a variety of reasons. It is unclear, for example, how unpleasant this is for an individual with impaired consciousness. Some argue that discontinuation is brutally cruel: would you like to be starved to death and to be deprived of fluid? Others have invoked the notion of "compassionate dehydration", arguing that fluid deprivation sometimes blunts the experience of other symptoms. The jury is out, but there is another reason why it has figured so much in ethical and legal debate over the past few decades, starting with the case of Tony Bland, a victim of the Hillsborough disaster, whose parents wished him to be allowed to die after many years in a persistent vegetative state. It is because artificial nutrition and hydration are a curious hybrid. The manner they are given is medical because it involves tubes and drips: they therefore count as "a treatment". But what is given through the tubes and from the drips is a basic necessity of ordinary life.

The fact that artificial feeding has this dual aspect may have made it difficult to handle in the law: artificial nutrition is seen as both a medical intervention, which can be appropriately discontinued, and as a human right, which is inappropriate to discontinue. Of course, human rights are a bit complicated when they hover round the nasogastric tube: there is the right to life, which sometimes favours continuation of feeding; and there is the right not to be subjected to undignified treatment, which sometimes favours discontinuation.

Even so, we have the intuition that medical treatment can be withdrawn if it is futile. Artificial nutrition and hydration under certain circumstances may be regarded as futile: ergo they may be withdrawn under those circumstances, although the legal framework still remains difficult.

The GMC discovered this to its cost, despite its earnest attempt to please or appease everyone, if necessary by giving conflicting advice. A Mr Leslie Burke, a patient with a progressive neurological condition, read the document from which I have just quoted and realized that his doctors might be permitted to withdraw artificial feeding and fluid if they deemed it futile to continue treatment. He could foresee a future time when he would not be able to communicate his wishes and challenged the GMC guidelines in the High Court. The judge upheld Mr Burke's demand that he should have artificial feeding and intravenous fluid for as long as he was alive. Now, this was important not only in itself but also because it set a precedent: for the first time it supported a person's right not only to determine in advance the treatment that could be refused but also to requisition treatment they did want. Because it potentially set this precedent, it was overturned on appeal.

Lesley Burke was concerned about controlling his medical treatment when he was no longer able to communicate his wishes. And this is relevant to our patient Mrs A: she lacks capacity or competence. Someone else would have to make decisions on her behalf. The challenge presented by incompetent patients is on the one hand to protect them from treatment that is hazardous, controversial or unnecessary, and on the other ensuring that they enjoy the best possible care. The "axiom of necessity" asserts that treatment that is necessary to preserve the life, health or well-being of the patient may be lawfully given without consent. So when Mrs A was admitted to the hospital and drips were put up and other treatments started without consulting her wishes, which could only be guessed at, this was entirely lawful. The application of the "axiom of necessity" is less clear when it is a case of withdrawing and withholding of treatment. There is no shortage of guidelines as to how to treat pneumonia but none as to when not to treat it, when the patient is not able to make her wishes known.

THE LAW AND BIOMEDICAL ETHICS

It is interesting at this point to think about the relationship between the law and ethics. It is not difficult to be a "legal" doctor – to remain within the letter of the law – and, indeed, much easier than to be a competent doctor. To be an ethical doctor is much, much more difficult. The law is about certainty, about bringing things to a conclusion; at any rate, it usually enables a decision to be arrived at in a timescale appropriate to the tempo of unfolding clinical situations. And for this we should be grateful. But we will sometimes need more than the confidence that our practice is within the law if we are going to feel entirely easy about some of the decisions we make. This is reflected in the feeling already referred to that, although legally there is no serious difference between withholding and withdrawing treatment without consent, it does really feel more ethically challenging than introducing treatment without consent.

In our search for something that takes us further than the law, we often appeal to the principles of biomedical ethics. The four principles most often invoked are: beneficence (doing what is in the objective best interests of the patient); non-maleficence (not deliberately causing harm); respect for autonomy (acting in according with the patient's wishes, so far as they can be determined); and justice (treating everyone equally). Unfortunately, these may not help us to decide what we should do in the case of Mrs A. Yes, we would want to act in accordance with Mrs A's wishes, but of course we can't access those wishes; we can't biopsy her soul to find out what she wants; so, in the interests of beneficence, we look objectively to see what is in her best interest. There is no guarantee that our judgement of the patient's best interests and what she may have wished for herself will coincide. All we can do is try to determine what Mrs A *probably* wants. How might we do that?

DETERMINING MRS A'S WISHES

Advance directives

There are various ways we might try to get a better idea of what Mrs A would want. Perhaps she left an advance directive or living will of some sort. Perhaps we should mobilize our general intuitions: "What would *I* like in this situation? What would I like for my mother?" Or perhaps we ought to seek the advice of those who know her best: her closest relatives.

Let's think first about advance information. Following the passing of the Mental Capacity Act 2005, advance directives have a much stronger legal status then they did hitherto: it affirms that people can make decisions to refuse treatment if they should lose capacity in future. Ignoring an advance directive and imposing treatment on a patient who has indicated clearly, when of sound mind, that they do not want it, is a criminal offence. This veto applies to treatments that the doctor considers necessary to sustain life only if strict formalities (including a witnessed signature) have been observed when the advance directive is drawn up.

Unfortunately, only a very small number of people have drawn up a living will. On the occasions when I have talked about them, I invariably ask the audience – usually a medical or legal audience – for a show of hands as to who has one. Very few hands go up. In part, this is because we are not very keen to think about the circumstances in which they might be required. Perhaps it is because we feel we have more urgent things to do, such as taking the children to football. Most probably it is because it is very difficult to frame a living will in such a way as to deal with the range and complexity of the situations that might arise. The best living will might seem to be a person whom we love and trust and who can speak on our behalf.

And there are other problems with living wills. For example, most of my pleasure in life comes from conversation, reading and writing. I can anticipate that if I lost all of those capacities, to the point where I could not communicate at even the most basic level, as a result of a stroke, I would be profoundly miserable and might even consider my life no longer worth living. This would be even more likely to be true if, in addition, I became demented and lost not only my capacity to use language but also large parts of my memory so that I became permanently disorientated, frightened and bewildered. Surely I should anticipate this by drawing up an advance directive specifying that, under such circumstances, I would not want to be actively treated even for a life-threatening disease.

This conclusion is less secure than it may seem. Supposing at the age of sixty I drew up an advance directive that specified that I would like to receive comfort-only treatment if I became seriously demented. Fast-forward twenty-five years: I am now eight-five and I have indeed become demented and have developed a serious chest infection. Shall I be denied treatment by my sixty-year-old self? Am I the same person as he? Have I become another person? Have I become a non-person? If I have become either another person or a non-person, what authority does my sixty-year-old self have over this successor self? Can I "enslave" a future different person or a non-person? And also how do I weigh my present interests at the age of eighty-five against the past wishes as enshrined in my advance directive?

Let me give an example of a famous case, that of a very high-powered mathematician, whose whole *raison d'être* came from doing mathematics. He had indicated to his nearest and dearest that if he could no longer do mathematics at the level at which he had hitherto done it he wouldn't want to continue to live. Anyway, he became demented and for the first time in his life his wife noticed he was (a) happy and (b) bearable to live with. He was no longer the tense, irritable, difficult person that he had been for all the previous years. So now what is to be done? His life is now worth living and he is worth living with.

This striking example highlights the distinction that many bioethicists, notably Ronald Dworkin, make between "experiential" interests (those that are connected with my present state of mind) and "critical" interests, which are those things, as with the mathematician's ability to do maths, that have given life its distinctive biographical meaning. When I decide on the criteria according to which my life is no longer worth living, should those who have to act on a living will take into account my current quality of life or give priority to those things that have mattered to me over my life?

This is not in any way to suggest that advance directives are not a valuable way to protect us against the unwanted assaults of aggressive unthinking medical treatment. But they have their limits.

Mobilizing our own intuitions

Advance directives were not an issue with Mrs A because, like most of the rest of the population, she didn't have one. We needed, therefore, to try some other way of accessing her wishes. There is the time-honoured – and now somewhat dishonoured – approach of mobilizing our general intuitions. There is a tradition of standing at the bedside and muttering: "God, poor Mrs A; it's pretty awful, it's pretty futile, isn't it? I mean, would I, if my mother...?", and so on, and so forth.

The trouble is that people are less accepting of clinicians' general intuitions, as we noted when we discussed the concept of medical futility. And in some circumstances they might be right to reject them. After all, they are potentially judgemental in a way we no longer entirely accept from the profession. We might say "Mrs A, you know, she has had a miserable life; she was alone, hardly saw her children, and was living on a diet of Valium and brown ale. And in future she will be even worse off because, if she survives, she will be severely disabled and perhaps her life will just not be worth living anymore." Without even noticing, we may have drifted into judging not only her present quality of life but her life as a whole.

There are dangers when you start judging the value of other people's lives. We have seen those dangers clearly expressed on a massive scale in the century that has just passed, when many millions of lives were deemed by others not to be worth living. Also there is the feeling that our intuitions might justify our deploying a rather crude utilitarianism by stealth: "Are we really wasting our time on this lady in ICU?"; "Could there be better use of resources or more deserving cases?"

Just how live this concern is has been illustrated recently by the hysteria the *Daily Mail* was able to whip up over the Liverpool Care Pathway, developed for the management of dying patients in the last few hours or days of life. This has represented a great advance in humane medicine based on the recognition that people who are actually dying need a different sort of care, with the withdrawal of active treatment, perhaps of food and fluid at times, and increasing levels of sedation. The *Daily Mail* headline reporting occasional unsatisfactory use of the pathway, however, suggested that 130,000 elderly patients were being killed a year.

There is also the problem of mobilizing empathy as a guide to evaluating the quality of life. Can we really empathize with what is valuable in other people's lives, how they might value their own lives, if we cannot speak with them? After all, we find it difficult to empathize with our own futures. If at the age of fifteen I woke up one morning and discovered I was sixty-six, I still had a mortgage, had not yet written the masterpiece I had imagined writing, I'd probably have slit my throat. As it is, I am actually much happier now than I ever was or could have dreamt of being at fifteen. If you can't even empathize with your own future and what a future self might value, how can you empathise with somebody else's life and what is valuable to them?

And then, of course, there are metaphysical limits to the validity of judgements on whether or not life is worthwhile. How do we value life? How do we value being alive? Well, Aeschylus (and Solon before him) said "Call no man happy until he is dead". This may have been simply a warning against judging a life to have been a good one until it is completed but it seems suspiciously like the assertion that we are all better off dead. There is no ambiguity in the case of the nineteenth-century German philosopher Arthur Schopenhauer who argued that suffering was inseparable from conscious life, that it was better not to have been born, and that, if one had made the mistake of being born, one should die as quickly as possible. This was reinforced by that rural pessimist and disciple of Schopenhauer Thomas Hardy:

> A time there was – as one may guess ...
> Before the birth of consciousness.
> When all went well. ("Before Life and After")

There must be something in the cider in Dorset.

On the other hand, William Wordsworth, in "Michael: A Pastoral Poem", wrote of "The pleasure which there is in life itself". I am not suggesting Mrs A was having pleasure, but you can just understand that perhaps just being conscious and aware may have a value in itself.

Perhaps the wisest view was that of Wittgenstein in the *Tractatus Logico-Philosophicus*, where he writes "The sense of the world must lie outside of the world" (§6.41), from which it follows that we cannot evaluate the world from within the world – or our lives from within life.

So when we're murmuring at the bedside, saying, "You know, is it really worthwhile for poor Mrs A to continue?", we're actually asking what Wittgenstein would regard as a question to which there is no answer, or not one which could be securely based on general intuitions.

Meet the family

So general intuitions, while they may be helpful, do not enable us to determine Mrs A's wishes in order that, despite the fact that she cannot exert it, we could respect her autonomy. We need help. The obvious place to find it is in the views of those who know the patient best: her children.

To do so is in accordance with the Department of Health guidance. This is prudent because any deviation from the script from the Department of Health or the GMC means tears before bedtime:

- *No-one* can give consent on behalf of an incompetent adult ...
- "Best interests" go wider than best medical interests, and include factors such as the wishes and beliefs of the patient when competent, their current wishes, their general well-being and their spiritual and religious welfare.
- People close to the patient may be able to give you information on some of these factors. (patient.co.uk)

And following the Mental Capacity Act 2005, the advice of others has much greater standing in law. A designated agent may act on behalf of the patient in respect of health as well as financial decisions. Such an agent can be identified in an advance directive.

But supposing no agent has been identified by the patient – and that is true in the vast majority of cases – or supposing there are several people who consider themselves agents and want to speak for the patient? Will the GMC come to the rescue? Alas, no. Consider this passage from the 2002 document I have already referred to: "It may be very difficult to arrive at a view about the preferences of patients who cannot decide for themselves, and doctors must not simply substitute their own values or those of the people consulted" (2002: para. 10). So where does the decision come from? Does it come down in a flaming pie from heaven? No human being – patient, relative or doctor – will suffice. So let us ignore the GMC's non-advice and return to the real world where decisions have to be made.

We had seen members of the family come and go and different members of the team had had conversations with different individuals. It was obviously high time that all parties met. Mrs A was getting increasingly chesty, and ethical decisions would have to be made.

We invited the family to a formal meeting. The first thing that struck me when I went into the rather small Relatives' Room on the ward was that it was very hot. This was because there was rather a large number of bodies metabolizing inside it. In addition to the staff, there were *nine* children, and unfortunately not only were there nine children but there were three views as to what should happen next.

Some family members were appalled with what we had done so far.

> My mother would not have wanted to have a tube up her nose, wouldn't have wanted to have had, you know, that sort of stuff in her arm. I mean, it is just disgraceful. She would have wanted to be left in peace. Whatever happened to death with dignity?

That was View 1. View 2, expressed with equal strength, was that the very thought of withdrawing treatment indicated that we did not value Mrs A, their mother. One very cross son suggested that we were not too distant in our attitudes from those individuals who had advocated euthanasia for the disabled. He spoke about "the slippery slope". Poignantly, there was a third view from the youngest child, who had learning disability. She didn't see the problem because "Mummy can't be ill because she isn't crying".

So there were three views and two of them were advanced quite forcefully. The meeting was characterized by heat and potential conflict and very little light. There was considerable hostility between the children and some of this was deflected towards the medical and nursing staff. It was easy to see why the children were angry: they were competing for their mother's love. Doubtless they had felt angry with their mother's failure to protect them adequately against their father's abusive behaviour, which was why they had neglected her in recent years. This was a chance to assert how much they loved their mother, notwithstanding their anger over what had happened in the past.

I could see that there would be little point in engaging in an abstract discussion about medical ethics. For example, it would not have been helpful to respond to the son who had talked about "slippery slope" by reciting some guiding principles such as: "Doctors will not unnecessarily prolong life when it is clear there is no benefit in continuing treatment". Or "Appropriate treatment decisions can be made in the interest of patients even where the foreseeable consequence of such actions may be the earlier death of the patient". It wouldn't have gone down well in that particular heated environment.

The reference to the "slippery slope" did upset me a bit, not just because I believe that the metaphor is actually extraordinarily unhelpful, although I believe that it is. It's worth taking a minute or two to consider why. Consider this quote from a nineteenth-century physician, Isaac Quimby: "A physician has no right to terminate the life of a patient, even when to prolong that life is to cause the most agonising tortures". I don't feel terribly happy about that. And I suspect I am not alone in regarding it as a poor model of the role of "the Good Doctor".

Anyway, if you are worried about slippery slopes, as I might have said, you can increase the coefficient of friction on the slope by many different means. Team-based decision-making is a corrective to eccentric, individual decision-making. Towards the end of my career as a doctor, I made sure that I tested my ethical decisions against the views of the most junior members of the team, to protect against group-think. The aim would be to develop a consensus as to the right thing to do not only within the healthcare team but also (where the patient is incapable of being at the centre of the decision) with the patient's family. The final safeguard would be an honest attempt to make sure that abandoning aggressive treatment should not lead to effective palliative care being withheld. If, for example, we decided not to treat a chest infection in this lady with intravenous antibiotics, we should still make all efforts to palliate her symptoms, by sucking out secretions if they were causing distress, providing oxygen, and so on.

WHAT NEXT?

The principles of biomedical ethics had not so far been very helpful in either our decision-making or in our discussion with Mrs

A's family. It would, however, be a serious mistake to dismiss them entirely: they are necessary to stop you straying too far from the path of virtue. They offer the most general reminders of the ethical underpinning of medicine. And they have also informed the debate around the reform of the law. Indeed, speaking as a non-lawyer, I have been impressed by the dialogue between biomedical ethics and evolving law. But they don't take you all the way to making a decision in a particular, that is to say singular, case.

The meeting with the family was both chastening and helpful. The knowledge that, whatever we did, we would upset one of her children was in some sense reassuring. They, too, had ethical intuitions and their collective understanding of the right thing to do did not prescribe a decision. We needed to think about other sources of guidance. One thing we all had in common was a wish to treat Mrs A in a way that we could all defend when we examined our consciences in the early hours. What was needed was something more subtle and specific than abstract principles: conversation.

On the other hand, it was perfectly obvious that there was not going to be a solution at the heated meeting I have described, so it was agreed we would leave things unchanged at present. If the chestiness turned into a chest infection, it would be treated in the conventional way. We would also continue with nasogastric feeding and subcutaneous fluids. The question of what to do if she had a cardiac arrest was not specifically addressed. However, I instructed the junior staff that if they were summoned to such an emergency they should hasten slowly and everyone who needed to know would make sure that futile and degrading heroics would be avoided.

A week later, we had a second meeting with the family. Significantly, fewer members attended. The temperature was rather lower; in particular, the hostility within the family and directed from the family to the staff was greatly diminished. I think they realized we didn't have horns sticking out of our heads: we were just people struggling to make a decent and humane decision in a rather difficult situation. It was explicitly agreed that CPR would be inappropriate and that the medical team could be allowed to make a decision as to whether or not intravenous antibiotics would be the right treatment if this lady developed a chest infection. Meanwhile we would continue with nasogastric feeding, although I wasn't too happy about that because Mrs A seemed to be signalling that the tube made her uncomfortable and frequently tried to pull it out. Finally, we agreed that we would continue with subcutaneous fluids.

A week later again, there was a further meeting, and the turnout on this occasion was even smaller, the temperature was much lower, and there was no hostility among those who turned up either to each other or to the clinical staff. It was agreed that we would not continue with the nasogastric feeding because of the discomfort it seemed to be causing. Sedation would be given liberally, even if it shortened her life. A few days later, she had a cardiac arrest and died.

THE LESSONS OF MRS A

I offer you this example to illustrate how, even in such seemingly straightforward cases, ethical decision-making is difficult. I am not sure that we did the right thing; after all, we may have simply prolonged the life and suffering of a patient in our care because we were too cowardly to stick by our sense of the right thing to do. Those extra weeks may have seemed like a very long time for the person forced to endure them.

When we make clinical decisions, we are always going to have to operate in an area of uncertainty, defined by the imprecision of clinical judgement, of the law, and the principles of biomedical ethics.

The clinical uncertainty, making judgement inevitably infallible, related most obviously to the prognosis and the extent to which different treatments would affect the outcome. Clinical guidelines are never going to tell you exactly what to do because clinical science is a probabilistic art. Even so, you have to make definite and irreversible decisions on the basis of incomplete knowledge. Then there might sometimes be an element of uncertainty about the appropriate application of the law, especially where there is (as there was) conflict between members of the family, none of whom had been identified as the patient's official spokesperson. And finally, and most worryingly, there was a clear uncertainty about the appropriate application of ethical principles in guiding our decision. In addition to this, there are all sorts of things that run through your mind when you are reaching a decision, influences of which you may not be completely aware: social pressures, unreflecting intuitions, custom and practice, and your own previous, particularly recent, clinical and personal experience.

And this is not going to change in the future. In the real mess of the real world, our decisions will fall short of being entirely defensible. We may have more precise clinical guidelines; we may have a mathematically more accurate idea of the likely outcome; but a serious margin of uncertainty will remain. The law is still going to give us guidance, but is not an exact prescription, as lawyers know to their benefit and their clients and the taxpayer to their cost. And the ambiguities, uncertainties and conflicts around the application of the principles of biomedical ethics will still remain. On top of that, clinicians will still be subject to (often conflicting) social pressures, and will have to reconcile warring intuitions within and between members of the care team, and these may become more difficult to deal with in a more diverse society.

So we have to operate in an area of uncertainty, and that means negotiation, rather than legislation; conversation supplementing rule or principle. In the case of Mrs A, we didn't achieve anything in terms of her outcome with our medical interventions. Perhaps we kept her slightly more comfortable with nursing care and a bit of fluid while we were thinking through the best way to deal with the consequences of our initial life-saving actions. If we did anything truly useful, it was to help her family to come to terms with her death and perhaps in consequence to come to terms with her life and with their own lives. We encouraged them to get on with each other and to talk to each other. I like to think that this was important.

At any rate, we need to supplement the abstract ethics that fills thousands of pages of books and journals published by the ever-expanding bioethics industry with an ethics that can address the aspects of the decision that sit in the unique interstices of individual cases, the parts of the real world that ethicists cannot reach. To some extent, this means that the clinicians and the patient and the family and the team are in territory that goes beyond the printed directions, beyond what can be defended under all circumstances and be proof against criticism.

I can envisage some people being very unhappy about how we managed this lady and her family. One of my closest colleagues was a devout Roman Catholic. He once presented a case of a patient with extremely advanced motor neuron disease and he discussed the circumstances in which he would consider withdrawing nasogastric feeding. (This was before new, less invasive and more effective feeding methods such as percutaneous endoscopic gastronomy were in common practice.) Two people stood up in the audience and said "You are a murderer". He was shocked and surprised but this to me illustrated the truth that when you make an ethical decision you won't please everyone. Once you go beyond, but not outside, the law and try and behave ethically in a way that goes beyond, but not outside, the principles of biomedical ethics, then you are a little bit on your own.

Good decision-making in every aspect of medicine requires mutual trust between those who are legitimately involved. This quotation from the bioethicist Arthur Caplan has the authentic ring of clinical truth:

> Numbers alone, even grim ones, derived from thousands of cases and years of experience, will not suffice.
> ... The greater the trust between physician and patient ... the more willing patients will be to refrain from pursuing long odds to achieve bad ends. (Caplan 1996)

And that is why trust in physicians is irreplaceable. "Trust me, I am a doctor" has almost become a standard joke; people are invited to translate it into "Trust me, I am Harold Shipman". But regulations and guidelines (with or without menaces) – and the GMC specializes in guidelines with menaces – can't fill a hole in trust. Lawyers, journalists and politicians – who may themselves be untrusted – are unlikely to compensate for any deficits in trusted doctors. Somebody has to make a decision and trust has to find a location somewhere.

That is why I am deeply concerned about the sustained attempt, especially in the first half of the noughties, to undermine trust in doctors. The assumption that you would find a locus for trust somewhere else is unfounded. Those who undermine trust in the medical profession to sell newspapers, to make a killing in fees, or to be voguishly postmodern are doing patients a great disservice.

Let's end with a final visit to the GMC. In the last paragraph of the unhelpful document from which I have quoted there is this warning:

> If you decide not to follow any part of the guidance in this document, you must be prepared to explain and justify your actions and decisions, to patients and their families, your colleagues, and where necessary, the courts and the GMC.
> (2002: para. 95)

"And the GMC". Message received.

FINAL REFLECTION

So how can one be an ethical doctor in the real mess of the real world? You must, of course, operate in accordance with broad ethical principles, as far as you can. If they are in conflict you must choose an overriding principle, and doing this involves consultation and the deployment of your imagination. You must remain within the framework of the law, which is not difficult, although sometimes remaining within the framework of the law makes you feel you have let the patient down. And, of course, you have a responsibility to optimize your knowledge of prognosis, evidence-based interventions and the latest clinical practice. Knowing what you are talking about is a fundamental ethical obligation.

After that, you simply do the best you can. And if you are still criticized, it is useful perhaps to remind yourself of a couple of thinkers who knew about the inescapability of uncertainty. The first is Nietzsche who pointed out that (very often) "Convictions are more dangerous enemies of truth than lies". And the second is W. B. Yeats, whose *persona* in *The Second Coming* reflected that "The best lack all conviction, while the worst/Are full of passionate intensity". If we remember this, we may be able to think a little bit more intelligently about ethical issues and making ethical decisions in the real mess of the real world.

13

On Caring and Not Caring

According to the philosopher Martin Heidegger, our very being-in-the-world, our *being there* or *Da-sein* as he called it, is characterized by *care*. It is not an occasional or episodic feature of our human being. Most of our care, of course, is devoted to ourselves: *Da-sein*, according to Heidegger, "is that being whose being is an issue for itself". We look after our being in a myriad different ways as we pursue a multitude of goals, creating or running away from narratives of ourselves; and of course we also care for those close to us – lovers, friends, relationships and dependents. And we care for the things we like – our possessions – and the parts of the environment that impinge on us. This care can be self-centred, as it mainly is, or other-centred, where we forget ourselves in thinking of the needs of others.

I am not going to say anything about this everyday kind of caring, huge and hugely important though it is. I am going to focus on another, also very important but rather problematic, form of caring: paid, professional caring for people who are often superficially the least attractive or glamorous of our fellow creatures and who may make very great demands because they are ill, or are for some other reason unable to take care of themselves, such as having learning disability, or suffering from dementia, and whose behaviour may test the sympathy we feel, or most certainly should feel, for their suffering. I am talking about this not only because it is topical but because it is something that affects, or should affect, us all. If we ourselves are not in need of care, it may only be a matter of time – less time in my case than in the case of many of you reading this book – and, anyway, we shall be very lucky if there is not already someone we care for, or should care for, who is needy in this unglamorous way.

THE OMBUDSMAN'S TALE

The stories are familiar and yet still beggar belief. Hospital patients: are starved because they are unable to feed themselves; become dehydrated because nobody thought to help them to drink, or could be bothered to do so; are left to rot in soiled or dirty clothes; are not bathed (in one case for thirteen weeks); and are denied pain relief. Families who try to make up for these terrible shortcomings in care are actively unwelcomed and are excluded from decisions about discharge.

These tales, reminiscent of reports from a Romanian orphanage, formed the substance of a shocking document published in 2011 by the NHS Ombudsman recording grossly abusive care of elderly patients in the NHS. In *Care and Compassion?*, Ann Abraham describes in detail ten of the 9,000 complaints investigated by her office between 2009 and 2010. Nine out of these ten patients died.

One wrong response to such ghastly stories is to minimize their significance. Ten patients, after all, is a small number compared with the many millions of people the NHS sees every year. In survey after survey, the overwhelming majority of patients are very satisfied with the care they are given. This defence won't wash. Would we feel relaxed about unnecessary deaths in custody because most policemen do a good job?

Besides, these stories illustrate a wider picture of neglect that many organizations, including the UK pressure group Patients Association, have flagged up. Many of us recognize this pattern from our own experience of the hospital care of elderly friends and relatives. Even I, a professor of geriatric medicine for many years, was unable to ensure that my mother, a hospital in-patient, and too ill to feed herself, was fed regularly in my absence. I lost count of the times I found a full plate of cold, no longer edible food out of reach.

Another wrong response is to see this report as a nail in the coffin of the NHS and of the very idea of a universal healthcare system free at the point of need, funded out of taxes, and directed and regulated centrally to a significant extent. On this issue, those impressive patient satisfaction surveys *are* relevant: the NHS is *not* broken. And those who think the answer lies in opening up healthcare provision more widely to the private sector should be reminded that abuse of older people and people with learning disability is equally well documented in that sector, notably private care homes. Two words – Winterbourne View – will be enough to establish my case. This privately run Gulag charged local authorities over £180,000 a year to bully and terrorize the residents until an investigation by the BBC television programme *Panorama* brought the cruel racket to an end.

Others will see *Care and Compassion?* as justifying the Health and Social Care Act 2012 bringing about radical changes in the way the NHS is organized, without explaining how yet another re-disorganization will help. Bringing in providers more explicitly motivated by profit is less likely to improve care for the most vulnerable and financially least attractive "clients" than to divert taxes to organizations whose interest in health is motivated primarily by the promise of rich pickings.

Indeed, the importation of a business ethos or business model into the NHS, in the name of efficiency, and the worship of throughput, may itself have contributed to downgrading the importance of things that matter but cannot be measured. An hour spent comforting a terrified, confused patient does not do much for the health of the balance sheet unless it can be separately invoiced. There has been much talk of "private sector values", but the assumption that only that which can be counted truly counts, and the narrowing of accountability to "accountantability", would only promote decline in standards of care.

The usual response to a scandal is to throw an inquiry at the relevant institution. With some exceptions, the track record of inquiries is dire. They are often worse than useless because they prescribe procedural, bureaucratic, legalistic answers to problems that lie elsewhere. Typically, they make vast numbers of recommendations – usually described as "rafts" or even "*whole* rafts" of proposals – as if the success of an inquiry were measured by the quantity of its recommendations. These translate in practice into boxes to be ticked documenting that certain procedures have been gone through, certain steps have been taken, and that these have been communicated and that the communication has been documented. Every box that has to be ticked carries an opportunity-cost. The exigencies of the computer screen compete with actual care, distracting health professionals from the needs of their patients. Each datum entered may be a kindness foregone.

We do not fill in a hole in basic humanity by regulating care more closely. Nor can it be filled with "more training", the other solution that is so often invoked. Training in what, for God's sake? In things that a four-year-old would understand? That older people need to eat and drink? That sitting in a puddle of urine is not pleasant? That it is wrong to allow an elderly patient to go unwashed for thirteen weeks on a hospital ward? More prolonged exposure, in an extended training course, to the rhetoric of "empowering" patients, and to educators who have degraded the word "dignity" to an empty mantra, will make little difference.

What is needed is reflection on the pressures, the permissions, the attitudes and the priorities that have made mistreating some patients so acceptable that it can take place in broad daylight. Genuine soul-searching and not just "measures", "procedures" and beady-eyed scrutiny is necessary. The simple question "How did we behave so horribly to this person?" would be a good place to start.

The answers will be complex and beyond the usual scope of inquiries. This should occur not only in those places where things have gone so wrong, but to other places where shortcomings are real but less headline-grabbing. And it would be equally important to learn from those many places where excellent care is given.

And reflection should look beyond healthcare institutions. They are, after all, a microcosm of a society at large and their values mirror society's values. Each society gets the carers and public servants it deserves. Devaluation of those unglamorous but supremely human, and invaluable, activities such as hands-on care of elderly people (who are often themselves undervalued) is the obverse of the overvaluation of empty glamour, which is currently pandemic. (Of this, more presently.) And the business ethos that has started to reduce health professionals from individuals pursuing a calling to sessional functionaries, replacing the covenant we have with the sick with a set of closely prescribed contractual arrangements, reflects wider unhappy trends in the world beyond the hospital.

The NHS should be fiercely proud of the care given to most people and deeply ashamed of the maltreatment of a minority. We are all part of the NHS and all of us in our different ways contribute to creating the context in which it operates and so shaping its record. That is why we must not allow our response to scandals to be confined to self-indulgent outrage or a call for more regulation of those who will care for us in our hours of greatest need.

NURSES

When a scandal breaks in a care setting, it is often nurses who are seen to be at the centre of events. This is not entirely fair, because it merely reflects the fact that they are responsible for the greater part of hands-on care: either providing it themselves directly or supervising others who do. The nursing profession was well represented among those who were convicted of extreme cruelty in the

Winterbourne View care home, although most of the care provided in this £180,000-a-year facility was given by care assistants.

In fact, nursing is one of the most admirable of all professions. I was very lucky, in my thirty-seven years as a hospital doctor, to work with some extraordinarily gifted nurses. They were knowledgeable, dedicated and hardworking, of course; but, on top of this, they had compassion, empathy, common sense, and a 360° solid-angle awareness of what was going on around them. And grace under pressure. It is not easy to keep your cool when several people at once are asking you questions, one or more phones are ringing, and you are reassuring a patient about to undergo an operation, trying to keep the drug round to time, and making sure the medical team knows what's going on.

But there are some nurses who are simply not right for the job. And there are wards where leadership is lacking. Here, information gets lost and practices are sloppy, and patients, treated with inappropriate familiarity, call in vain for bedpans. The staff appear too busy to care or to show that they care, and seem to spend more time chatting to each other than talking with anxious patients. Not infrequently, elderly people who are immobile become malnourished and dehydrated because food and drink are placed out of reach.

A year or so ago, the then junior Health Minister Ann Keen announced a measure that she believed would "raise the quality of patient care". This would seem to be welcome. But the measure she described may not have been precisely what the patient ordered. By 2013, anyone wishing to be a nurse will have to have taken a degree course lasting up to four years. The reasons given for this, the most radical change in nurse training since the NHS was founded, are not entirely persuasive or encouraging. It is designed "to raise the *status* of nursing" (my emphasis). This, alas, is a story we have heard many times before to justify reforms in the profession, particularly in the development of new career pathways. It no longer seems relevant. The ghost of the nurse as "the doctor's handmaiden" has long since been exorcised, not least because of the increasing proportion of nurses who are male and the fact that the medical profession is becoming increasing female. In many cases, nurses are the leaders of the multidisciplinary team.

The then Chief Nursing Officer Christine Beasley argued that, as more young people than ever are studying for a degree, this will make nursing more attractive. The logic is not compelling. A four-year course may put off some individuals who have all the necessary qualities for nursing either because they do not feel academically inclined, or because they may not wish to accumulate large debts. Besides, one would hope that people would enter the nursing profession because they are motivated to care for others rather than simply because they want to enter a degree course. It has also been argued by the Department of Health that graduates would "be able to deal more readily with increasingly complex care in an increasingly challenging health and social care system". It is not at all clear that the difference between a degree course and the existing diploma will necessarily equip nurses to function better in complex situations. The kind of multitasking I have just referred to requires quite different qualities. What is more, there is no evidence that the 75 per cent of nurses who currently lack degrees are less capable than the remainder who have them.

Many nurses have successfully extended their roles – acting as specialists in different contexts – without a degree. I have a particular reason for being grateful to specialist epilepsy nurses, who vastly improved the care I was able to give to my patients when we worked together to deliver a service to older people with seizures. Most simply took on the extra training. Requiring all nurses to have a degree seems to be a blunt, poorly targeted instrument for enabling some nurses to acquire new skills and take on new roles. There is no reason why, of course, some nurses should not choose to proceed to a degree after they have acquired a diploma.

There is, however, a deeper concern that has made the Patients Association lukewarm about this development. It will not address the failures of basic care that it has documented and all of us have witnessed when we visited the bedsides of our friends and relatives in hospital. Indeed it may exacerbate the problem. The emphasis on the academic aspects of nursing, rather than practical skills and the deeply humane activity of hands-on care, may constitute a kind of "dumbing up". Focusing on more abstract, theoretical issues, which a degree course, as opposed to vocational training, would seem to demand, might diminish commitment to basic nursing, a fear captured in the much-used phrase "too posh to wash". This is dangerous, particularly at a time when such care is undervalued – although not by those who receive it.

One could be forgiven for thinking that the rewards and prestige of nurses rise in proportion to the distance they maintain from the bedside. Already, we are seeing core nursing activities being handed over to healthcare assistants who require only a National Vocational Qualification (NVQ) or similar. Such individuals are often deeply caring and highly skilled but it cannot be good for patients to have their nursing care divided between yet more professionals or an iron wall erected between different aspects of nursing. Experienced nurses know that they are often able to learn much more about the patient's needs and indeed their condition during the course of giving a blanket bath than through a structured interview in which many boxes are ticked.

One can only hope that this latest development in nurse training will not simply place more distance between nurses and the patients who need their care. Ann Keen's talk of providing "new nurses with the decision-making skills they need to make a high-level judgement in the transformed NHS" doesn't awaken the expectation that the reforms will do much for the lonely, frightened, thirsty patient sitting in a pool of urine.

DEPENDENCY

My concern for such a patient is not exactly disinterested. One day it will be me. Or you.

You wake up, leap out of bed, rush into the shower, drag on your clothes, run down the stairs two at a time, bolt your breakfast, and drive off to work. Thus an ordinary start to an ordinary day. Ordinary, that is, until one ordinary day, disaster – a car crash, a fall from a horse – picks you out. Your legs, paralysed by spinal injury, are no longer obedient to your will; they have become items to be lugged around, almost as if they were part of the external world. *Almost* – because the price of not looking after these engines-turned-into-passengers may be very high.

Everything changes. You no longer leap from your bed but work your way out of it; the journey to the shower is on wheels that get stuck in the pile of a thick carpet; washing demands cutting-edge gymnastics; and dressing, the painstaking construction of a house of cloth around your body, is a sequence of ingeniously solved problems, enacted in the teeth of the spasms of your wilful limbs. The stairs are now as unassailable as a glass cliff. Breakfasting, once performed in an absent-minded hurry, breaks down into an infinite number of calculated steps. Things that seemed to happen almost by themselves, requiring little or no attention, have to be enacted in all their tedious detail.

And when you leave your front door you enter an unfriendly place of physical obstacles, hazards, frustrations. In the great outdoors you face the ever-present risk of being left stranded, or taunted by things just out of reach, in a world made more hostile by the carelessness, thoughtlessness and gawping rudeness of others. There is no "nipping back" to collect something that is forgotten. Daily living demands D-day levels of organization.

In her brave, brilliant and witty despatches from the front line, Spinal Column in *The Times*, Melanie Reid describes how her spinal injury (she fell from a horse) "threatens the death of daydreams", the displacement of personal narratives of chosen futures by other stories that are unchosen and impersonal, although they have to be lived personally. Dreams of losing those pounds, completing a marathon, securing that promotion, are put seemingly permanently on hold. At any rate, they are squeezed out by other more urgent goals: getting your left leg to lock long enough at the knee so you can stand; learning the best ways of ensuring continence; mastering the art of safely mounting a recalcitrant pavement in an unstable wheelchair.

While we are not identical with our bodies, or even our nervous systems, a body and, in particular, a brain and a spinal cord, in some sort of working order, are essential for normal life. Neurological damage, in particular, may turn the theatre of daily life into a strange and often hostile land. Medicine has much to offer, even in the case of serious spinal injury: most importantly, ways of minimizing the initial damage to the spinal cord and preventing some of its secondary consequences (such as pressure sores and bladder infections and dealing with those fiendishly impertinent spasms). It may one day offer techniques such as stem cells to repair the spinal pathways. Even more important are the knowledge, intelligence and skill of therapists and nurses, whose marvellous hands and heads and hearts can be all-transforming, giving training, guidance and advice, dispensing the right balance of hope and realism as you retrace the journey back from a dependency you had not experienced since you took your first few tottering infant steps. It is hardly surprising that psychological and spiritual support so hugely influence outcome in people who are trying to construct new ways of engaging with the world. But even when it encompasses moral support, intelligent understanding, tact and encouragement, medicine is not enough. The wider world has its part to play.

It is perhaps because events such as stroke and spinal cord injury change your world with an appalling abruptness, allowing no time for adaptation and mental preparation, that they are such a dramatic *exposé* of the illusion that we are ever truly independent. Throughout our lives, we are borne up by millions of visible and invisible hands, creating a safe, warm, hunger-free, meaningful world. Disability does not make us more dependent but makes visible that large part of our dependency that is normally concealed through being so obvious: the normal working of a body that we take for granted. Having an intact nervous system means that we do not have to know how to move our legs in order to walk; they do the walking. If I had to run my own body, I would be dead in minutes, if not seconds.

The cliché that "we are all in it together" is connected with a truth upon which civilized society is based: our profound mutual dependency. Mutual support mitigates our dependency on our always vulnerable and sometime capricious bodies that never particularly had our lives in mind. The experience of those who are forced in midlife to fashion a new, liveable world from scratch, underlines this. Melanie Reid's journey from the "helpless blob" she felt herself to be immediately after her accident to a rich and rewarding life constructed on her own terms requires a world that is as supportive to her as it is to those of us who have not, or not yet, suffered damage to the bodily infrastructure that we rely upon at every moment of our lives.

NOT CARING ABOUT ANYTHING THAT MATTERS

And yet we have grounds to fear the future that will await us if we are foolish enough to fall seriously ill and look to our fellow citizens for help. The most obvious grounds for terror are the manifold, wall-to-wall consequences of the translation of value into price; of the marketization of social consciousness; of the replacement of those complex covenants that underpinned mutual responsibility with an ever denser network of contracts. Caring, healthcare, support may in future be delivered according to service-level agreements that will be determined by multinational business entities whose primary responsibility will be to their shareholders while the gap between minimal care and true kindness will be finessed by PR agencies. But there are less obvious, and possibly even more important, influences at work. I am talking about the cult of the celebrity, whose malign effect goes far beyond the devaluation of care.

I first began brooding over this one weekend when the late unlamented *News of the World* devoted several pages to a woman dishing the dirt on her ex-hubby, once a footballer of some renown. At the same time, the magazine shelves of WHSmith were offering six different versions of the state of play in the circulation war that was the relationship between Katie Price (aka Jordan) and *her* hubby, Mr Peter Andre. Amy Whitehouse was waiting in the wings to make a comeback to or from scandal. This is the celebrity culture and, some will tell you, if it makes you vomit, or rage, *just get over it*. Even Canute (that one-factoid celebrity) gave up when he saw the ice cream vans floating in the sea. Besides, there are, surely, worse curses: violence, greed, poverty and – looking further afield – civil war, dictatorship, plague. Even so, it is a curse; it is a cognitive malaise that affects us all and erodes many of the things that we hold dear.

The heart of the celebrity culture is an individual emptiness gawped at by a collective emptiness. (Think of the face of Kate Moss, which amounts to nothing other than the face of Kate Moss, attached to a thousand photo shoots and a million magazine articles purveying things that would be uninteresting even if true.) OK, so it's not very edifying but isn't it all a bit of harmless fun? No it is not; and the harm has many dimensions.

First and foremost, there is the opportunity-cost of interminable second-hand gossip: preoccupation with celebrities is an appalling squandering of human consciousness. The centuries of prattle, of airtime and screen-time, the miles of column inches, are a sickening misuse of the gift of life, of health and adequate nutrition, of freedom from oppression, of the access we now have to the world of knowledge and the arts. They are stolen from thought about things that are truly important or worthwhile: fighting poverty, disease and the iniquities and injustice of the world; the profound joy afforded by literature and the arts; questions about the meaning and purpose of life; and caring about those who need and deserve our care. Celebrity culture is a black hole sucking up the light. It is not only a manifestation of the cretinization or tabloidization of our culture but also further cretinizes it.

This culture spreads like a stain. It engulfs even those whose fame is rooted in real achievement or real responsibility. As the empty are valued, so the valuable are emptied. They are treated as if they were as vacuous as pop idols. Scientists, artists and politicians become defined in the collective consciousness not by the serious, complex matters they deal with or with their real achievements but, increasingly, by their sex lives, their personal traumas, their peccadilloes. Never mind the general theory of relativity and those field equations that are one of the greatest monuments of the human intellect. What the punter wants to know is whether Einstein shagged his dog. This is what we might call, after Alan Bennett's play, the *Kafka's Dick Syndrome*. Don't bore me with the fact that Kafka had one of the great imaginations of the last century: tell me what he was like in the sack.

Another damaging aspect of celebrity culture is the increasing tendency to treat celebrities as oracles. This goes beyond unscrupulous product endorsement. I lost count of the number of household names whose ignorant, innumerate opinions clouded the debate on the MMR vaccine. The expertise of the empty reached its climax when a certain pop-star who has, to distract from the poverty of her music by (to use my late mother's phrase) "prancing half-naked round a stage", commanded attention for her opinion that mystic Kabbalah fluid could decontaminate radioactive sites.

It must be wonderful when people hang on your every ill-considered opinion, your choice of lipstick, every twist and turn of your turbulent relationship with Mr Not Right. So it's hardly surprising that so many young people declare that they wish to be famous as a primary aim rather than as a by-product of true achievement, or as a result of making a difference to the world. Victoria Beckham is an exemplar that awakens aspirations that are at once worthless and, for the vast majority of people, beyond reach.

And then there is the disgusting endgame. When those who have been elevated to divine status stumble, the pack smells blood. The erstwhile worshippers, in the grip of *Schadenfreude*, rejoice to see the Photoshop-enhanced body fall over, with pooh on its knickers (or, in the case of Britney Spears, visible menstrual blood), rowing with its partner, throwing up in the gutter or checking in and out of rehab.

All right, it may be conceded, celebrity culture is harmful in many ways; but surely it is not new. Mark Bostridge's brilliant biography reminds us of the extraordinary cult that surrounded Florence

Nightingale. But at least she earned her fame on the basis of a fundamental contribution to making the world a better place. She was not just a pair of big tits attached to a savvy PR machine. And the celebrity culture is now more efficiently mediated than it was in Victorian times: it is wall-to-wall.

It is, perhaps, a touch Utopian to imagine a society in which people are preoccupied by the large, practical problems of the world, immersed in the richness of art, and exercised by the mystery of human nature. But surely we do not have to settle for a diet of eternal gassing about tenth-order ephemera reported at third hand? Celebrity culture degrades, and indeed endangers, us all. The conversation we have with ourselves about things that matter is immeasurably impoverished and our lives are lost to lifestyle. No one who cares for the world we live in should "just get over it". The empty glamour of celebrity steals glamour from those things that matter, are truly worthwhile, and address our deepest needs.

SURGEONS

Foremost among those who address such needs are surgeons. Placing your anaesthetized body in the hands of someone who is charged with opening it up and removing diseased parts without damaging the rest is the supreme expression of trust in others. And it makes appalling demands on those at the other end of the knife. An old friend once told me that, in the years he was training as a surgeon, he would wake his wife regularly with nightmares in which he would shout "Stop the bleeding!"

The evidence over the past few decades is that surgery in the UK has become progressively safer with fewer avoidable errors. This is a tribute to the passionate determination of surgeons to achieve ever better results by a series of initiatives, including a multitude of clinical trials, improved training, education and self-education, and increasing accurate documentation of outcomes and errors. Candour and transparency have gone hand in hand with scientific and technical advance. The attitudes and behaviour of surgeons are now far from the seemingly ineradicable Lancelot Spratt stereotype. Yes, studies show surgeons to be extraverts but this must be a good thing: one would not wish for them to be paralysed by Hamlet-like introspection – to cut or not to cut.

It would, however, be dangerous to assume that everything is well. The career of the late Rodney Ledward, a cavalier gynaecologist who damaged the bodies and lives of hundreds of women before he was finally stopped only a decade ago, and more recently of Ian Paterson, a breast surgeon who operated on people who did not require operations and operated inadequately on those who did, are terrifying examples of what it is still possible to get away with. And there is still a small minority of practitioners who are not signed up to the ethos of modern surgery.

The story of one such surgeon was sufficient to sweep the Eurozone crisis off the front pages of *The Times* a couple of years ago ("Scandal of Killer Doctors Allowed to Stay in the NHS"). Gideon Lauffer, a Consultant General Surgeon, had been temporarily suspended from clinical practice by the GMC. The GMC found that he had acted outside his competence in two cases that had ended disastrously for the patients. His period of suspension over, he was employed in an A & E department, acting in a junior capacity and closely supervised, although these limitations on his practice have recently been relaxed.

Hardly the kind of thing, you might think, to relegate the possibility of a global recession to the middle pages of *The Times*. But there was an extensive hinterland to the story. Concerns about Lauffer's competence had been raised by an admirably persistent whistle-blower as long ago as 2000. It is possible that he had killed or seriously injured up to twenty patients through botched operations. Over the decade, there have been several out-of-court settlements, involving in one case a gagging order. What is more, the GMC was itself deeply unhappy with the decision of its Fitness to Practice Panel (which, it should be noted, has a majority of lay members) to recommend temporary suspension rather than permanent erasure from the medical register. The case of this one surgeon raises many issues.

It would be inaccurate and unfair to suggest that Lauffer's behaviour was typical of his profession. The attitude of the vast majority of surgeons is entirely appropriate to the gravity of the responsibilities they carry; and their competence is not in doubt. It is astonishing, therefore, that Lauffer was able to continue operating for so long. The unfunny joke that doctors bury their mistakes overlooks the fact that, if they do, they exhume them in their hearts when they face the court of conscience that meets at 3am. This may be why medics have sometimes been reluctant to report the failure of colleagues: "There, but for the grace of God, go I". That sentiment has long been a thing of the past and the GMC's *Good Medical Practice* requires doctors to "protect patients from risk of harm posed by another colleague's conduct, performance or health". Concealing another's incompetence is as much a dereliction of duty as concealing your own.

Deciding to blow the whistle is never easy. It may require setting aside loyalties to someone who may be a close colleague. You also need to be sure that their performance really is off the scale and that a succession of poor outcomes is the result of incompetence rather than bad luck. And those who have to respond to the whistle-blower have an equally difficult task. They have to pick out the signal of a real problem from the noise of acceptable variation in outcomes in a surgeon who may have conducted thousands of operation on patients whose risk profile (including frailty and concurrent illness) may be quite different from that of other practitioners. There is also the sometimes difficult task of distinguishing whistle-blowing from grudge-bearing, although this hardly applied to the Lauffer case, where clear evidence of malpractice was not just an illusion of hindsight.

The unbearable suffering of those affected by surgical incompetence and the refusal of some surgeons to acknowledge it may make it seem unfeeling and crass to urge that the failings of a few doctors, however serious, be kept in proportion. But it is important for the sake of other patients that the cases of Ledward, Lauffer and Paterson should not prompt the usual blanket response to medical scandals. The GMC must pursue its intention to seek to extend its powers to appeal against the decision of the Fitness to Practice Panel.

But treating all surgeons as potential miscreants and demanding ever closer monitoring, documentation and regulation of everyday practice will not make the world safer for patients.

Harry Cayton, the Chief Executive of the Council for Healthcare Regulatory Excellence, the umbrella organization that oversees the various health professions, once observed that "leaders of medical colleges and organisations are resolutely and seriously self-critical in a way that no other groups of employers, experts, workers or advisors has shown itself to be" (Royal College of Physicians 2005: 6). And this is certainly true of surgeons.

What is needed is to support the present culture of candour that makes it possible to admit mistakes, and near-mistakes, to apologise where necessary, and to look at what it was in the doctors or the system within which they work that predisposes them to otherwise avoidable error. Above all, it is important to remember that while surgery may kill or otherwise damage people, sometimes avoidably and sometimes negligently, it is hugely beneficial and practised by dedicated professionals who carry burdens of responsibility that few of us could withstand, and who meet extraordinary demands made on their skill, knowledge and decision-making ability, and their moral courage, on a day-to-day basis.

Why, in a world where money and celebrity are now valued above everything else, would anyone want to undergo long training to meet those demands? Why would anyone want to give themselves to a caring profession where the rewards are delayed and relatively small and the pressures are often unbearable? Ruthlessly self-promoting celebrities and rapacious bankers tell us that there is a much better way to live. Caring is a mug's game.

NOT *THE TRUMAN SHOW*: TRUE CARING

Dementia is a stark reminder of how, as Philip Larkin said, "our flesh/ Surrounds us with its own decisions" ("Ignorance", in Larkin 1964). Brain processes we may not even have heard of, and certainly could not understand, eat into our ability to think, and our capacity to grasp who and what and why. Until we lose our agency altogether, we act in ways that hitherto would have horrified us. Our memories are pruned and the rich connectedness of the "I" is pulled apart. The future shrinks along with the past and we are confined to an eternal present in which (to quote Larkin again) we sit "through days of thin continuous dreaming", trying, with what remains of our self, to make sense of a world that has become warped into a permanent and often terrifying question mark.

Little wonder, then, that it is difficult to look unflinchingly at this condition, in which we see mirrored our most radical vulnerability, or even to think clearly about how we should respond to, support, manage, care for and protect those who suffer from it and whose ranks we may well ourselves join. So when we hear of a purpose-built village in the Netherlands populated almost entirely by people with dementia, we may have rather confused reactions.

In Hogeway, which was opened in 2009, there are 152 residents living in groups of six in houses that have been specially designed to correspond to a variety of Dutch lifestyles, ranging from rustic to Indonesian, so that they look like home. The domestic spaces are customized to match the memories, culture, interests and hobbies of the residents, which is important since, when factual and other explicit memories are lost, the material environment is an even more crucial prop for orientation. Residents are free to do largely as they wish: to dress when and how they like, to eat whatever they fancy, to walk out into the streets rain or shine, enter each other's houses, to participate in cultural activities, even to go shopping without their wallets and return with dozens of cans of food they do not want or need. One key to reconciling this remarkable freedom with ensuring safety is the lavish provision of carers – four to each resident – available day and night to bring people home, to ensure that they do not neglect or hurt themselves, and even to return food to the supermarket.

The Hogeway experiment – which has attracted European-wide attention – sounds imaginative and deeply humane. The description of the atmosphere as "serene" is not implausible and a great improvement on the anguished indignity and frustration that often characterizes the life of residents in even the best-run and respectful institutions, where the focus is primarily on provision of basic care and any ambition to establish a truly therapeutic community is constrained by risk assessments, often made more cautious by staff shortages. Daily life in some institutions consists of dozing in chairs in front of meaningless television screens, and/or being subjected to unchosen music, punctuated by futile attempts to go home that may be rewarded by an increase in sedation. The contrast with Hogeway – where residents take themselves to the hairdresser, have a drink, and do their shopping, all under the careful but unobtrusive guidance of care staff – could not be greater.

Even so, some have found the very idea of the village rather chilling, even if it does replicate the amenities of everyday life, and offers the residents the possibility of self-expression that may lead to striking improvements in their condition. The sequestration of people with dementia may seem a cognitive apartheid or waken memories of earlier rejected approaches to chronic illness: colonies for people with epilepsy; asylums for the mentally ill hidden in the depths of the countryside; remote isolation hospitals for infectious diseases; and other "total institutions". To be transferred to a place where you are surrounded by other people who do not understand you, or acknowledge you, just as you do not comprehend or acknowledge them, might seem to reinforce the sense that dementia is taking you to a world with no outside. And there is the deception practised on patients by treating as normal behaviour that is nothing of the kind and then discreetly heading off its adverse consequences. In some cases, the deceit is quite elaborate, with better-off residents being encouraged to believe that the carers are their servants, the delusion being reinforced by expensive decor. The analogy with *The Truman Show* – the film that portrays the life of a man unaware of living in a constructed reality television show broadcast worldwide – has been invoked.

These reservations are compelling only if we underestimate the extent to which dementia remorselessly unscrambles every aspect of ourselves. To a person with the drastically shrunken life-space of advanced Alzheimer's disease, a conventional care home is much more of a ghetto than Hogeway, particularly as the latter's world, free of the locks and doors and proscriptions of most institutions, keeps its walls hidden. And the village is not cut off from the outside world. Visiting by friends, acquaintances and loved ones is open. The key to the whole enterprise is a sustained attempt to empathize with the experience of the residents, motivated by a profound respect that sees people with dementia as being as singular beneath their general symptoms as they were when they were cognitively intact.

And – ah yes – resources. At £50,000 per person per year, this publicly funded facility is not cheap. In the light of the coming privatization of the NHS, which will divert more taxpayers' money into the pockets of health entrepreneurs, similar developments in the UK may seem utopian. (Recall, after all, Winterbourne View, run by a private company, which charged the state £3,500 a week for a regime marked by "cruel, callous and degrading abuse" of disabled patients.) We should, however, see Hogeway as a benchmark against which what is typically on offer for people with dementia should be judged; and we should not allow the malign forces currently circling the NHS to cause us to lose sight of what is possible or to despair of realizing it (see Tallis & Davis 2013).

Because I know where I would like to be cared for when I no longer have any idea who Raymond Tallis is or was: somewhere like Hogeway, where I would not be a mere instance of a disease but still a person. But please, please don't call my new home town "Dementiaville".

AFTERTHOUGHTS

> We perish'd, each alone:
> But I beneath a rougher sea
> And whelm'd in deeper gulfs than he.
> (William Cowper, "The Castaway")

It is as important to reflect on how it is that things have gone well – when they do go well – as it is to think about what happened when they go horribly wrong. The deep humanity of Hogeway may tell us as much about how we may translate the hot-and-cold running rhetoric of a "caring society" into actual care for those who need it. It is striking that it is in the Netherlands that we see this experiment in state-sponsored kindness. This is a country that has legalized euthanasia and, according to those who oppose liberalizing our present laws around assisted dying, must be a place where life is devalued and the lives of those who are intimately and globally disabled are devalued even more profoundly. But that is a theme for another place (see Chapter 16, "The Right to an Assisted Death").

Hogeway is a beacon and it shows what is possible. But if the possible is going to become more generally actual, and excellence is to be the norm, we need to think more honestly about the barriers to caring for those who are most vulnerable: the measure, we endlessly repeat to ourselves, of a civilized society. And this must begin with looking not outwards at the dereliction of duty that we see all around us but inwards at ourselves. This is an important corrective to the easy finger-pointing that, however justified it may be in terms of those whom we single out for blame, is far too easy on ourselves. The moral high ground is a very comfortable place; no wonder it is so densely populated.

The truth is that we rarely care for those who need care unless they are our own nearest and dearest. We know in principle that we ought to do so, that we should treat others as we ourselves would wish to be treated and that "others" should not be confined to friends and family. We don't require the principles of ethics and biomedical ethics and metaethics to remind us of this. If we appeal to these principles, it is probably because we don't experience the compassion that we think we ought to feel; or we know that we are guilty of outsourcing compassion to professionals – professionals who will care for those who are strangers or from whom we are estranged by the demands they make on our capacity for love or even concern. Philosophizing – even home-spun philosophizing such as invoking the golden rule that we should treat others as we ourselves would wish to be treated – is remote from the existential realities that may contribute to making some people treat those in their care insensitively, negligently or with deliberate cruelty. Very few of us would be able to respond with undiminished courtesy and kindness to repeated calls to be taken to the toilet, or would be able to deliver a comforting bed bath for someone who has been faecally incontinent for the fourth time in a day, or calm a lost soul who is endlessly wandering in search of her long-dead mother.

Most of those who have commented on, and moralized over, the delinquency of carers are not themselves full-time professional carers. They have jobs that they value, and where they are valued, not low-paid jobs taken on by workers for whom there is simply no alternative. While one must applaud investigative journalists who have exposed abuses that would otherwise have remained hidden and continued unchallenged, we have to remember that they, and most of us who are outraged by what they have revealed, are remote from the bedside, from the urine and faeces, from the repetition of reassurances, from endless unsatisfactory communication with people who have suffered the tragedy of aphasia or dementia.

The immediate response is to resort to ever-tighter regulations governing the behaviour of professional carers and ever more complete documentation of what is going on. It assumes that conscience has shrunk to a little voice that tells you that a closed-circuit television (CCTV) camera is watching everything you are up to. Perhaps more regulations are necessary, more standards have to be set, and more boxes have to be filled in so that obedience to the regulations and measuring up to the standards can be monitored. But this cannot be the solution and may add to problems. The emphasis on what can be recorded and measured and the presupposition that coercion will make people care more so that they care better – rather than simply mandate the external appearance of caring – is mistaken. Such behaviourist approaches leave out what it is that lies at the heart of care: the sense that this needy, confused, terrifying and, yes, unappetizing and unglamorous person is myself.

We need to begin by reminding ourselves that most of us do not fill most of our waking hours caring intimately for, behaving lovingly towards, a succession of strangers who place huge demands on us and often are unable to give anything in return. Yes, professional carers get paid for doing what they do, but payment (often scarcely above the minimum wage) is not sufficient to awaken the attitude of a true carer. It has to be supported by an ethos, within the institute and, more importantly, within the community where the caring institutions are located. A society that cares about everything other than those of its members who need care, a society fixated on self-advancement, that measures lives by material success, that values glamour above everything, will be implicitly hostile to those who need care; and the low status of the infirm, the disabled, the cognitively impaired will rub off on those who are charged to care for them. This will be reinforced when what they have to offer is noticed only when something goes wrong: when they are increasingly defined by scandals prompted by revelations of failure.

We need to be hard on such failures and on those who have failed. But we need also to be hard on the conditions that have led to us not to care about care, so long as it does not impact on ourselves or our loved ones. We need to be hard on ourselves.

14

Coinages of the Mind: Hallucinations

Until the French psychiatrist Jean-Étienne Dominique Esquirol gave them their current name, hallucinations – seeing or hearing things that are not there – were called "apparitions". This captures their profoundly disturbing nature, an eeriness that is not fully reflected in the definition Oliver Sacks quotes from William James's classic *The Principles of Psychology* (1890): "An hallucination is a strictly sensational form of consciousness, as good and true a sensation as if there were a real object there. The object happens to be not there, that is all" (2012: x). Unlike mental images, hallucinations do not remain obediently inside your head – they are projected into the world that surrounds you – and they can surprise. Having a life of their own, which reinforces their compelling reality, they are intimate invasions that break into your chosen biography rather than belonging to it.

Their power to terrify may be, in part, due to their content: a giant spider irradiating venom meant just for you or something like W. H. Auden's "lean horror flapping and hopping" closing in on you "with inhuman swiftness" (*The Sea and the Mirror*). But even the most benign hallucination is deeply unsettling precisely because, as Sacks says, there is no "consensual validation". Nobody else can see, hear, feel, smell or taste what you are experiencing. To be in the grip of such incorrigibly private experiences is to be sequestrated in the most profound solitude. Hallucinations italicize the separateness that haunts the shared daylight of the community of minds to which we belong, confirming that each mind is a universe communicating only imperfectly and intermittently with other minds.

Hallucinations, in short, subvert our social self at the deepest level. The profoundest human need to live in a shared world underpinned by shared experiences is evident even in infancy. Before we learn to speak, we will point out things that we see and desperately want to share with others. Joint attention to items that we all agree are before us is the ground floor of a common human world woven out of countless cognitive handshakes. The involuntary perceptual dissidence of the one who hallucinates reminds us how frail and transient is our occupancy of this world; and how, even when you and I are side by side in the sunlight, each of us may be sealed in the privacy of our minds.

Because such reminders are deeply unwelcome, we fear hallucinations not only in ourselves but in others. Attitudes may vary from cruel mockery directed at those who are "dippy" or "bonkers" to a concern for their well-being, which historically has often resulted in confinement to an institution. Hallucinations are regarded as the most important – the so-called "first-rank" – symptoms of mental illnesses such as schizophrenia. In a famous experiment in the 1970s, eight "pseudopatients" with no history of mental illness and the single complaint that they "heard voices" were hospitalized for up to two months, despite otherwise normal behaviour. There are, of course, cultures in which, under certain circumstances, seeing or hearing things that are invisible or inaudible to others may be the mark of the priest or shaman with a privileged access to the realm of the sacred: an egregious case of being "kicked upstairs". More often, however, hallucinations are treated as elementary untruths rather than higher truths and those who suffer from them are pitied or despised rather than looked to for deeper understanding.

It is scarcely surprising, therefore, that the isolation they impose on those who suffer from hallucinations is compounded by a reluctance to speak of them. Telling others that you can see squirrels dancing in the dark will scarcely advance your job prospects or even the chance of being taken seriously as a conversational partner. And yet they are extremely common, as Sacks points out in his opening chapter, when he talks about the "silent multitudes" of visual images that may fill the gathering darkness when eyesight starts to fail. Charles Bonnet syndrome – named after the polymath physician who first described it in the eighteenth century – is characterized by extraordinarily complex and variable images. This is how, Rosalie, a blind ninety-year-old lady in a nursing home described what she "saw":

> People in Eastern dress! ... In drapes, walking up and down stairs ... a man who turns towards me and smiles, but he has huge teeth on one side of his mouth. Animals, too. I see this scene with a white building, and it is snowing – a soft snow, it is swirling. I see this horse (not a pretty horse, a drudgery horse) with a harness, dragging snow away ... but it keeps switching ... I see a lot of children ... walking up and down stairs. (Sacks 2012: 3–4)

She is greatly relieved when Sacks tells her that "her hallucinations represented a recognized condition, one that even had a name" (*ibid.*: 5). She was keen for him to tell the nurses that she had Charles Bonnet syndrome.

There is an intuitive explanation of why perceptual loss – as in blindness and in experimental sensory-deprivation tanks – should be associated with hallucinations: that nature, the brain, the mind, abhors a vacuum. This, however, does not explain why, as in Rosalie's case, the symptoms began only many years after she had gone blind. Nor does the "running on empty" notion account for the wonderful, if disconcerting, richness of her hallucinations. The general propensity to hallucinate, however, is unsurprising, given the complexity of the processes – cerebral and mental – that underpin ordinary perception and the extent to which the world we experience around us is a construct that goes far beyond the raw material of sensation.

Nor is it surprising that they can be induced in so many different ways. Sacks's masterly *catalogue raisonné* of these coinages of the mind encompasses the effect of drugs (prescribed and recreational), migraine (where there are transient alterations of the blood flow to parts of the brain), epilepsy (in which there are massive spontaneous neural discharges), delirium (associated with fevers and toxins of various sorts), sleep (normal and abnormal), disturbances of body image (following loss of a limb or a stroke), near-death experiences (after cardiac arrest) and direct stimulation of the brain (in waking subjects undergoing epilepsy surgery). In doing so, he draws on his previous writing and in some respects this could be seen as the *summa neurologica* of this supreme observer of the phenomenology of neurological disease. His humanity – informed by the sense that "this patient is potentially me" – is evident throughout.

In some cases he literally is the patient. His interest in the subjective experience, as opposed to the objective account, of neurological disease that normally dominates textbook descriptions was triggered by a lifelong experience of migraine. His first attack, when he was three or four years old, took the form of a shimmering light, which expanded to an enormous arc stretching from the ground to the sky, and underwent a series of brilliant transformations before his left visual field emptied. He was lucky that he had a medically qualified mother who recognized what this was – a prodromal migrainous aura, which in his case was not succeeded by a headache – and was able to reassure him that he was not going either blind or mad. Many years later, he immersed himself in the nineteenth-century treatise on megrim and other "nerve-storms" by Edward Liveing, which, aided and abetted by the amphetamines he was currently popping, induced a state of ecstasy in which he saw "migraine shining like an archipelago of stars". A more lasting effect was the realization of the vocation that made him world famous. He would, he decided, be the Liveing of the twentieth century.

He describes the migrainous auras, as he does other hallucinations, with the loving attention of a naturalist or a collector. He looks beyond the standard fare of the medical literature on migraine, which tends to focus on diagnostic signs, such as zigzag lines ("fortification spectra") to more exotic visual phenomena such as that experienced by a patient who reported "a fly's eye made of millions of light blue Mickey Mouses". These and other effects seem to show, by default, Sacks argues "what a colossal and complicated achievement normal vision is" – where a world is constructed in which "colour and movement and size and form and stability are all seamlessly meshed and integrated" (2012: 129). The aura of migraine, like that associated with certain forms of epilepsy, was, as the nineteenth-century astronomer George Airey said, "a sort of photograph" of the brain in action.

In the 1960s, Sacks extended his neurophenomenological explorations by taking an extraordinary variety of recreational drugs; not only amphetamines but also pot and, of course, LSD. The results were occasionally ecstatic, sometimes merely weird and often utterly terrifying. Conversations with a friendly spider – who, after an opening exchange of pleasantries, discussed whether Bertrand Russell had, with his famous Paradox, irreversibly damaged Gottlob Frege's system of thought – and studying key moments from the Battle of Agincourt enacted on his dressing-gown sleeve, were not atypical episodes in the picaresque pharmacological dramas unfolding in his head. He fought off panic by carefully transcribing the "craziness" inside himself, writing "for dear life" as "wave after wave of hallucination" rolled over him. These were not quite as crazy as the experience of a student, Daniel Breslaw, a subject enrolled in a formal study of LSD, who entering an elevator, passed "a floor every hundred years" and, when back in his room, swam "through the remaining centuries of the day. Every five eons or so a nurse arrives (in the aspect of a cougar, a differential equation, or a clock radio) and takes my blood pressure". As if this were not enough, Breslaw experienced synaesthesia, or a fusion between the senses, reporting gems such as "the smell of a low B flat, the sound of green" (ibid.: 98–101).

233

The varieties of hallucinations are protean. While vision predominates, hearing, smell, taste, touch, memory, altered body image and strange emotions seeking an object, often figure. Phantosmia (hallucinations of smell), analogous to Charles Bonnet syndrome, may occur in people who have lost this sense. Auditory hallucinations, in addition to those bothersome, frightening voices, take many forms. The unremitting mental junk of tinnitus is a huge source of suffering but musical hallucinations following damage to the brain may be just as distressing. Imagine hearing Bing Crosby, friends and orchestra singing "White Christmas" for days on end: a thousand times worse than the musical phrases or "earworms" that stick limpet-like to the normal mind. Tactile hallucinations can be compelling, as in the case of one of Sacks's subjects on drug treatment for Parkinson's disease. The surfaces of objects seemed to be covered by a film of peach fuzz, cotton candy or spider's webs and the film sometimes became very "lush" as if the items were submerged under a pile of "stuff" (*ibid.*: 82). Hallucinations can sometimes be multisensory. When Rosalie, the very old blind lady with Charles Bonnet syndrome, became ill and thought she was dying, she had visions of her mother and heard her welcoming her into heaven. These were completely different from her usual hallucinations: as well as being multisensory, "they were personal, addressed to her, and steeped in warmth and tenderness" (*ibid.*: 253–4).

The most "respectable" hallucinations are those we are all prone to on a daily or more usually nightly basis, associated with sleep – namely, dreams – and we accept their occurrence. We do not hesitate to tell others about our dreams; indeed, we wish some people would hesitate a little more. However, there are experiences on the fringes of sleep that are less easy to talk about. Hypnagogic hallucinations seen on the threshold of sleep may take the form of faces or presences charged with malign intent. And hypnopompic hallucinations, which occur on waking, are often seen with open eyes: the terrified gaze populating the darkness with evil faces, spiders, snakes and devils. For many years I suffered from sleep paralysis. Half way between sleep and waking, feeling unable to move, even to breathe, I was threatened by a figure at the end of my bed, sculpted out of the darkness. Such experiences did not affect my life but, for some people, "night hags", sometimes associated with abnormal propensity to dream sleep – so-called "narcolepsy" – may interfere with their waking life. Occasionally they are a dark secret they dare not share with others.

Of a book that is so rich and so respectfully attentive to the particulars of neurological illness and the people who suffer from them, complaint may seem churlish, but it is disappointing that *Hallucinations* scarcely touches on the philosophical questions raised by its subject. This omission is particularly striking in Sacks's discussion of epileptic seizures (where he surprisingly relies on outdated terms such as "grand mal") in which part of the brain has massive synchronized, spontaneous activity. While many of the epileptic manifestations he discusses are not strictly hallucinations they are nonetheless of the greatest interest. They include a sense of déjà vu, out-of-body experiences, and even episodes of ecstasy. Some patients have interpreted these as revelations of the presence of God and undergone, as a result, religious conversion. The very rough correlation between the brain area affected by the abnormal activity (more precisely defined by EEG and fMRI brain scans) and the kinds of experiences patients have has misled some writers into imagining that the experiences are identical with the neural activity (or even, in extreme cases, that religious beliefs are epileptic phenomena). This neuralization of consciousness – according to which brain activity is not only a necessary but also a sufficient condition of awareness and indeed is identical with it – has seemed to some to be justified by the famous observations made by Wilder Penfield, discussed by Sacks (see also Chapter 1, "Am I My Brain?").

One avenue that Sacks could perhaps have explored is the astonishing *organization* of hallucinations, as in the case of spiders that talk analytical philosophy. This would be inexplicable if they were purely coinages of an activated brain freewheeling independently of an extra-cranial reality. It is evident that they involve a top-down shaping, and sense-making, activity of the mind, which eludes the kinds of understanding available to currently fashionable reductionist accounts of the conscious mind as being identical with neural activity, seen ultimately as the effects in a material brain wired into its environment of material events impinging on sense endings.

Hallucinations have long interested philosophers of perception. They are invoked to challenge what is called "naive realism": that what we see is not always out there reminds us that our idea of what is out there is *mediated* – at the very least by our senses. This has raised questions of whether what is there exists independently of our senses. The argument from illusion (or hallucination) leads to the view that even items we regard as the basic furniture of everyday life – material objects – are merely constructs out of sense experience. These venerable views are no longer mainstream. As we have seen (in Chapter 5), Gilbert Ryle pointed out that illusions cannot undermine the truth of other experiences because "there can be false coins only where there are coins made of the proper materials by the proper authorities". More recently, disjunctivist philosophers have reasserted what the rest of us suspected: that true perceptions and hallucinations – howsoever similar – are not the same kinds of mental entities. Even so, hallucinations are a deeply disturbing reminder of how what we take for reality is underdetermined by the sense experiences upon which our taking is based. And the profound puzzle of the relationship between our perceptions, the objects we individually perceive, and what we all agree is "out there", remains.

The richness, complexity and infinite variety of hallucinations are the underside of the richness, complexity and variety of "ordinary" perception. And they are a reminder of the miraculous extent to which our sense experience normally coheres at and across times. This is extraordinary, not least because the items that are brought together, in and between moments of consciousness, are also kept tidily apart, so that I can experience items in the visual field separately, sounds distinctly from sights, emotions and thoughts and memories from the immediate data of sensation, and can attend separately to, and report, the colour, size and location of an object while experiencing all of them at once. Hallucinations betray their nature by not fitting into the seamless fabric of the field of experience and meaning unfolding over time until they become so insistent that they have an apparent reality comparable to that of the objects that others can also see.

Although philosophical issues are largely bypassed by Sacks, *Hallucinations* is nonetheless a superb synthesis of the literature on these arresting, disturbing and sometimes terrifying phenomena. It is a profound work of humanity – reaching out to all those who are prone to hallucinations – in short to all of us. I hope it is widely read so that many people, like Sacks's fortunate patients, will take comfort in knowing that, in undergoing these most solitary of experiences, they are not alone.

15

Becoming the Prisoners of Our Free Choices

TRAGEDY

Nothing could be worse than losing a child who has died in her twenties, after a career of alcoholism and drug-taking documented in prurient detail by the tabloids. But the suffering endured by Amy Winehouse's parents must be made worse by the judging voices echoing in the aching emptiness she will have left behind. The sheer number of explanations of the addiction that accompanied her journey from a brilliantly successful artist to a tragic figure betrays the poverty of our understanding.

Given the increasing fashion for seeking biological bases for human behaviour, it is not surprising that genetic explanations for addiction have been sought. It is true that the children of addicts may be more likely to become addicts themselves; and comparisons of genetically similar twins brought up either together or apart suggest that environmental influences do not entirely account for this association. But the evidence of a hereditary contribution to addictive behaviours falls far short of that sufficient to support the kind of genetic fatalism made popular by Émile

Zola when he explored the doomed Rougon-Macquart family in a mighty cycle of novels.

Just how remote some biological approaches are from human life is betrayed by the fact that one of the favourite animal models for studying alcoholism is the fruit fly. Like us, they lose postural control and sexual inhibition when they are exposed to alcohol. What is more, they can be bred to be alcohol-resistant or alcohol-sensitive, and this has been used to investigate the genetic basis of alcoholism. But we know little, after all, of the social attitudes of these minute creatures (approximately 2.5 millimetres long) towards public displays of drunkenness by fruit flies that have become bar flies and they seem to have little to tell us about the combination of circumstances that turn the life of a drug-user to one dedicated solely to addiction.

For many, the link between genes and addictive behaviour is the brain. Nearly all addictive drugs tickle up the so-called "reward" system and cause it to be flooded with neurotransmitters such as dopamine. Genes are claimed to influence the "reward circuitry" that makes an individual want to take drugs in the first place, to desire to continue taking them, and to experience difficulty discontinuing them. This is the basis of the developing consensus that addiction is "a brain disease". The Washington-based American psychiatrist Sally Satel has pointed out, however, that if it is a brain disease, it is quite different from undoubted brain disorders such as Alzheimer's or Parkinson's. A twelve-step programme modelled on the Alcoholics Anonymous approach would hardly have any impact on the course or outcome of Alzheimer's disease. What is more, people tend to recover from addictions more effectively if there is something in their lives that they value that is at stake. Incentives work in these cases but they don't do much for dementia. Telling a person with dementia that he won't get his job back if he does not recover his memory would be futile and cruel.

The notion of addicts as diseased or as passive victims of their addiction is a gross simplification. Of course, in the late stages, psychological dependency and physical dependency may make it impossible to break the habits of years without external help; and the motivation to give up the guaranteed pleasure, or at least relief, of the next hit or the next drink must be greatly diminished by the knowledge that you will return to a world reduced to a landscape of wreckage, marked by the damage you have done to your prospects or to the lives of others. Guilt, emptiness and a huge and daunting task of reconstruction face the recovering addict.

In the early stages, however, it is a different story. In his classic account of addiction to laudanum (opium dissolved in alcohol), *Confessions of an Opium Eater*, Thomas de Quincey speaks of the decade in which he was a voluntary consumer of a drug that was an "assuaging balm" for his troubles, taking it no more than weekly. Eventually, however, he became a hopeless addict and the overriding theme of the remainder of his long life was his struggle to break free from "the bondage of opium". His story illustrates how, in the case of addictive drugs, we ultimately become prisoners of our earlier free choices.

Our uncertainty as to why someone might progress from the recreational use of drugs to a life defined by them should make us hesitate to pass judgement. The poignant comparison of the pictures of the little girl with the beautiful voice who dreamed of fame and of the hunted young woman who fled from her disastrous final concerts in Serbia should at least put paid to the romantic notion that "a systematic derangement of the senses" will be the making of a great artist. As The Verve sang in their haunting song, "The drugs don't work".

TRAGI-COMEDY

The notion of helpless addiction has also been invoked in the less tragic case of another celebrity, Tiger Woods. He is, of course, addicted to golf: an appalling condition given the futility of this pastime. I suspect that God, if he had existed and had seen the game coming, would have appreciated the positive qualities of the void and left it alone, uncontaminated by the Creation. But there are times when even golf gets interesting. The brouhaha surrounding Tiger Woods's exertions in the nineteenth hole and his break up from his wife made for such a time.

Apparently this extraordinarily handsome, fabulously rich, wonderfully talented man had been having sex with a number of beautiful women, only one of whom was his wife. This caused shock and amazement to those who seem to be entirely unacquainted with the history of the world. From Solomon (300 wives and 700 concubines, according to the anonymous gossip columnist of Kings 11:1–3) to Warren Beatty (an estimated 12,775 lovers) we know that those who have the power to pull will usually pull. And the inappropriately named "Wilt" Chamberlain, a basketball star of the twentieth century, claimed in his autobiography *The View from Above* that he had bedded 20,000 woman, or approximately 1.15 a day from his fifteenth birthday onwards, demonstrating how much can be achieved when the maximum of temptation is combined with the maximum of opportunity. Against these heroic numbers, Woods's alleged total of nine liaisons (although there may be more to come out of the woodwork) looks like celibacy.

And yet he underwent treatment for "sex addiction". This may have been a way of reinventing himself after a brutal re-badging from Mr Clean to "Love-Rat" and of squaring things not only with a very angry Mrs Woods but also with the advertising industry that had hitherto paid him so handsomely. Sex-addiction clinics model themselves on other institutions that deal with addictions. They prescribe psychotherapy (to get to the bottom of the mystery of why a grown man could ever wish to shag a beautiful woman), drugs to control mood, libido and other drivers to transgression, and a self-help regime modelled on the famous twelve-step approach used by Alcoholics Anonymous.

The first of the twelve steps is revealing: "We admit that we are powerless over addictive sexual behaviour". It is this claim that seems to justify the deployment of the white coat and the questionnaire rather than the wagged finger. The propensity to use the power one has to attract the most attractive members of the opposite sex is turned on its head and becomes powerlessness. Others would regard seduction as the supreme exercise of power. At any rate, it seems odd to classify it as behaviour for which medical treatment is appropriate. After all, in Woods's case, there was no question of sexual deviancy or the need to coerce partners. Everything that happened was between consenting adults. Nor did it look like the genuinely pathological promiscuity of a teenage girl with low self-esteem due to parental neglect engaging in the physical intimacy of sex as a substitute for the love she craves.

The existence of a specific "sex-addiction disorder" has been contested. Although Patrick Carnes, the leading expert in the area and editor of the journal *Sex Addiction and Compulsivity*, claims that it is suffered by as much as 6 per cent of the population, it has not yet made it to the psychiatrist's Bible, the *Diagnostic and Statistical Manual of Mental Disorders* (DSM). (DSM lists pukka illnesses for which there are accepted diagnostic criteria, treatment pathways and, most importantly, billing arrangements.) For sex addiction is unlike alcohol addiction: there are no clear guidelines as to what count as safe levels of sexual activity, and preoccupation with sex seems to be nearly universal in males of a certain age, although being physically unattractive and/or hard up somewhat restricts translation into action in most cases. Nor is there evidence of the kind of physiological dependence that makes withdrawal from alcohol and other drugs so unpleasant. John F. Kennedy's claim that "If I don't have a woman for three days, I get terrible headaches" has to be treated with caution because Mrs Kennedy, while indubitably a woman, was not quite what he had in mind.

And this suggests that, if there is an addiction, it is not to sex but to sexual conquest. However powerful Woods's sex drive, nobody would have suggested treatment if he had satisfied it entirely with Mrs Woods. "Sexual conquest addiction" or "New Birdism" seems even less plausible as a medical condition than horniness *per se*, although novel syndromes are coined everyday by doctors – and by lawyers wanting to uphold the claim of diminished responsibility on behalf of their clients. Computer-addiction syndrome, parental-alienation syndrome, self-victimization syndrome, and UFO-survivor syndrome are recent American examples that would make "sexual-addiction syndrome" as robust a diagnosis as depression or bronchitis.

Setting aside (with some difficulty) a certain amount of scepticism, we might think about the significance of medicalizing Woods's predicament. The latter seems to have less to do with sex than with getting caught (and perhaps we shall see the emergence of getting-caught syndrome); and less to do with the power of the physical sex drive than the multiplicity of its targets. Although rebranding it as a medical disorder may seem to be sympathetic, liberal, indeed progressive, this move may not be quite so benign. It is not so long since the medical approach to people who were thought to be too sexy involved treatments rather less kind than psychotherapy. And when homosexuality was expelled as a mental illness from DSM in 1973, this was rightly thought to be progressive. To gather up more of human sexual behaviour into the clinic has sinister undertones.

It's also rather insulting to the sexual partners of the putative addict, who are reduced to the equivalent of the bottle of whisky (or meths) downed by an alcoholic and it undermines the patient's standing as a free agent. It is interesting in this respect how ambivalent Woods was, admitting personal responsibility for his actions with a touching humility, and at the same time making them into a condition to be treated, as if they were something that happened to him rather than actions he performed.

At any rate, his true fans, eagerly awaiting his return, will be hoping that treatment aimed at helping to weaken one drive will not also weaken the other. In the meantime, some of us are grateful to him for making golf a little less mind-numbingly boring.

WAR

Wars on nouns – such as Terror – have a dismal track record. With their targets ill defined, they inevitably cause mainly collateral damage and are unwinnable, interminable and expensive. Thus it is with the war on drugs, first declared in 1971 by that disinterested benefactor of humanity Richard Nixon. Nixon's war, joined by a coalition of the willing, has recently been declared a "trillion dollar failure" but the loss of life, of health, of freedom, of rights is even more important than the loss of dollars. Last year the Global Commission on Drug Policy declared that the war had not only failed but "had had devastating consequences for individuals and societies round the world".

That this should be a surprise to anyone is a depressing tribute to the irrationality that can dominate public debate. The anticipated consequences of criminalizing drugs, and consequently those who consume them, must be evident to anyone prepared to engage in two consecutive minutes of thought. Prohibition causes the prices of drugs to skyrocket and makes a life of dealing, if always dangerous and often short, attractive to those for whom there seem to be few other opportunities for self-advancement. Addicts, at the mercy of suppliers who have an interest in maximizing the needs of their clients, have to devote every hour of the day to finding means to pay for their highs, and frequently resort to criminal activity. The lack of quality control of drugs and associated kit such as syringes means illness and death on a vast scale. Police time is squandered on hunting down people who are often not even harming themselves, as well as those who harm others in pursuit of their fix. The prison population – where there is a more reliable access to drugs – explodes, at huge cost to the consumer nations. And the effect on supplier nations such as Mexico and Columbia has been catastrophic. The Mexican government crackdown on drug cartels, backed by the US, launched in 2006, has resulted in over 60,000 murders and the bloodletting is continuing.

That legalizing drugs would ruin drug-pushers, that regulating the supply through licensed outlets would protect the life and health of drug-takers, and that more people would come forwards for treatment and rehabilitation to seek a life not centred on pharmacological vacations from an increasingly unbearable existence: these are things that those who are morally opposed to drugs do not want to hear. They do not recognize that the truly moral position is the pragmatic one that will favour whatever course of action minimizes the suffering of their fellow humans.

They cover their ears when discussion turns to jurisdictions where liberalizing drug policy has brought benefits. In 2001, Portugal abolished all criminal penalties for personal possession of drugs including marijuana, cocaine, heroin and methamphetamine. Dreadful consequences were predicted, but a report by the Cato Institute in 2009 found that the use of hitherto illegal drugs by teenagers had declined, the rate of HIV infections among drug-users had halved, and the number of people seeking help for drug addiction had doubled. The policy was brave but could have been even braver, with proper authorities taking over the sourcing, the distribution and the sale of drugs, as in Uruguay, where a state monopoly of the production and sale of cannabis is proposed.

The contrast between the successful consequences of even partial legalization and the dismal outcomes of hard-line approaches makes the call by the Home Affairs Select Committee for a review of current policies welcome indeed. The UK spends more on drug policy than any other European country and, by the criterion of the consumption of Class A drugs, has the worst results, suggesting that resources are not being well spent, although in the UK, as elsewhere, there has been some decline in the use of hard drugs among teenagers. The recommendations in the House of Commons Home Affairs Committee report *Drugs: Breaking the Cycle* (2012) focus on reducing the damage caused by drugs by a greater emphasis on treatment than criminal sanctions, improved support in prisons and society at large and early intervention with better education and preventative work, and more use of residential rehabilitation. The committee recommended that UK drugs policy should be comprehensively reviewed by a Royal Commission to report in 2015.

These modest recommendations have already been dismissed by government sources. The Home Office says that its drugs policies are working and it has no intention of changing them. Should anyone be surprised at this lightning response to a report? Governments view rational debate on drugs with terror. Politicians know that it is dangerous to dabble in these substances, particularly if they are cut with factual accuracies and coherent arguments.

So when Alan Johnson, one of the most sensible politicians of the past decade, learned that his chief drug adviser, Professor David Nutt, had been caught telling one or two truths – such as that tobacco causes more harm than cannabis, ecstasy and LSD, even without the assistance of criminal gangs – Nutt was sacked. But the professor had shown form. He had annoyed Johnson's predecessor, Jacqui Smith, by blurting out another truth – namely that horse-riding caused more deaths (100) than were linked to ecstasy (30). The first casualty of war – whether it is a war on a neighbouring country or the war on drugs – is the truth. And it is soon joined in its grave by reason. The instinct of obedience to the party ensures that no politician would lay a wreath on their joint headstone.

The harm caused by illegal drugs, unlike that caused by fish and chips (against which no war has been declared), is largely a consequence of their illegality. It is this that is most responsible for those aspects of an addict's life that leads them in some cases to wreck others' lives. For a politician to admit this, and to suggest or support policies that would ruin a trade that has had such a calamitous impact on the world beyond our borders, and make the world safer for all of us by helping addicts to live less precarious lives, would require vision and courage. To imagine that such a politician could survive in a climate where public discourse is debased to reflex responses, facts are boring, arguments are tedious, and moral outrage is delicious, is perhaps fantasy.

To speak such a fantasy out loud may provoke the accusation that I am on something. I could even be arrested for being in possession of that most feared and loathed psychoactive substance: namely, my wits.

16

The Right to an Assisted Death

Dedicated to the memory of Dr Ann McPherson

I have been preoccupied for nearly a decade by the need for a change in the law to legalize the choice of physician-assisted dying for mentally competent people with terminal illness who have expressed a settled wish to die. In summer 2011, I was elected chair of a new group – Healthcare Professionals for Assisted Dying (HPAD) – whose immediate aim is to represent the views of doctors, nurses and other healthcare professionals who favour a change in the law. I took over this role from Dr Ann McPherson.

I was privileged to know Ann, sadly only for a short time, before she died in June 2011. By a bitter irony she had a hideous death, which her daughter – a consultant dermatologist – described in harrowing detail in a "Personal View" in the *British Medical Journal* (2012). Despite her unbearable symptoms, which had resisted the best possible palliative care, any physician assisting her to die (by, for example, writing a prescription for life-ending medication) would have been prosecuted for manslaughter, and been liable to a fourteen-year gaol sentence.

That anyone could oppose such a humane ambition as decriminalization of assisted dying may seem astonishing. But there has been highly organized opposition to a change in the law. Some opponents have appealed to religious principles such as "the sanctity of life", but more often than not wrap up their opposition in a cloak of pragmatic concerns intended to instil fear. They frequently talk of "the slippery slope", arguing that if Ann had been allowed her wish, people with disabilities would be pressurized to choose death against their wishes and "burdensome" older people would be advised that they were surplus to requirement.

THE CASE IN FAVOUR

I shall come to these objections presently but let me first very briefly state the case for legalizing assisted dying. Unfortunately, most of the energy in winning the argument will have to be directed at countering the bad and sometimes dishonest arguments that are already in play. And it these false arguments – and making a case against the case against rather than the positive case for – that I will focus on. It would, however, be remiss of me not to remind you of the core of the positive case. And here it is.

First, unbearable suffering, prolonged by medical care, and inflicted on a dying patient who wishes to die, is unequivocally a bad thing. From this it follows that not doing (or worse still, forbidding) what has to be done to prevent this is unacceptable cruelty. I add this because I believe it is not those who support assisted dying but those who oppose it who have the moral case to answer, and should be on the defensive. And, second, respect for individual autonomy – the right to have one's choices supported by others, to determine one's own best interest, when one is of sound mind – is a sovereign principle.

And that's it.

THE CASE AGAINST: RELIGIOUS OPPOSITION

So much for the positive case. Unanswerable one would think. But, of course, it has been answered and I want to devote the remainder of this essay to dealing with the objections that have been raised by opponents of assisted dying. They are made more difficult by the tendency of many opponents to conceal what really lies behind their views.

Here it is, set out with exemplary candour in the speech given by Baroness Richardson of Calow when the House of Lords gave Lord Joffe's Assisted Dying for the Terminally Ill Bill its second reading: "There is no doubt that the [Joffe] Bill has shocked the religious communities ... It has undermined the security some of us have felt that God is to be in control of life and death". Most of those who are religiously opposed to assisted dying are sufficiently savvy to know that this would cut little ice in a present-day British society. Even among those who profess religious beliefs there is little opposition to assisted dying. The data from the most recent British Social Attitudes Survey (and consistent with findings over many years) reveal that religious belief seems hardly to reduce the tendency to be in favour of assisted dying, with 82 per cent in the general population and 71 per cent of those who designate themselves as having religious belief supportive of assisted dying. And indeed, for many people, religious belief is a key factor in their support for assistance to die on the grounds of compassion.

Mary Warnock, in her book *Dishonest to God: On Keeping Religion out of Politics* (2010) has described how religiously motivated opponents will duck and weave between absolutist arguments based on faith and pragmatic or consequentialist arguments that appeal to empirical "evidence" about anticipated adverse consequences for society.

> When the bishops switch from their impregnable argument that God is the giver of the sacred gift of life (impregnable in the sense that it is theological and not supported by evidence

or capable of proof), it is to the vulnerability of the terminally ill or otherwise suffering that they turn. (*Ibid.*: 63)

This is what we might call the "belt and braces" or, better perhaps, "belt and gaiters" approach, slithering between arguments from principle and arguments based on what are presented as facts. It is reminiscent of the Groucho Marx quip: "These are my principles, and if you don't like them ... well, I have others". What applies here is: "These are my (inviolable) principles but if you don't like them I have some facts that will bring you round to the same conclusion as me". The facts, however, are not as convenient as opponents of assisted dying would wish. So they resort to principle-warped factoids; and we must examine these head-on.

In dealing with the religiously motivated case against assisted dying, I shall also examine a couple of principles that enshrine fundamental values: one religious and one secular. The religious principle will be that of *the sanctity of life* and I shall recall how it has never been regarded as unassailable in any society– it has always been applied inconsistently – so it is irrelevant to the case for or against assisted dying. Most importantly, it has no relevance to the question of the value of life as invoked in this context. The secular principle I shall look at will be that of the right to have respect for decisions that affect only one's own welfare – *the principle of autonomy* – and I shall show that while there are problems with this, which have been pointed out by religious opponents, such problems as it has are common to all ethical principles when applied in real life.

FACTS AND FACTOIDS

I am not an epidemiologist of error but it seems to me that the commonest objection is that assisted dying is actually *unnecessary*, or would be unnecessary if optimal palliative care were universally available. This is not true, as my experience as a doctor for over thirty-five years made clear, when I was responsible for patients whose symptoms were uncontrolled even when they had first-rate palliative care. And Ann's own death – typical of so many others (including those of my mother and father) – is eloquent, if terrible, testimony to the failures of palliative care in some patients. The description of Ann's protracted death by her daughter is compelling in its awfulness:

> Mum was diagnosed with pancreatic cancer in 2007. For at least three years her life with cancer was worth living. She put up with many "new normals" as she called them. A new normal to take regular morphine to control pain … a new normal to have a chest drain in situ which she herself drained daily; a new normal to eat only baby food. She put up with these and other trials, and was grateful always for the medical support and interventions which made her life possible. To continue her work, to spend time with friends and family, to enjoy the days she knew were so precious.
>
> On 3rd May 2011 Mum had had enough. A recent scan had confirmed that the cancer had spread to around the gastric outlet so that she could no longer eat anything solid and even fluids were difficult. Her chest drain had started to leak and was pouring out fluid to drench dressings. She had lost so much weight. She was getting pressure sores.
>
> She wanted to die, she needed to die. Her GP was wonderful and set up a morphine drip to control the now uncontrollable pain and discomfort. Mum said that she hoped to drift away that night. But there was no drifting away. What followed were three weeks of unbearable agony. She had become highly tolerant to morphine.
>
> We would try to dress and move her but it became increasingly difficult. By now she had two morphine drips, one in each wasted leg which needed re-siting often. Her drain site poured fluid, her bed clothes were drenched. Her last spoken words to me three days before dying (while I was trying to change her night dress with a lovely carer) were … "HOLD …

MY ... HEAD". There was no dignity. There was no Mum; just a wounded animal who needed drips changed.

Night after night we would expect that she would not wake up. She could not receive the medicines that would relax her tiny gasping frame. My brother and sister were up and down from their homes and families. They were not coming to say goodbye: that had been done weeks earlier, just to sit hopelessly. It is an honour to care for someone you love but it no longer felt honourable to try to care for someone who wants to be dead. (2012: 35)

Her body hung on to the (very) bitter end:

Even as she died, her body seemed furious with its final fight, gasping to the end, and in a desperate haunting shudder I found myself sitting in pools of expelled fluid. That was not what she wanted. Mum had seen this happen before and wanted to avoid it, for future patients and their families. (*Ibid.*)

Thus the testimony of a loving daughter. So much for palliative care as a panacea. And Ann's case was not unusual. Many patients still have bad deaths, despite the best palliative care, as indicated by the 560 suicides by seriously ill Britons in 2010, and the nearly 200 Britons who have undertaken dreadful journeys to Dignitas clinics in Switzerland to end their suffering in the past decade.

International experience also confirms that palliative care fails some patients. To take one example, for the past ten years assisted dying has been legal in Oregon under the Death with Dignity Act. Oregon has among the best palliative care of the fifty states in the US and yet nearly 90 per cent of those seeking assisted dying are in receipt of hospice care. This is not to belittle the importance of palliative care, which can help a great many dying patients achieve a dignified death, but to acknowledge honestly that it, like other modes of healthcare, has its limitations. The eminent palliative care physician and opponent of assisted dying Baroness Finlay has admitted in the House of Lords that "palliative care is not a blanket panacea in all cases".

There are those who state that the availability of assisted dying as an "easy" option has inhibited investment in palliative care. I have heard it claimed by someone on several occasions – name withheld for the sake of the family – that palliative care does not exist in countries where there is legislation in favour of assisted dying. International experience, of course, does not support this. The usual pattern is that liberalization of the law (in some countries, such as the Netherlands, far beyond anything I would support) has been accompanied by *increasing* investment in palliative care services. In Oregon, the proportion of people dying in hospice care – a marker of the availability of palliative care – has more than doubled since the Death with Dignity Act was introduced. A recent authoritative report by the European Association of Palliative Care (2011) came to this conclusion:

> The idea that legislation of euthanasia and/or assisted suicide might obstruct or halt palliative care development thus seems unwarranted and is only expressed in commentaries rather than demonstrated by empirical evidence ... There is scant evidence of the supposed underdevelopment of palliative care.
> (Quoted in Commission on Assisted Dying 2012)

It is also dogmatically asserted by those who oppose it that liberalizing the law will break down trust between doctor and patient. This is not borne out by the evidence. A Europe-wide survey put levels of trust between doctors and patients in nine European countries highest in the Netherlands (Kmietovicz 2002) and 97 per cent of patients were confident in their GP. More recently, it has been noted that the present law permitting euthanasia and physician-assisted dying is supported by 92 per cent of the population in the Netherlands ten years after the law was introduced. (Commission on Assisted Dying 2012). None of this should come as any surprise: in countries with assisted dying, discussion of end-of-life care is open, transparent, honest and mature, not conducted in a cloud of ambiguity, as it is in the UK. And the knowledge that your doctor will not abandon the therapeutic alliance with you at your hour of greatest need will foster, not undermine, trust.

THE SLIPPERY SLOPE: FACTS

If these factoids don't deliver the results that are desired, then the antis up the antes: more quasi-facts, rumours and urban myths are mobilized. Legalization of assisted dying, opponents assert, will set us on a road that leads inevitably to assisted dying for people who aren't dying but have a non-terminal chronic illness or disability; and then to such people who do not wish to die and/or cannot express their wishes either way. In addition, the slippery-slopers tell us, the law will create or legitimize a culture in which when you are frail, infirm and judged to be a burden to others you will be expected out of decency to seek assistance to die. And it is implied that this is what is already happening somewhere or other.

The first step in dealing with such claims is to reiterate certain distinctions. A law to permit mentally competent, terminally ill adults who are suffering unbearably to receive assistance to die at their considered and persistent request would not at the same time legalize assisting people with non-terminal illnesses to commit suicide or legalize *voluntary euthanasia*, in which people can have their lives ended by someone else. Assisted dying would not apply to people with disabilities who are not terminally ill; elderly people who are not terminally ill; people with non-terminal illness; or people who are not mentally competent, including those who have dementia or depression. These distinctions are not vague or ambiguous and they are clear to the general public; for example, while a consistent 80 per cent-plus people support assisted dying, the support for assisted suicide for the non-terminally ill runs at only 40 per cent.

What is more, there is international experience to which we may refer to settle the argument about the inevitability of the slippery slope. The most relevant is the experience in Oregon. It is most relevant because the Death with Dignity Act, which was introduced over a decade ago, is very close to the laws that have been considered in England, although the Bill proposed by Lord Falconer (and debated in the House of Lords in 2013) has more safeguards. The proportion of deaths that are assisted has never risen above 0.2 per cent (Oregon Health Authority 2013). The average age of those who have assisted dying is *lower* than the average age of deaths, so elderly people are not disproportionately represented when you take into account the fact that the overwhelming majority of deaths take place in old age. The typical profile of a person who avails himself or herself of assisted dying is a strong-willed, middle-class person used to getting his or her way: hardly representative of groups traditionally depicted as "vulnerable" (Battin *et al.* 2007). What is more, there is no evidence in Oregon of extension of assisted dying to assisted suicide for people with non-terminal illnesses, nor is there any public appetite for this.

Needless to say, the Oregon experience, being so inconvenient for opponents of assisted dying, has been misrepresented. In a debate Mary Warnock and I had with him on BBC Radio 4's *Start the Week*, Lord Gummer reported that the rate of assisted dying in Oregon had increased by 300 per cent in the first few years of legislation. This was true, but it was meant to suggest that this was something out of control. The full picture was that the number of assisted deaths increased over a few years as the law began to be implemented in practice, from a minute figure of 16 to 64, and that since then the percentage has remained, as I mentioned, low at 0.2 per cent.

I am going to come back to the slippery slope when I talk about principles and values, but I want to make a couple more points on this issue. If there is a slippery slope, legislation – with all the safeguards envisaged in a Bill such as the one proposed by Lord Joffe – would, to borrow the ethicist John Harris's metaphor – "apply crampons rather than skis". The Dutch experience, frequently misrepresented by those against assisted dying, illustrates this. Rates of non-voluntary euthanasia (i.e. doctors actively ending patients' lives without having been asked by them to do so) *decreased* from 0.8 per cent of all deaths in 1991 (approximately 1,000 deaths) to 0.4 per cent in 2005 (approximately 550 deaths) (Van der Heine et al. 2007). In the UK, a study published in *Palliative Medicine* in 2009 found that in 0.21 per cent of deaths attended by a doctor, life was ended with an explicit request from the patient (in other words, voluntary euthanasia) and in 0.3 per cent of cases, life was ended without an explicit request from the patient (in other words, non-voluntary euthanasia) (Seale 2009). This means that approximately 2,600 people in the UK are being given direct help to die, with or without their explicit request, outside any relevant legal framework.

We may treat the claim made repeatedly by the *Daily Mail* in the latter half of 2012 that 130,000 elderly people are being killed each year as a result of being placed on an end-of-life care pathway (the Liverpool Care Pathway) – in order that hospital trusts will be financially rewarded and managers and doctors can work together to clear beds and improve turnover – as, well, the *Daily Mail*. Even so, we may still maintain that the present clinical, ethical and legal fudge, in which ploys such as continuous sedation, and starvation and dehydration, are in some cases used to get round the prohibition on assisted dying, is unacceptable. Those who are concerned for the safety of patients, far from opposing a change in the law, should support legalizing assisted dying in view of the scrutiny it would bring to bear on medical practice. Not only is it possible to devise a law with sufficient safeguards against abuse, but also a law regulating assisted dying would itself be a mighty safeguard.

MISTAKES

Let me wind up my tour of factoids with a final group that are generated by the fear that *mistakes* would be made: mistakes that are of particular concern since, in the case of assisted dying, they are irreversible. Opponents often treat their audiences to tales of individuals who asked to be assisted to die, and then, after talking to an understanding physician, one who is (to appropriate the catchy name of a campaign group) into "Care not Killing", change their minds and subsequently live long, happy, contented lives. The caring not killing physician (quite unlike a homicidal character like me) will receive a postcard from their patient announcing that she has just climbed the North Face of the Eiger single-handed without ropes ten years after requesting assistance to die. I exaggerate, of course, but some of the stories beggar belief. However, they carry huge potential weight and lead people to draw very large conclusions. As Bertrand Russell said, "popular induction depends upon the emotional interest of the instances, not upon their number".

How shall we address the concern that physicians may not read the patient's mind correctly and/or his or her ability to make a rational decision? Well, it is easy to build in time for reflection in any law: it should include ample opportunity to change one's mind. And people do change their minds. The experience in Oregon is compelling: only a tiny minority of those people who discussed assisted dying with their doctors actually received, cashed and took the prescription. This is the principle of emotional assurance. Many people will have taken comfort from having banked a prescription and many more from knowing that this option is available. Lord Falconer's Bill includes a period of reflection between being granted, and implementing, assistance to die. Where there is doubt about the patient's mental competence or about the absence of a treatable depression, psychiatric advice can be sought. This is less easy to sort out in the case of trips to Dignitas or self-administered suicide, given that, as the law stands at present, patients cannot even discuss assisted dying with their doctors. I suspect that once you have embarked on a journey to Switzerland it is very difficult to change your mind. You have boarded a train you cannot get off. And as for the rationality of a decision, there are ways of testing competence and the presence or absence of reversible depression. Patients experiencing a horrible death may well be depressed but this does not mean that they are not competent to make a decision. What is more, in every other area of medicine there is *a presumption of competence*: the patient is presumed to be of sound mind and able to make a rational decision unless there is clear evidence to the contrary.

What about the other worry: that the diagnosis could be wrong? In most cases, this seems highly unlikely. A candidate for assisted dying will have widespread advanced illness, clear objective reasons for suffering, in which palliation has failed, and the ultimate outcome will not be in doubt. Rejecting legalization of assisted dying will not, of course, save the occasional misdiagnosed patient from unnecessary death from medical error; it will simply ensure that that avoidable death – as well as that of all those correctly diagnosed – will be more prolonged. What is more, raising the possibility of an assisted death will prompt review of the case and this may turn up the very rare example where clear-cut, advanced disease turns out to be nothing of the sort.

Much attention has been paid to errors doctors make in prognosis. In fact, again, the likelihood of the prognosis being seriously wrong will be considerably less in very advanced disease. Most studies have shown that doctors overestimate the prognosis, expecting patients to live longer than they do. What is more, doctors already rely on estimates of prognosis when they move to management plans that will shorten life, such as withdrawing life-supporting medical care (insulin, artificial ventilation), exploiting the so-called "double effect" (of which more presently), colluding in the patient's death by starvation and dehydration, or initiating continuous deep sedation.

The truth is that medicine is a probabilistic art. This is evident when we look at the outcomes for elective or non-emergency surgery in patients who may, in many cases, be reasonably fit. One very large study showed a significant mortality – up to 5 per cent – in very elderly patients receiving elective surgery to prevent future problems. We accept that as an occasional consequence of trying to alter the natural history of disease. So why do we set impossibly high standards of certainty and clinical accuracy in the case of patients who wish to die when we settle for much lower standards for patients who do not wish to die? Why do we raise the bar above the balance of probabilities, above "beyond reasonable doubt", to "beyond, beyond reasonable doubt"?

Why, in this context, do we believe, as we do not elsewhere in medicine, that it is better that thousands should suffer unnecessarily than that a very rare mistake might be made? *Why can't the fully informed competent patient make the decision*? Why is it better that nature should take its cruel course than that a doctor should hasten the death of a patient? A cynic would say that doctors oppose assisted dying because *they are trained to hasten death only by accident*. Or accidentally on purpose – the so-called "double effect". I shall return to this, and the medical profession, in due course.

RELIGIOUS OPPOSITION: THE SANCTITY OF LIFE

Life, we are told by people who believe this kind of thing, is a gift of God. Consequently, we may not take away a life God has created, even at the request of the person whose life is at issue. This principle is absolute, non-negotiable. But is it? Can it be? In actual practice, the history of those religions that explicitly profess the sanctity of life as an absolute, basic principle – Christianity, Judaism, Islam – shows that it is (to put it politely) inconsistently applied. The notion of the "just war", where people will be killed in large numbers and against their will rather than individually at their request, is accepted; in many explicitly religious countries, judicial execution is commonplace and this may not only be for murder but for lesser crimes, or for non-crimes such as apostasy or blasphemy or being gay. And, to pre-empt the claim that this is evident only in distant countries about which we have only prejudices, let me give you two examples nearer home: the Anglican response to events in the Second World War and, more recently, the rhetoric around the recent Iraq War.

In 1944, George Bell, the Bishop of Chichester, condemned the area-bombing of civilians in German cities: it was, he said, an unjust pursuit of a just war. He was opposed by his fellow bishops, including the Archbishop of York, who said, "It is a lesser evil to bomb [i.e. kill] the war-loving Germans than to sacrifice the lives of our fellow countrymen ..., or to delay the delivery of many now held in slavery". It appears that it is better to kill others directly in order possibly to save others indirectly. There are circumstances, it would appear, under which orthodox opinion allows a utilitarian calculus to trump the "inviolable" principle of the sanctity of life, illustrating Warnock's point about the slithering between absolutist principles and pragmatic considerations.

And let me take an example even nearer home. Rowan Williams, until recently Archbishop of Canterbury, has led the Anglican Church in its violent opposition to legalizing assisted dying in response to the Falconer Commission. It goes against Christian values: "We are committed as Christians to the belief that every life in every imaginable circumstance is infinitely precious in the sight of God". Assited dying would be "a major shift in the moral and spiritual life in which we live" (Christian Institute 2012). Now contrast that forthright response with his statement on the eve of the Iraq War. "Doubts persist", he said, in his joint statement with the Archbishop of Westminster "about the moral legitimacy of a war with Iraq" (BBC News 2003): this muted response to a war in which predictably large numbers of people were killed who had no wish to be – over 600,000 as it turned out (Burnham *et al.* 2006) – was at a time when 2,000,000 of his fellow citizens had taken to the streets to protest out loud this clearly unjust and criminal war.

One could be forgiven for thinking that there is a strain in religious belief that sees assisting the death of someone who is dying and wants to die as morally more hazardous than raining death on a city filled with people who want no such thing. One could be forgiven even for concluding that the sanctity-of-life principle, while supporting the position that it is always wrong to assist someone to die who is terminally ill and longs to die, will suggest that is less wrong to kill a perfectly healthy man, woman or child who does not wish to die.

But we need to dig a little deeper. Why do the opponents of assisted dying invoke a clearly vulnerable principle whose theological resonance would be rejected by most people, even though they are usually less than candid and invoke the factoids we examined earlier? I think it is because it seems to them to be the only way of defending, standing up for or protecting something that we would all wish to defend, stand up for or protect: the fundamental ethic of valuing human lives – our own and those of others – as infinitely precious. This is reflected in the reason given in his presidential address to the General Synod by Rowan Williams for his rejecting legalization of assisted dying: "It will create an ethical framework in which the worthwhileness of some lives is undermined by the legal expression of what feels like public impatience with protracted dying and 'unproductive' lives".

Behind the appeal to the supposedly absolute (but in fact negotiable) principle, there is the implicit assumption or claim that the religious principle of the sanctity of life is the only source of the value we place upon life, as much in a secular as in a religious society; if we question it, we shall devalue life; and we shall particularly devalue the lives of those who are powerless or are already likely to be devalued. Elderly people, people with disability, people who have mental illness, will be at risk.

Most of us can see that this is nonsense but it is nonetheless worthwhile spelling out the obvious. Let me personalize this to make it clear. My wife and I have been happily married for over forty years. We can imagine a time when one of us is terminally ill, nearing the end and in unbearable misery and wanting to die. We would both like there to be a law to make it possible for us to get the help one or other of us may need. Let us suppose that I become terminally ill first and I ask her to seek help from a physician to help me to die and she complies with my wish. This cannot imply that she is colluding in my devaluation of my own (and consequently our shared) life. If I *am* devaluing any part of my life, it is only the next two suffering-filled weeks – not the preceding seventy or (better) eighty years or (better still) ninety years. Neither of us is devaluing human life in general or the irreplaceable preciousness of human beings. Neither she nor I is devaluing anyone else's life: the lives of old people, of people with disability, of people from minority groups. She is respecting my judgement of the value of the last few days of a life: days filled with unbearable suffering. Indeed, we are enhancing the value of life by doing our best to prevent our own lives being diminished by the sustained horror of unbearable and pointless suffering. We are respecting those things by which we judge our lives and our shared personal experiences.

The assertion that legalizing assisted dying would erode the value we place on each other's lives – in particular those who are vulnerable and dependent on our good will – is, of course, an empirical claim. It may be tested by looking at social trends in places where the law has been liberalized. The evidence, such as it is, is in the opposite direction. The care for people with dementia in the Netherlands – see "Not the Truman Show" in Chapter 13 – is superb and places such as Hogeway are moral exemplars that put other countries, including UK, to shame.

FIBBING FOR GOD

The irrelevance of the sanctity-of-life doctrine to determining whether or not the law should be changed is evident to many religious opponents of assisted dying which is why so many factoids are mobilized to try to influence opinion by instilling fear. There are other ways of influencing opinion both directly by appealing to the public and indirectly through influencing bodies that themselves carry considerable clout with those who are in a position to change the law, most notably the medical profession, where organizations such as Care Not Killing and the Christian Medical Fellowship are punching above their numerical weight.

The Catholic Church played a prominent role in the formation of Care not Killing, via the Catholic Bishops' Conference of England and Wales. In the document "Faith in the Future: 2006–2008", they state:

> The work of the Church supporting and promoting pro-life issues has been given a real boost through Faith in the Future.

> The Care Not Killing Alliance was established in 2005 to work with other faith groups, palliative care organisations and disability rights groups, forming a broad coalition of parties concerned with the legalisation of euthanasia ...

Only four of the known thirty member organizations of Care Not Killing are non-religious. So much for "a broad coalition". Dr Peter Saunders, CEO of the Christian Medical Fellowship and Campaign Director of Care not Killing, made the strategy clear:

> As Christian doctors we oppose euthanasia and assisted suicide because we believe in the sanctity of human life made in the image of God ... But to win the debate on assisted dying we need to be using arguments that will make sense to those who do not share our Christian beliefs ... Christian doctors need to play a key role in this debate; and they will do so most effectively by learning to put what are essentially Christian arguments in secular language.

The conflation of euthanasia, assisted suicide and assisted dying is not accidental: it is an essential element in a strategy intended to further the idea that legalizing assisted dying has a built in slippery slope.

In parliament, opponents of change are even more effective in cloaking a principled objection to change in the clothes of pragmatic concern. Resistance to change, specifically in the House of Lords, is organized by the supporters of Living and Dying Well, co-chaired by Lord Carlile QC and Baroness Finlay. Launched in 2010, they describe themselves as "a public policy 'think tank'" whose aim is to "promote reasoned discussion and to publish evidence-based information on the laws relating to euthanasia and assisted suicide" (from Lord Carlile's page at www.9-12bellyard.com). A former part-time Press Officer of Living and Dying Well, and researcher to Baroness Finlay, now Associate Editor of *The Catholic Herald*, recently wrote about the need to separate pro-life campaigns:

One key group would defend the rights of the unborn child and the other would focus on opposing the legalisation of assisted suicide and/or voluntary euthanasia.

Both groups would take a strictly evidence-based approach to influencing and resisting future legislation. Religious sentiments or distracting arguments about sexuality would be kept out of the equation. (Teahan 2012)

We have already seen the "strictly evidence-based approach" referred to by Living Well and Dying Well in action. But we have not touched on one aspect of this approach: namely, the occasional fabrication of the required evidence. Prompted by a poll in May 2012, which found that 62 per cent of doctors were in favour of the British Medical Association (currently opposed to assisted dying) adopting a stance of neutrality, the *British Medical Journal* (*BMJ*) published a leader from the editor Fiona Godlee calling for this stance at their upcoming Annual Meeting, where it was to be debated. The *BMJ* invited its readers to respond to the editorial by voting for or against neutrality. Astonishingly, over 80 per cent of those who voted were *against* neutrality: quite different from what had been found in the scientific poll. This surprising result prompted an analysis of voting patterns. In a two-day period, there was a huge surge in votes. During this time, there were many anomalies, the most striking being one individual, apparently located in Iceland, *who voted against neutrality 168 times*. One could not have clearer evidence of how the debate against assisted dying is being hijacked. This was a re-run of what happened in 2006 when Lord Joffe's Assisted Dying for the Terminally Ill Bill was being debated in the House of Lords. The Euthanasia Prevention Coalition – an international body based in Canada – flooded two polls of British public opinion, one run by Bath University and one by the *Evening Standard*, with "No" votes from Canada and the US.

MEDICAL OPPOSITION TO ASSISTED DYING

One might expect the leaders of the Church to be opposed to assisted dying (although they are at odds with the majority of their flocks); it is of a piece with the kind of heartless, even brutal, confusions that often characterize religious attitudes to matters of life and death. More surprising, and more shocking, is the seemingly strong opposition from the medical profession. The leading medical Royal Colleges, such as the Royal College of Physicians, the Royal College of Surgeons and the Royal College of General Practitioners, are currently against assisted dying, as is the British Medical Association, although Clare Gerada, Chair of the Council of the Royal College of General Practitioners, has called for her college to move to a position of neutrality (Gerada 2012). It was this position of the "representative medical bodies" that provoked Ann McPherson, along with her friend Professor Joe Collier, and supported by Dignity in Dying, to establish Healthcare Professionals for Assisted Dying (HPAD) in October 2010. The most modest of its aims was to send out a signal that the medical profession was not unanimous in its stance towards assisted dying.

This is, in fact, an understatement. Many resent how the debate has been hijacked by special-interest groups inside the profession as well as without. Recent polls have supported this view. For example, the most reliable information suggests that between 30 per cent and 40 per cent of doctors are in favour of liberalization of the law (Lee *et al.* 2009; Seale 2009). What's more, only a third of 1,000 doctors in a survey in October 2011 were opposed to having assisted dying *for themselves*. I have already referred to the study published in May 2012 of 1,000 GPs, which found that 62 per cent of respondents felt that the representative medical bodies should adopt a stance of neutrality towards the issue: that is to say, should be actually representative. This study clearly worried opponents of assisted dying, to judge by the sharp practice it triggered, which I mentioned earlier. No surprise, therefore, that the British Medical Association refused a request in 2013 (from Healthcare Professionals for Assisted Dying) for a survey of its members' views. It might deliver the "wrong" answer.

It is important to question the legitimacy of the medical profession's extension of its authority to matters that are for society as a whole to decide. Individual doctors are, of course, entitled to express and campaign for their views on the ethical case for, and the potential social impact of, liberalizing the law. So long as no healthcare professionals are obliged, against their conscience, to help a dying patient achieve an assisted death, the role of their representative bodies should be confined to speaking on those areas where they have special expertise: for example, the safeguards and codes of practice necessary should any law be implemented and more explicitly medical matters, such as determining prognosis and setting guidelines for optimal end-of-life care. For the profession to go beyond this is a gross example of paternalism, or, given that a large proportion of the profession is female, "parentalism".

At this point, it is important to set aside an objection to this argument that I have often encountered. Is it not sometimes the duty of the medical profession – and indeed parliament – to be paternalistic and to ignore public opinion? After all if there were a referendum on the death sentence today, we would find that the majority of the British public would be in favour of bringing back hanging. The analogy is not valid because those who are seeking to restore the death penalty do not envisage themselves or their loved ones being strung up. Those in favour of assisted dying are advocating something they would want for themselves or for those they care for. This is why the paternalism argument is relevant. Whatever happened to "patient-centred care" and "no decision about me without me" – the mantra that Andrew Lansley placed at the heart of his Health and Social Care Act?

Given that there are physicians of good will, deep religious convictions or none, and expertise in palliative care, with passionate views on both sides of the debate, the proper stance of medical bodies is one of neutrality. This does not mean indifference; rather, what the American physician Timothy Quill has called "studied neutrality". This is what the Royal College of Nursing has chosen, after a survey of its members that produced 49 per cent of responses in favour and 40 per cent against. The fact that the nurses are more in tune with the public on this issue is not entirely surprising. As Joyce Robins, co-director of Patient Concern, has written (pers. comm.), "Nurses ... are likely to be at the bedside of the dying and hear and understand patients' and relatives' feelings. Doctors appear briefly so it is easier for them to stick to ... the *status quo*"; to put it bluntly, it is easier for the less imaginative among the medical profession to bear the sufferings of others heroically as they do not have to experience it minute by minute, hour by hour, day by day. Until the colleges and the BMA adopt a position of neutrality, there will be a serious obstacle to a full, open and honest debate on assisted dying.

Doctors wishing to avoid assisted dying and yet humanely committed to achieving the same end already make liberal use of ploys such as: the double effect, where the primary intention is to control symptoms, although this may accidentally hasten death; withdrawing treatments such as artificial ventilation in someone who has lost their respiratory drive, which will ensure death with 100 per cent certainty; the institution of continuous sedation, which reduces a person to a breathing body; or, worst of all, standing idly by while a patient has an unassisted death by thirst or starvation. So what is behind this anomalous and, it seems to me, in some cases unacceptable behaviour, which exploits distinctions without real differences? After all, C. Everett Koop, the former US Surgeon General, described withdrawal of dialysis in terminally ill patients as "euthanasia by omission". Something is clearly at work here, making people think irrationally.

For some, it is the incorrect belief that assisting a terminally ill person to die would be contrary to the very ethos of medicine. The BMA's opposition is defended by the argument that "it is alien to the traditional ethos and moral focus of medicine". Repeatedly, one hears it said by doctors that they went into medicine "to save lives not to end them". Behind this kind of statement – which, as Marcia Angell (2012) said in a recent article, focuses too much on the physician, and not enough on the patient – is the feeling that to participate in assisted dying is to contravene, even to betray, the solemn undertakings of doctors entering the medical profession.

In its classical form, the Hippocratic Oath includes this promise: "I will not give a lethal drug to anyone if I am asked, nor will I advise such a plan". But it also adds (in the same paragraph) "and similarly I will not give a woman a pessary to secure an abortion". In other words, doctors involved in abortion would also be in breach of the oath but this does not cause problems for the vast majority of the profession. It also enjoins doctors to be chaste and religious. Well you may judge my chastity from the fact that I have two children and the fervour of my religious belief from the fact that I am a strong supporter of the British Humanist Association. In neither instance do I feel that I have betrayed my professional calling.

So the classical oath is an anachronism. The oath has been brought up to date in various ways. One widely used version introduced in 1964, has this key paragraph:

> Most especially must I tread with care in matters of life and death. If it is given to me to save a life, all thanks. But it may also be within my power to take a life; this awesome responsibility must be faced with great humbleness and awareness of my frailty.

This seems to allow for assisted dying. And the Declaration of Geneva, adopted by the General Assembly of the World Medical Association at Geneva in 1948, and most recently amended in 2006, says only that: "I will maintain the utmost respect for human life". This is consistent with supporting assisted dying under the circumstances we envisage. It does not say anything about not taking life. In short, the claim that support for assisted dying violates the fundamental ethos of the medical profession is unfounded.

Indeed, the opposite would appear to be the case. Charles Bulman, a retired surgeon, commented in his written evidence to the Falconer Commission on Assisted Dying (2012): "As a professional, I can recall numerous examples of patients who have requested assistance to die and in almost every case I have felt that I denied my professional duty of care by my refusal to help". It may well be the case that medical opposition to assisted dying, far from originating in moral concerns is due to moral laziness: the unavailability of assisted dying spares doctors from making decisions. Without a law in place, the decision is already made: "I can't help you". In the meantime, a certain amount of life-shortening help is offered to patients outside of the safety of the law under the cover of darkness.

THE SLIPPERY SLOPE REVISITED: AUTONOMY

In making the case for legalizing assisted dying, I invoked the patient's right to choose, behind which lies the principle of autonomy. This principle has been singled out for attack by opponents of legalization. Most of the reasons for attacking the appeal to autonomy may be set aside. Here are a couple. The first, that we do not belong to ourselves but are God's possessions, does not get much traction in a secular society. Most of us happen not to believe this. If it were true, however, it might lead us to deny ourselves the right to *any* autonomy. The second is an inescapable truth and one that, again, does not point to any particular conclusions except a reinforcement of what is called the harm principle. Let me say a word about this principle. It is difficult to improve on its first formulation by John Stuart Mill:

> That the only purpose for which power can rightfully be exercised over any member of a civilized community, against his will, is to prevent harm to others. His own good, either physical or moral, is not a sufficient warrant. He cannot rightfully be compelled to do or forbear because it will be better for him to do so, because it will make him happier, because, in the opinion of others, to do so would be wise, or even right.
> (1859: 22)

And he spells this out clearly enough for everyone to understand:

> The only part of the conduct of anyone, for which he is amenable to society, is that which concerns others. In the part which merely concerns himself, his independence is, of right, absolute. Over himself, over his own body and mind, the individual is sovereign.
> (*Ibid.*)

Opponents of assisted dying have argued that this is not something that concerns only the individual who is directly affected. There will be effects on society as a whole through, they claim, the devaluation of human life. I have dealt with this already.

But there is another challenge that I think requires more thought. It relates to the question of the consistency with which the principle is applied. If you argue for assisted dying on the basis of respect for autonomy, why do you restrict its availability simply to people who are terminally ill, are deemed to be mentally competent, and so on? Why do you oppose a law that would go beyond assisted dying and permit assisted suicide for people who are not terminally ill, even though they request it? Surely a human right is a human right? Doesn't consistency demand of us that we accede to the request of anyone of sound mind who seeks our assistance to die, even if the reason is something as nebulous as being "tired of life". It may not lead down to the involuntary slaughter of people who are seen as undesirable, surplus to requirement or merely unproductive, as Rowan Williams suggested. But it may take us to a place where none of us would like to be. Let me explore this.

Supposing you come across someone about to jump off a bridge. You establish that he is not being forced to do this at gunpoint. Do you then say "Good luck" and let him get on with it? Of course not. Even less would you be willing to accede to his request for assistance in jumping off. There are several practical reasons why one would treat this case differently from that of a dying patient seeking assistance to die. We have no history of what has led up to his despair; we have no idea of the cause; he could well have an entirely solvable problem; we could save him for a happy life. To say "Get on with it" would be a callous indifference to human life.

And we don't have to look at such an extreme example to see that we do not simply accede to people's wishes, even over things that seem to affect directly only themselves. This may seem to be a retreat from the assertion of the primacy of autonomy. Should the invocation of autonomy authorize the progressive extension of the cases in which dying could be assisted? If it did *not* lead to this slippery slope, wasn't this because the principle of autonomy was being applied *inconsistently*? Haven't I joined the Groucho Club along with my religious opponents?

I think it is possible to deal with this problem entirely honestly, as follows. In all cases, the application of a non-religious ethical principle – as opposed to an absolutist religious one – has to be put in context; it is right to begin with the principle but it may not always be right to apply it without limit; this applies to every aspect of human life. Assisted dying respects autonomy and it has a clearly defined scope. Assisting anyone who wishes to jump off a bridge will have clear-cut adverse consequences, spreading an ethos of cruel indifference to what may be remediable suffering: precisely this devaluation of human life that opponents of assisted dying say they fear. So this presents us with a challenge: we have to judge the place where the gain in individual autonomy is offset by harms to society as a whole. To some extent this will be a calculus of benefits, harms and risk of harm.

This apparent retreat from the boundless application of the principle of autonomy is entirely different from the appeal to, and deviation from, the principle of sanctity of life for which I criticized some of the religiously motivated opponents. For their deviations are from a principle that is claimed to be absolute and inviolable; and their deviations are into killing in war, and other modes of behaviour that require further justification; and the original principle sits ill with a utilitarian calculus of greater and less benefits. The harm principle that limits autonomy is a utilitarian principle that makes up part of a coherent picture that weighs autonomy and harm in the same scales.

The need to restrict the application of the principle that supports it is not a problem unique to assisted dying. It is present throughout our judgements of the correct thing to do. We have to do something that I have called "dichotomizing over a continuum" (see Tallis 2012c). Take, for example, free speech, which gives me right to express my views without censorship. This sounds fine – an unquestionably Good Thing – but it may have unintended consequences that require us to mobilize a second principle to modify the first: the harm principle. If someone exploits the principle of free speech to indulge in hate speech – say, making anti-Semitic remarks designed to stir up hatred – the harm that is caused has to be reined in by invoking another principle banning the use of speech that causes harm. Anyone who is considered to cause such harm will have their claim to exercise their autonomy overridden and is justly charged with a criminal offence.

There will, however, be a continuum, rather than a natural break, between totally acceptable and totally unacceptable speech and yet we have to draw a line at right angles to this at a point that will seem to some arbitrary: we have to divide a continuum in two. *This* side of the line is a legitimate exercise of free speech, we judge; and *that* side of the line is an illegitimate and criminal abuse of the principle of free speech.

And the same applies to considering the age of criminal responsibility; or where we judge a medical treatment to be futile and withdraw life-extending treatments such as kidney dialysis or artificial respiration; or, indeed, as to what counts as an appropriate application of the doctrine of the double effect, in which treatments aimed at symptom relief are permitted to be used even if they shorten life – just as much as to the decision to assist dying. There is, in short, nothing uniquely flawed about limiting the application of the principle of autonomy when we use it to support the case for assisted dying.

The fundamental point is that the legalization of assisted dying is *extending* the application of the principle of autonomy, even though it is not rendering it boundless. There remains the fact that any good principle – such as that we should not hold immature human beings to the adult level of accountability for crimes – cannot determine from within itself the scope of its application and it could always be (ab)used to justify actions we do not wish. We have to decide on an age of criminal responsibility; the sharp cut-off is an artefact. In the case of assisted dying, the continuum of the application of the principle of respecting autonomy has clear points at which it can be considered no longer to be sovereign. There are distinctions between terminal and non-terminal illness; between people who do and people who do not have a serious illness; between people who have and people who do not have mental competence; between assistance to die and euthanasia; and between voluntary and involuntary euthanasia. If there is a slope downwards from one to the other, it has a high coefficient of friction.

BUT IS A CHANGE IN THE LAW NECESSARY?

Some of those who accept the facts and the arguments that I have presented may still oppose legislation on the grounds that only a small minority of dying people would seek assistance and an even smaller number would use the prescription. Wouldn't legislation prove a sledgehammer to crack a nut, a leap in the dark that threatens all of us, for the sake of a few people? Even if it did not have the dangerous consequences our opponents claim, it would most certainly upset flocks (I think that is the collective term) of prelates (although not their congregations), something not to be lightly dismissed. Well, I happen to believe that even small numbers of people going through unbearable hell are important and there is something wrong in a society that cannot see that. What is more, the availability of assisted dying would bring much comfort to many more sufferers than actually use it because it brings an all-important sense of having some control, as we know from the Oregon data I referred to.

It has been argued that, since the Director of Public Prosecutions (DPP) has not, in the two years since he introduced his guidelines for prosecution of those who have assisted another to die, referred any cases sent to him for prosecution, things are fine at present. No law is needed. Let us muddle on in the usual British way. This will not do. First, assisting someone to die remains a criminal offence: the relative or friend is the "suspect" and the patient the "victim". Since "suspects" usually spend months under investigation before being told whether or not they are to be prosecuted, there is huge anxiety and stigma at an already intensely distressing time. Thus a *de facto* history of sensible decisions so far is not as good as a law that permits assisted dying within clear limits and safeguards. What's more, a future more hawkish DPP may have a quite different attitude and use the current sixteen tests of motivation – yes, sixteen tests – to draw different conclusions as to whether assistance has been compassionate or motivated by criminal intent.

Most importantly, it remains a criminal offence for any medical qualified practitioner or other healthcare professional to give advice. Assistance is, therefore, delegated to amateurs, who have to assume a huge responsibility at a time when they are already greatly distressed, and may well be incompetent to carry it out. This morally repugnant situation, imposing a final cruelty on those who have seen their loved ones suffer an appalling death, is unacceptable. That cruelty will be compounded by the investigations that must take place after an assisted death. This is illustrated by this story from a grieving husband, former test cricketer Chris Broad: "Michelle had organised the end of her life remarkably well – left little gifts for her tennis club members and notes for me and the children ... And [the police] just swooped up all those things and took them away" (quoted in Chorley 2012).

We therefore need a change of the law – and soon. I am an optimist and I believe that, even if the Church and the representatives of the medical profession continue to disrespect the considered opinions of their respective memberships, their views will eventually be discredited as unrepresentative. With this obstacle out of the way, parliament may indeed come to support legislation in favour of assisted dying.

Indeed, my optimism extends to the belief that rational argument, rather than pre-rational opinions, will win the day and the law changed. For this to happen, a small but vocal minority, prepared to tolerate other people's suffering heroically for the sake of their idea of God and of his will, must be challenged. Opponents of change make a lot of noise. It's time that the relatively silent majority made more, so that, as Ann McPherson hoped, "needless suffering at the end of life would become a thing of the past".

EPILOGUE

And So to Bed: Notes towards a Philosophy of Sleep from A to Zzzzzzz

This epilogue is at least in part the result of an accident: a happy one, I hasten to add. A little while back, I was sitting on a panel with the philosopher Christopher Hamilton, discussing the question of whether a world without pain is an appropriate goal for mankind or whether pain serves some additional positive purpose other than the obvious biological one of directing us away from things that might harm us (a topic, perhaps, for a future essay). Meeting Christopher after a long interval reminded me of his excellent book *Living Philosophy* (2001). The volume includes a fascinating essay entitled "The Need to Sleep", where he notes that philosophers have not paid sufficient attention to this extraordinary phenomenon. Well, a decade on, this is the beginning of a response to Christopher's wake-up call.

For sleep *is* rather extraordinary. If I told you that I had a neurological disease which meant that for eight or more hours a day I lost control of my faculties, bade farewell to the outside world, and was subject to complex hallucinations and delusions – such as being chased by a grizzly bear at Stockport railway station – you would think I was in a pretty bad way. If I also claimed that the condition was infectious, you would wish me luck in coping with such a terrible disease, and bid me a hasty farewell.

Of course, sleep is not a disease at all, but the condition of daily (nightly) life for the vast majority of us. The fact that we accept without surprise the need for a prolonged blackout as part of our daily life highlights our tendency to take for granted anything about our condition that is universal. We don't see how strange sleep is because (nearly) everyone sleeps. Indeed, the situation of those who do *not* suffer from TRHDS (Tallis's Recurrent Hallucinating Delusional Syndrome) is awful. They have something that truly deserves our sympathy: chronic insomnia.

Since all animals sleep, we assume it has a biological purpose. The trouble is, we don't know what that purpose is. There are many theories – energy conservation, growth promotion, immobilization during hours of darkness when it might be dangerous to be out and about, consolidation of memories – but they are all open to serious objections. William Dement, one of the leading sleep researchers of the past century, concluded from his fifty years in the forefront of the field that "the only reason we need to sleep that is really, really solid, is that we get sleepy".

PHILOSOPHERS ASLEEP

It is easy to see why philosophers have, on the whole, avoided talking about sleep. Those who see the aim of philosophy as being to cultivate the most unpeeled mode of wakefulness are likely to treat sleep as an enemy. *Hypnophobia* was a striking theme in existentialist thought. "Blessed are these drowsy men", Nietzsche said sarcastically, "for they shall soon drop off". And he sometimes endeavoured to do without sleep, on one occasion trying to live on four hours sleep a night for a fortnight. (I read this unimpressed when I was a junior doctor in the 1970s, and my 104-hour-week included periods of up to forty-eight hours continuously on call.) Jean-Paul Sartre's Antoine Roquentin, the anti-hero of *Nausea* (1938), expresses his contempt for the landlord of the cafe he frequents by observing that "when this man is alone, he falls asleep" (2000: 16). And I seem to recall that a character in one of his other novels observes with horror the person opposite him on the train, fast asleep, passively swaying in time to the movement of the carriage, reduced to a material object. This continuation of our lives in the absence of our waking self, in which the living daylights are replaced by half-living nightlights, is a creepy reminder of the unchosen automatisms upon which our chosen path through life depends. It is a reminder of our ultimate helplessness and of how circumscribed a place coherent thought (never mind philosophical thought) plays in our lives.

Of course, there is no reason – other than fear of contagion – why the mind should not think about its antithesis, nor why super-mindful philosophers should not take an interest in our regular spells of compulsory mindlessness. After all, physicists have devoted much of their extraordinarily brilliant intellectual exertions to clarifying the nature of matter: of what is there, stripped of the kinds of meanings that fill their own consciousnesses. Philosophers, however, have a particular fear of one kind of sleep: the sleep that their own works may induce. Those carefully crafted arguments, the painstakingly revised sentences, expressing insights, so they hope, into the most fundamental aspects of the world, seem less able than a strip cartoon or a gossip column to hold back the reader from a world-dissolving snooze.

Honest philosophers know they cannot complain about casting their own philosophical pearls before drowsy swine because they, too, have fallen asleep over the works of philosophers greater than themselves. I speak as a minor player who has sometimes dozed off while reading Martin Heidegger's *Being and Time*, possibly the greatest philosophical work of the past century and the subject of a monograph I published a decade ago, and over which others too, I suspect, have dozed off. (Not many, judging by the sales.) On other occasions I have woken with a start to discover that Kant's *Critique of Pure Reason* has fallen from my slackening hand. There could be no more profound critique of reason, pure or impure.

For Descartes, cessation of thinking meant ceasing to be an "I", so thoughtless sleep was vexing indeed: a vegetable, organic gap in our spiritual life. As James Hill (to whom I owe much of what follows in this and the next paragraph) pointed out in "The Philosophy of Sleep" (2004), Descartes' view of the mind as a *substance* did not allow for any pause in the continuity of thought. If the mind were the kind of thing that could be extinguished by the sound of a lecturer's voice and rekindled by a wet flannel, it would not be worthy of the status of a substance, which should be immune from mere accidents. Descartes, therefore, concluded that we never stop thinking, even in the deepest sleep; however, in our deepest sleep we do not lay down any memories of our thoughts.

Ad hoc or what? John Locke would have none of it. Empirical evidence, he says, tells us that we do not think when asleep, and that's the end of the story: "every drowsy Nod shakes their [the Cartesian] Doctrine" (*Essay* Bk II, ch. 1, §13). Leibniz, anticipating the confusions of Herr Professor Freud, argued that Descartes was right: we *are* thinking during dreamless sleep, but our thoughts are unconscious, rather like the perceptions we have without noticing them. I leave the reader to referee the discussion, but its unsatisfactory nature offers another reason why most philosophers have shied away from sleep.

PERCHANCE TO DREAM

Dreams, of course, have figured more significantly in philosophy. Since they are a mode of consciousness – prompting Aristotle to say that "the soul makes assertions in sleep" (*On Dreams* 458b) – dreams seem one step up from the mere putting out of zzzs. More to the point, they place a philosophically interesting question mark against our confidence in the nature of the world we apparently have in common with others. Your dreams, so long as you are dreaming them, may be as compellingly real as the fact that you are reading this book (and possibly dozing off over it). "There are no certain indications", as Descartes pointed out in his *Meditations*, "by which I can clearly distinguish wakefulness from sleep". The glib response to this – that we should not be looking for mere "indications", because we do not rely on mere indications to find out whether we are awake or sleep – doesn't work; so we are embarked on an endless, and endlessly fascinating, journey in pursuit of the kind of certainty that only our philosophical selves want, or pretend to want, or need, or seem to need.

There is certain pathos in our vulnerable, gullible, sleeping selves, and the dreams that something – that is ourself and yet not ourself – puts together in order to make narrative sense of what is going on in our brains and bodies when they are almost completely disconnected from the world. To meet our insatiable appetite for coherent meaning, we unpack a whole scene out of a sensation, or make sense of a sudden movement of a limb by inventing a cliff down which we are falling. (No expense spared!) The fact that we can confect a sort of sense out of whatever is served up to us casts an interesting light on the question of the relationship between the real and the rational: whatever we can rationalize may seem real to us, and whatever seems real to us we try to rationalize – with impressive rates of success. The division within our (mind-constructed) dreams between the "I" that is making sense of what is there, and the "there" that is made sense of – so that we can even wait tensely for what happens next – is particularly striking.

Paul Valéry invented the character Monsieur Teste. "A mystic without God", Teste was committed to uninterrupted, undistracted thought. His whole life's work was "to kill the puppet", the automaton, inside himself. In the famous *An Evening with M. Teste* (1896), Valéry leaves his hero drifting off to sleep, observing the stages of his own gradual extinction, and murmuring "Let's think very closely … You can fall asleep on any subject … Sleep can continue any idea", as his self-awareness fades into suspension points.

Valéry himself kept a diary for over fifty years (collected as the *Cahiers* [Notebooks]). One of his central preoccupations was to capture the successive phases of his awakening, as in the early hours of the morning he annotated his mind-rise. Naturally, dreams preoccupied him as much as the daily resurrection of the self. He suggested dreams might be an attempt to make sense of the body's passage from sleep to wakefulness. Like me, he was unimpressed by Freud's evidence-impoverished claims about dreams being the "royal road" to the Unconscious: that multi-storied jerry-built word-castle that so many otherwise intelligent people have taken for a scientific idea. Nor did Valéry buy the notion that dreams could be prophetic, the mind slipping along loops in time to enable us to see the future of the world or the will of God.

These nightly adventures, spun out of a consciousness permitted to free-wheel by disconnection from a perceived world, are of compelling interest when we are in the grip of them as lead actor or as the helpless centre of events. Yet by an irony, nothing is more sleep-inducing than the egocentric tales of someone else's solipsistic dreams. We long to hear that magic phrase "And then I woke up".

I could go on, but I won't, lest I cause your copy of *The Reflections of a Metaphysical Flâneur* to fall out your lifeless hand as you slip from the philosophy of sleep to the thing itself and are drowned in the object of your thoughts.

Good night, reader.

Bibliography

Abraham, A. 2011. *Care and Compassion? Report of the Health Service Ombudsman on Ten Investigations into NHS Care of Older People*. www.ombudsman.org.uk/care-and-compassion/home (accessed March 2013).

Angell, M. 2012. "May Doctors Help You to Die?" *New York Review of Books* (11 October).

Auden, W. H. 2005. *The Sea and the Mirror: A Commentary on Shakespeare's The Tempest*, A. Kirsch (ed. and intro.). Princeton, NJ: Princeton University Press.

Baron-Cohen, S. 2003. *The Essential Difference: Men, Women and the Extreme Male Brain*. London: Penguin.

Baron-Cohen, S. 2011. *Zero Degrees of Empathy: A New Theory of Human Cruelty*. London: Penguin.

Battin, M. P., A. van der Heide, L. Ganzini, G. van der Wal & B. D. Onwuteaka-Philipsen 2007. "Legal Physician-Assisted Dying in Oregon and the Netherlands: Evidence Concerning the Impact on Patients in 'Vulnerable' Groups". *Journal of Medical Ethics* **33**(10): 591–7.

BBC News 2003. "Archbishops Doubt Morality of Iraq War". http://news.bbc.co.uk/1/hi/uk/2781783.stm (accessed April 2013).

Bishop, K. M. & D. Walsten 1997. "Sex Differences in Human Corpus Callosum: Myth or Reality?" *Neuroscience and Biobehavioural Reviews* **21**: 581–601.

Blackburn, S. 2011. "Morality Without God". Review of *The Moral Landscape* by Sam Harris. *Prospect* (April).

Blood, A. J. & R. J. Zatorre 2001. "Intensely Pleasurable Responses to Music Correlate with Activity in Brain Regions Implicated in Reward and Emotion". *PNAS* **98**(20)(25 September): 11,818–23.

Bradley, F. H. 1893. *Appearance and Reality: A Metaphysical Essay*. London: Swan Sonnenschein.

Burnham, G., R. Lafta, S. Doocy & L. Roberts 2006. "Mortality After the 2003 Invasion of Iraq: A Cross-sectional Cluster Sample Survey". *The Lancet* **368**(9,545): 1,421–8.

Caplan, A. 1996. "Trust and the Debate over Medical Futility". *Annals of Internal Medicine* **125**: 688–9.

Carnap, R. 1963. "Intellectual Autobiography". In *The Philosophy of Rudolf Carnap*, P. A. Schilpp (ed.), 1–84. Peru, IL: Open Court.

Catholic Bishops' Conference of England and Wales 2008. "Faith in the Future: 2006–2008". London: Catholic Bishops' Conference of England and Wales.

Chakrabarti, B., F. Dudbridge, L. Kent *et al.* 2009. "Genes Related to Sex Steroids, Neural Growth, and Social-Emotional Behaviour are Associated with Autistic Traits, Empathy and Asperger Syndrome". *Autism Research* **2**: 157–77.

Chalmers, D. 1995. "Facing Up to the Problem of Consciousness". *Journal of Consciousness Studies* **2**(3): 200–219.

Chalmers, D. 1996. *The Conscious Mind: In Search of a Fundamental Theory*. Oxford: Oxford University Press.

Chalmers, D. 2010. *The Character of Consciousness*. Oxford: Oxford University Press.

Chorley, M. 2012. "Change 'Unsafe' Law on Assisted Dying, Says Ex Police Chief". *Independent* (1 January).

Christian Institute 2012. "Archbishop Warns of 'Disaster' if Assisted Suicide is Legalised". www.christian.org.uk/news/archbishop-warns-of-disaster-if-assisted-suicide-is-legalised/ (accessed April 2013).

Churchland, P. 1988. *Matter and Mind: A Contemporary Introduction to the Philosophy of Mind*, rev. edn. Cambridge, MA: MIT Press.

Commission on Assisted Dying 2012. Report. www.demos.co.uk/publications/thecommissiononassisteddying (accessed March 2013).

Crick, F. 1994. *The Astonishing Hypothesis: The Scientific Search for the Soul*. New York: Charles Scribner's Sons.

Damasio, A. 2012. *Self Comes to Mind: Constructing the Conscious Brain*. New York: Vintage.

Davies, P. 1993. *The Mind of God: Science and the Search for Ultimate Meaning*, Harmondsworth: Penguin.

Davis, W. 2011. *Into the Silence: The Great War, Mallory, and the Conquest of Everest*. New York: Alfred A. Knopf.

Deacon, T. W. 2012. *Incomplete Nature: How Mind Emerged from Matter*. New York: W. W. Norton.

Dennett, D. 1991. *Consciousness Explained*. Boston, MA: Little Brown.

Eliot, L. 2010. *Pink Brain, Blue Brain: How Small Differences Grow into Troublesome Gaps – And What We Can Do About It*. Oxford: OneWorld.

Eliot, T. S. 2001. "Little Gidding". In *Four Quartets*. London: Faber & Faber.

Feigl, H. 1958. "The 'Mental' and the 'Physical'". *Minnesota Studies in the Philosophy of Science* II: 370–497.

Fodor, J. 2007. "Headaches Have Themselves". *London Review of Books* **29**(10) (24 May): 9–10.

Gefter, A. 2012. "Bang Goes the Theory". *New Scientist* **214**(2,871) (30 June): 32.

General Medical Council 2002. *Withholding and Withdrawing Life-prolonging Treatments: Good Practice in Decision-making*. London: GMC.

Gerada, C. 2012. "The Case for Neutrality on Assisted Dying: A Personal View". *British Journal of General Practice* **62**(605) (December): 650.

Global Commission on Drug Policy 2011. *War on Drugs: Report of the Global Commission on Drug Policy*. www.globalcommissionondrugs.org/wp-content/themes/gcdp_v1/pdf/Global_Commission_Report_English.pdf (accessed March 2013).

Godlee, F. 2012. "Assisted Dying: Legalization is a Decision for Society not Doctors". *British Medical Journal* **344**: e4075. www.bmj.com/content/344/bmj.e4075 (accessed April 2013).

Gray, J. 2002. *Straw Dogs: Thoughts on Humans and Other Animals*. London: Granta.

Halvorson, H. 2011. "The Measure of All Things: Quantum Mechanics and the Soul". In *The Soul Hypothesis: Investigations into the Existence of the Soul*, M. C. Baker & S. Goetz (eds), 138–67. New York: Continuum.

Hamilton, C. 2001. *Living Philosophy: Reflections on Life, Meaning and Morality*. Edinburgh: Edinburgh University Press.

Hawking, S. & L. Mlodinow 2010. *The Grand Design*. London: Bantam.

Hazlitt, W. 1819. "On Wit and Humour". In *Lectures on the English Comic Writers*. London: Taylor & Hessey.

Hill, J. 2004. "The Philosophy of Sleep: Descartes, Locke and Leibniz". *The Richmond Journal of Philosophy* (Spring): 20–26.

House of Commons Home Affairs Committee 2012. *Drugs: Breaking the Cycle*. London: Stationery Office. www.publications.parliament.uk/pa/cm201213/cmselect/cmhaff/184/184.pdf (accessed March 2013).

Hurley, M., D. Dennett & R. Adams 2011. *Inside Jokes: Using Humor to Reverse-Engineer the Human Mind*. Cambridge, MA: MIT Press.

Kelly, S. 2012. "Art and Science Don't Mix". http://m.scotsman.com/lifestyle/visual-arts/stuart_kelly_art_and_science_don_t_mix_1_2034135 (accessed March 2013).

Kent, A. 1990. "Against Many-Worlds Interpretations". *International Journal of Modern Physics* A5: 1745–62.

Kmietovicz, Z. 2002. "R.E.S.P.E.C.T. – Why Doctors are Still Getting Enough of It". *British Medical Journal* **324**(7,328): 11–14.

Koch, C. & F. Crick 2001. "Consciousness, Neurobiology of". In *The MIT Encyclopedia of the Cognitive Sciences*, R. A. Wilson & F. C. Keil (eds), 193–4. Cambridge, MA: MIT Press.

Krauss, L. 2012. *A Universe from Nothing: Why There is Something Rather Than Nothing*. New York: Free Press.

Kuhn, R. L. 2007. "Why This Universe? Toward a Taxonomy of Possible Explanations". *Skeptic* **13**(2): 28–39. www.skeptic.com/magazine/downloads/skeptic13-2_Kuhn.pdf (accessed March 2013).

Kuhn, R. L. 2013. "Why not Nothing"? In *The Mystery of Existence*, J. Leslie & R. L. Kuhn (eds), 246–78. Oxford: Wiley-Blackwell.

Larkin, P. 1964. *The Whitsun Weddings*. London: Faber.

Lee, W., A. Price, L. Rayner, M. Hotopf 2009. "Survey of Doctors' Opinions of the Legalisation of Physician-Assisted Suicide". *BMC Medical Ethics* 10: 2.

Lehrer, J. 2012. *Imagine: How Creativity Works*. New York: Houghton Mifflin.

Le Poidevin, R. 2003. *Travels in Four Dimensions: The Engimas of Space and Time*. Oxford: Oxford University Press.

Lévi-Strauss, C. 1969. *The Raw and the Cooked*, J. Weightman & D. Weightman (trans.). New York: Harper.

Locke, J. [1690] 2004. *An Essay Concerning Human Understanding*. London: Penguin.

Macfarlane, R. 2012. *The Old Ways: A Journey on Foot*. London: Hamish Hamilton.

Mannes, E. 2011. *The Power of Music: Pioneering Discoveries in the New Science of Song*. New York: Walker.

Marks, J. 2011a. "Marks on Animals". *Philosophy Now* **86** (September/October). http://philosophynow.org/issues/86/Letters (accessed March 2013).

Marks, J. 2011b. "Veterinarian, Heal Thy Profession!". *Philosophy Now* **85** (July/August). http://philosophynow.org/issues/85/Veterinarian_Heal_Thy_Profession (accessed March 2013).

Marks, J. 2011c. Review of *What Animals Want* by Larry Carbone. *Philosophy Now* **85** (July/August). http://philosophynow.org/issues/85/What_Animals_Want_by_Larry_Carbone (accessed March 2013).

McPherson, T. 2012. "Mum Wanted Assisted Dying but We Watched Her Die Slowly and in Pain". *British Medical Journal* 344 (14 June): e4007.

Meillassoux, Q. 2008. *After Finitude: An Essay on the Necessity of Contingency*. London: Continuum.

Mill, J. S. 1859. *On Liberty*. London: John W. Parker and Son.

Musser, G. 2002. "A Hole at the Heart of Physics". *Scientific American* (September): 48–9.

Neale, B. M., Y. Kou, L. Liu *et al.* 2012. "Patterns and Rates of Exomic De Novo Mutations in Autism Spectrum Disorders". *Nature* **485**(7,397) (5 April): 242–5.

Neighbour, R. 2005. "The Little Mushroom and the Blighted Twin". In *I'm Too Hot Now: Themes and Variations from General Practice*, 107–18. London: Radcliff Publishing.

Nietzsche, F. [1878–79] 1996. *Human, All Too Human*, R. J. Hollingdale (ed. and trans.). Cambridge: Cambridge University Press.

Nietzsche, F. [1895] 2013. *Die Götzen-Dämmerung – Twilight of the Idols*. From the original German and translations by W. Kaufmann and R. J. Hollingdale. www.handprint.com/SC/NIE/GotDamer.html (accessed April 2013).

Oregon Health Authority 2013. "Death With Dignity Act". public.health.oregon.gov/ProviderPartnerResources/EvaluationResearch/DeathwithDignityAct/Pages/index.aspx (accessed April 2013).

O'Roak, B. J., L. Vives, S. Girirajan *et al.* 2012. "Sporadic Autism Exomes Reveal a Highly Connected Protein Network of De Novo Mutation". *Nature* **485**(7,397) (4 April): 246–50.

Pinker, S. 1997. *How the Mind Works*. New York: W. W. Norton.

Prideaux, S. 2012. *Strindberg: A Life*. New Haven, CT: Yale University Press.

Putnam, H. 1967. "Time and Physical Geometry". *Journal of Philosophy* **64**: 240–47.

Ramachandran, V. S. 2012. *The Tell-Tale Brain: Unlocking the History of Human Nature*. London: Random House.

Rosenberg, A. 2011. *The Atheist's Guide to Reality: Enjoying Life Without Illusions*. New York: W. W. Norton.

Ross, J. 2012. *Orwell's Cough: Diagnosing the Medical Maladies and Last Gasps of the Great Writers*. London: Oneworld.

Ross, S. 1991. *Nineteenth-Century Attitude: Men of Science*. Dordrecht: Kluwer.

Royal College of Physicians 2005. *Doctors in Society: Medical Professionalism in a Changing World*. Technical supplement to a report of a Working Party of the Royal College of Physicians of London. London: RCP.

Russell, B. 1927. *The Analysis of Matter*. London: Kegan Paul.

Russell, B. [1927] 2009. *An Outline of Philosophy*. London: Routledge.

Ryle, G. 1949. *The Concept of Mind*. Chicago, IL: University of Chicago Press.

Ryle, G. 1954. *Dilemmas*. Cambridge: Cambridge University Press.

Sacks, O. 2012. *Hallucinations*. New York: Alfred A. Knopf.

Sanders, S. J., M. T. Murtha, A. R. Gupta *et al.* 2012. "De Novo Mutations Revealed by Whole-Exome Sequencing are Strongly Associated with Autism". *Nature* **485**(7,397) (4 April): 237–41.

Sartre, J.-P. [1938] 2000. *Nausea*. Harmondsworth: Penguin.
Saunders, J. 2001. "Perspectives on CPR: Resuscitation or Resurrection?" *Clinical Medicine JRCPL* 1: 457–60.
Schlosshauer, M. (ed.) 2011. *Elegance and Enigma: The Quantum Interviews*. Berlin: Springer.
Seale, C. 2009. "Legalisation of Euthanasia or Physician-Assisted Dying: Survey of Doctors' Attitudes". *Palliative Medicine* 23(3): 205–12.
Searle, J. 1998. *The Mystery of Consciousness*. London: Granta.
Sellars, W. [1963] 2007. "Philosophy and the Scientific Image of Man". In *In the Space of Reasons: Selected Essays of Wilfrid Sellars*, K. Sharp & R. B. Brandom (eds), 369–408. Cambridge, MA: Harvard University Press.
Seung, S. 2010. "I Am My Connectome". Video. www.ted.com/talks/sebastian_seung.html (accessed March 2013).
Sheldrake, R. 2005. "The Sense of Being Stared At, Part 1: Is it Real or Illusory?" *Journal of Consciousness Studies* 12(6): 10–31.
Simpson, W. 2012. Unpublished introductory comments, Philosophy of Physics Conference, 11 September, University of St Andrews.
Smolin, L. 2006. *The Trouble with Physics: The Rise of String Theory, the Fall of a Science and What Comes Next*. London: Penguin.
Stecker, M., A. T. Cheung, A. Pochettino *et al*. 2001. "Deep Hypothermic Circulatory Arrest: I. Effects of Cooling on Electroencephalogram and Evoked Potentials. *Annals of Thoracic Surgery* 71: 14–21.
Stern, J. P. 1959. *Lichtenberg: A Doctrine of Scattered Occasions Reconstructed from his Aphorisms and Reflections*. Bloomington, IN: Indiana University Press.
Stroud, B. 2002. *Understanding Human Knowledge*. Oxford: Oxford University Press.
Tallis, R. 1995. "The Difficulty of Arrival". In *Newton's Sleep: The Two Cultures and the Two Kingdoms*, 126–208. London: Macmillan.
Tallis, R. 2003. *The Hand: A Philosophical Inquiry into Human Being*. Edinburgh: Edinburgh University Press.
Tallis, R. 2004. *Why the Mind is Not a Computer: A Pocket Lexicon of Neuromythology*. Exeter: Imprint Academic.
Tallis, R. 2005. *The Knowing Animal: A Philosophical Inquiry into Knowledge and Truth*. Edinburgh: Edinburgh University Press.
Tallis, R. 2008. "Medical Ethics in the Real Mess of the Real World". *Medico-Legal Journal* 76(3): 95–112. http://mlj.rsmjournals.com/content/76/3/95.full.pdf+html (accessed February 2013).
Tallis, R. 2010a. "How Can I Possibly be Free?" *New Atlantis* (Summer): 120.
Tallis, R. 2010b. "What Neuroscience Cannot Tell Us About Ourselves". *New Atlantis* (Fall). www.thenewatlantis.com/publications/what-neuroscience-cannot-tell-us-about-ourselves (accessed March 2013).
Tallis, R. 2011a. *Aping Mankind: Neuromania, Darwinitis and the Misrepresentation of Humanity*. Durham: Acumen.
Tallis, R. 2011b. "What Consciousness is Not". *The New Atlantis* (Fall). www.thenewatlantis.com/publications/what-consciousness-is-not (accessed February 2013).
Tallis, R. 2012a. "Wit and Wickedness: Is It All in the Brain?" *Brain* (17 October). http://brain.oxfordjournals.org/content/early/2012/10/17/brain.aws214.extract (accessed February 2013).
Tallis, R. 2012b. "An Introduction to Incontinental Philosophy". *Philosophy Now* (July/August). Reprinted in *In Defence of Wonder*, 88–94. Durham: Acumen.

Tallis, R. 2012c. "My Bald Head: The Ethics of Hair-Splitting". In *In Defence of Wonder*, 132–8. Durham: Acumen.

Tallis, R. 2013. "Oliver Sacks on Drugs". *Times Literary Supplement* (13 February 2013). www.the-tls.co.uk/tls/public/article1213308.ece (accessed February 2013).

Tallis, R. & J. Davis (eds). *NHS SOS: How the NHS was Betrayed and How We Can Save It*. London: Oneworld.

Teahan, M. 2012. "The Pro-life Movement Needs to be Divided if it is to Win Battles in Parliament". *Catholic Herald* (3 July). www.catholicherald.co.uk/commentandblogs/2012/07/03/the-pro-life-movement-needs-to-be-divided-if-it-is-to-win-battles-in-parliament/ (accessed March 2013).

Valéry, P. [1896] 1989. *Monsieur Teste*. Princeton, NJ: Princeton University Press.

van der Heide, A., B. D. Onwuteaka-Philipsen, M. L. Rurup, H. M. Buiting, J. J. M. van Delden, J. E. Hanssen-de Wolf, A. G. J. M. Janssen *et al.* 2007. "End-of-Life Practices in the Netherlands under the Euthanasia Act". *New England Journal of Medicine* **356**: 1,957–65.

Wallace, A. R. 1871. "The Limits of Natural Selection as Applied to Man". In *Contributions to the Theory of Natural Selection*. New York: Macmillan.

Wallace, D. 2008. "Philosophy of Quantum Mechanics". In *The Ashgate Companion to Contemporary Philosophy of Physics*, D. Rickles (ed.), 16–98. Aldershot: Ashgate.

Warnock, M. 2010. *Dishonest to God: On Keeping Religion out of Politics*. London: Continuum.

Weinberg, S. 1994. *Dreams of a Final Theory*. New York: Vintage.

Index

Abraham, Ann 207
access unity of consciousness 105–6
accountability 209
Adams, Douglas 176
Adams, Reginald 74–7
addiction
  drugs and alcohol 238–40
  explanations for 238–40
  sex 240–43
  war on drugs 243–6
advance directives/living wills 192–4
affordances 8–12
agency 44
The Analysis of Matter (Russell) 101
An Evening with M. Teste (Valéry) 280
"An Introduction to Incontinental
  Philosophy" (Tallis) 126–7
Angell, Marcia 267
animals
  consciousness 126–8
  exploitation 128–9
  medical research 129–30
  and music 54
anti-neurophilosophy 45
Antinomy of Time (Kant) 170, 173–4
*Aping Mankind: Neuromania,
Darwinitis and the
Misrepresentation of Humanity*
(Tallis) 111
apparitions 229
appearance 33, 36–8
appearances 111–12
Aristotle 107–8, 144, 148, 279
art 58–64
artificial feeding 189–90
artificial intelligence (AI) 75
artificial mouse consciousness 91
assisted dying 226
  autonomy 269–73
  case in favour 248
  Catholic Church 262–3
  context of debate 247–8
  discussion of 253–4
  facts and factoids 250–54
  medical neutrality 266–7
  medical opposition 265–9
  mental competence 257–8
  misdiagnosis 258
  mistakes 256–9
  need for change of law 273–5
  Netherlands 253
  non-voluntary euthanasia 255–6

289

Oregon 252–3, 255, 257
organizational/institutional lobbies 262–4
prognosis 258
religious opposition 249–50, 259–62
sanctity of life 250, 259–62
slippery slope argument 254–6
trust 253
valuing life 261–2
asymmetry, ethical 184
The Atheist's Guide to Reality (Rosenberg) 36
Atkins, Peter 149
atomism 145
attention 22
Auden, W. H. 3, 229
Augustine 163
Austin, J. L. 34
authority, suspicion of 182
autistic spectrum disorder (ASD) 66–7
automatism 16
autonomy
 assisted dying 269–73
 of machines 78–9
axiom of necessity 190–91

Barbour, Julian 153
Baron-Cohen, Simon 66–8, 72–4
basket-weaving 141–2
Battin, M. 255
Bayne, Tim 105
Beasley, Christine 212
"Before Life and After" (Hardy) 196
behaviour, not unified 107
beliefs, and experiences 113–15
Bell, George 259–60
Bergson, Henri 41
Big Bang 170, 171, 172
binding problem 40–41, 105
biography, and bodies 17
biology, denigrating humanity 164
birds 3
birdsong 55–6
Blackburn, Simon 160
Bland, Tony 189
bodies, and biography 17
body, human relationship to 134–5
bonnes à penser 3
Bradley, F. H. 161

Bragg, Lawrence 153
brain
 as conscious machine 78, 80–84
 consciousness of 80
 freezing 91–2
 labelling/classifying of functions 84
 location of empathy 70–71
 as machine 79–80
 musical 49–50
 spatial differentiation 39–40
 see also consciousness; personhood
brain in a vat 123
brain injury/dysfunction 30–31
brain stimulation experiments 31–2
brains, identification with 29–30
Breslaw, Daniel 233
British Social Attitudes Survey 249
Broad, Michelle and Chris 274
Bulman, Charles 268–9
Burke, Leslie 189–90
Butler, Samuel 101
Byzantine empire, silk 139–40

Cahiers (Valéry) 280–81
calculus 146
Camel Estuary 18
Canada geese 10
Caplan, Arthur 203
cardiopulmonary resuscitation (CPR) 186
care
 afterthoughts 225–8
 barriers to 226
 everyday 206
 see also professional care
Care and Compassion (Abraham) 207, 208
Care not Killing 262–3
carers, demands on 227–8
Carlile, Lord Alex 263
Carnap, Rudolf 153
Carnes, Patrick 242
Cartesian dualism 99
causal connections 12–13
causal sequences 13–14
causality 88
Cayton, Harry 222
celebrity culture 216–19
Chalmers, David

INDEX

The Character of Consciousness 94ff.
The Conscious Mind: In Search of a Fundamental Theory 93–4
Charles Bonnet syndrome 231
childhood 5
China, silk 139
choice, and obligation 6
Churchland, Patricia 147
Churchland, Paul 84
classifying, of functions 84
clinical decisions, as ethical decisions 184–5
clothes 135–6
co-consciousness 104–5
coherence 11, 12–14, 236–7
Coleridge, Samuel Taylor 23
Collier, Joe 265
common sense 147–8
communication 179–80
compassion, outsourcing 226
competence, and medical ethics 190–91
complexity 43–4
computational processes 116
computational theory of mind 99, 156–7
computiverse 79
conceivability 109–12
concepts 115
conceptual analysis 147
conceptual art 23
conditions of satisfaction 119
Confessions of an Opium Eater (de Quincy) 240
Confessions (Rousseau) 1–2
connectomes 29, 82–3
  replicating 85–9
  responses to critique of connectome theory of self 89–90
conscience, medical ethics 266
conscious machines 78, 80–92
conscious unity 104–8
consciousness 31–3
  animals 126–8
  appearance 33, 36–8
  "binding" problem 40–41
  of brain 80
  as brain's experience of itself 35–6
  concepts and contents 113–16

easy and hard problems of 95–8
intentionality 33–5, 42, 44
layeredness 121
and neural activity 38
neural correlates 103–4
neuralization of 235
and physics 151–2
place in nature 98–102
selective denial 44
sharing 142–3
unity of 104–8
consciousness meter 106
consumerism 181–2
contents, of consciousness 113–16
contracts 6–7
coordination, and timing 177–8
Copernicus 163–4
correspondence 118–19
"Could an Artificial Mouse Be Conscious? Artificial Consciousness: How to Build a Conscious Brain" (Shanahan) 89
Council for Healthcare Regulatory Excellence 222
creativity, neurobiology of 56–8
Crick, Francis 30, 103
criminalization of drug use 244
critical interests, and experiential interests 193–4
Critique of Pure Reason (Kant) 169–70
crossing the road 4–8
cruelty 67–9
cultural dependence 69

Da-sein 206
Damasio, Antonio 128–9
Davies, Paul 79
Davis, Wade 129
Dawkins, Richard 159
de Quincey, Thomas 240
Deacon, Terrence 43
death, reminders of 17–18
Death with Dignity Act (Oregon) 252–3, 255
deception, by perception 124
Declaration of Geneva 268
deep time 176
Dement, William 277
dementia 222–5

291

dementia care, Netherlands   223–5, 226, 262
denial   44
denigrating humanity   163–6
Dennett, Daniel   32–3, 44, 74–7, 94
Department of Health   196–7
dependency   213–16
Descartes, Réné   279, 280
detection devices, and observers   157–8
Diagnostic and Statistical Manual of Mental Disorders (DSM)   242
dichotomizing over a continuum   272
disconnection   12–13
discreteness   11
Dishonest to God: On Keeping Religion out of Politics (Warnock)   249–50
disorder   17
DNAR orders   182
doctors
  regulation   6–7
  trust in   203–4
dog, urination   126–7
dopaminergic pathways   52–3, 54
double effect   258, 259, 267
dreams   234, 279–81
drug policies   245–6
drugs
  criminalization   244
  legalization   244–5
Drugs: Breaking the Cycle (House of Commons Home Affairs Committee)   245–6
du Bois Reymond, Emil   32
dualism   99
Dworkin, Ronald   193

e-ttenuation   180
easy problems of consciousness, vs. hard   95–8
Edelman, Gerald   103
Edenic content   122–3
EEG   90
egocentric space   167
Einstein, Albert   42, 153
embodiedness   18, 59
emergence   43–4
emotions   62–3
empathy   67–9
  explaining deficiency   71–2
  judging quality of life   195–6
  locating in brain   70–71
empathy circuit   70–72
empathy gene   72–3
empathy quotient (EQ)   69–70
Emperor Huang Ti   139
entanglement   155, 158
epilepsy   235
epiphenomenalism   98, 100
Esquirol, Jean-Étienne Dominique   229
The Essential Difference: Men, Women and the Extreme Male Brain (Baron-Cohen)   66
eternity   170
ethical asymmetry   184
ethical decisions
  clinical decisions as   184–5
  ideal   182–3
  implicit   184–5
  team-based decision-making   199
ethical principles   271
European Association of Palliative Care   253
euthanasia   226, 255–6
Euthanasia Prevention Coalition   264
evil   67–9, 73
existential reality, of personhood   39–41
experience
  pooling   166–7
  problems of   96
experiences
  and beliefs   113–15
  experiencing   180
  making sense of   86–9
  shared   230
  unity of   39–40
experiential interests, and critical interests   193–4
experimental philosophy   150
explicitness   23
eyes, as visible objects   18

factual memory   85
"Faith in the Future: 2006–2008"   262–3
Falconer, Lord Charles   255
Fall   122
Faraday, Michael   146
farewell   16
Feigl, Herbert   35

INDEX

Feynman, Richard 151
Finlay, Baroness Ilora 252–3, 263
First Antinomy (Kant) 170, 173–4
first-person being 39
Flaubert, Gustave 1
form, of music 63
frame problem 75
free speech 272
freedom 9, 58–9, 61–2
Frege, Gottlob 146
Freud, Sigmund 281
fruit flies 238–9
functionalism 118
futility, of medical intervention 185–8

Galileo 146, 148, 152
Garden of Eden 122
gaze 35, 59, 166
Gellner, Ernest 147
General Medical Council (GMC) 196–7, 204, 221
  Fitness to Practice Panel 220, 221
  medical ethics 187–9, 190
genetic fatalism 238–9
genetics, of empathy 72–3
genius, explanations of 47–8
Gerada, Claire 265
Godlee, Fiona 264
golf 240
Good Medical Practice (GMC) 221
Gray, John 164
greeting 14–16
Grillparzer, Franz 46
Gummer, Lord John 255

habit memory 85
hallucinations 229
  fear of 229–30
  isolating 229–30, 231
  and mental illness 230
  organization of 235–6
  and perceptual loss 231–2
  religious and cultural significance 230
  varieties of 234–5
Hallucinations (Sacks) 229–37
Halvorson, Hans 148, 155, 156, 160, 161
Hamilton, Christopher 276
handwaving 43

hard problems of consciousness 95–8, 124–5
Hardy, Thomas 196
harm principle 271–2
Harris, John 255
Hawking, Stephen 149, 164, 172–3
Hazlitt, William 77
head injury 88
Health and Social Care Act 2012 208
healthcare assistants 213
Healthcare Professionals for Assisted Dying (HPAD) 247, 265
Heidegger, Martin 206, 278
Heraclitus 10–11
higher-order thought (HOT) theory 106–7, 108
Hill, James 279
Hippocrates 30
Hippocratic Oath 268
Hogeway 223–5, 226, 262
Holocaust 68
Horatio 20
hospital care 207–8
Human, All Too Human (Nietzsche) 74
human beings, individuality 85
human rights, and medical ethics 189–90
humanity, denigration 163–6
humans, relationship to body 134–5
humour 74–5
hungers 61
Hurley, Matthew 74–7
Husserl, Edmund 146
hydration 189
hypnophobia 277
hypothermic circulatory arrest 89–90

ideal conceivability 109–10
ideal ethical decisions 182–3
ideas, carried along Silk Road 142
"Ignorance" (Larkin) 222
images, of the world 161
immortality 81
Incomplete Nature: How Mind Emerged From Matter (Deacon) 43
India, silk 139
individuality 85
inflaton 159, 171
information 116, 157

Chalmers's use of term 99–100
ink 20
Inside Jokes: Using Humor to Reverse-Engineer the Human Mind (Hurley et al.) 74–7
insincerity, of materialism 41
intentionality 33–5, 41, 44, 114, 118, 120, 158
interactionism 99
interconnectedness 28
interests, experiential and critical 193–4
interpretosis 8
Iraq War 260
it-from-bit doctrine 116

Jains 129
James, William 229
Joffe, Lord Joel 249, 255
Johnson, Alan 246
jokes 74–5
judgement, marginalizing of 7
just-in-time spreading activation (JITSA) 75
just war 259
Justinian I 139–40

Kafka, Franz 50
Kant, Immanuel 169–70, 173–4, 278
Keen, Ann 211, 213
Kelly, Stuart 54
Kierkegaard, Søren 2
Kirk, Robert 108
knowledge 60–61, 166–8
Koch, Christian 103
Koop, C. Everett 267
Kripke, Saul 110
Kuhn, Robert Lawrence 160

labelling, of functions 84
language 147
Lansley, Andrew 266
Larkin, Philip 222, 223
Lauffer, Gideon 220–21
laughter 76–7
law, and medical ethics 191
layeredness, of consciousness 121
Le Poidevin, Robin 169
Ledward, Rodney 220

legalization of drug use 244–5
Lehrer, Jonah 57–8
Leibniz, Gottfried von 279
Lévi-Strauss, Claude 50–51, 55, 65
life, valuing 194–6, 261–2
light 19–20
"The Little Mushroom and the Blighted Twin" (Neighbour) 47–8
Liveing, Edward 232
Liverpool Care Pathway 195, 256
Living and Dying Well 263, 264
Living Philosophy (Hamilton) 276
living will/advance directives 192–4
location 14–15
Locke, John 279
looking 2, 8–12
  and thinking 26
  vs. thinking 21–4
looking back across the lake 24–7
Lucas, J. R. 173

Macfarlane, Robert 1–2, 3
machines
  autonomy of 78–9
  defining 78–9
making sense 86–9
man on the park bench 18–21
many worlds hypothesis 155
maps 141–2
Marks, Joel 126ff
marriage 27
Marx, Groucho 250
Mary's room 114–15
material objects, perception of 34–5
material world 152, 158
materialism 33, 34, 36–8, 41, 109
mathematics 13
The Matrix 123
Matter and Mind (Churchland) 84
matter, and physics 154–5
McPherson, Ann 247, 251–2, 265, 275
meaning, desire for 280
measurement, and experience 37
measurement problem 154–5, 158
medical ethics
  advance directives/living wills 192–4
  axiom of necessity 190–91
  clinical decisions as ethical 184–5
  and competence 190–91

Department of Health 196–7
family wishes 196–9, 200–201
futility 185–8
General Medical Council (GMC) 187–9, 190, 196–7
and human rights 189–90
ideal ethical decisions 182–3
implicit ethical decisions 184–5
intuition 194–5
issues of conscience 266
and law 191
lessons of Mrs A 201–4
Mrs A 183–4, 190, 196–201
nutrition and hydration 189–91
patient's wishes 192–9
problems of 181–2
reflection on 204–5
team-based decision-making 199
trust 203–4
value judgements 194–6
withdrawal of treatment 184–5
see also professional care
medicalization 242
Meditations (Descartes) 280
memory 41–2, 85
fake 87, 90
of neural networks 85
neural theory 87–8
retrieval 88–9
transferability 88
Mental Capacity Act 2005 192, 197
mental illness, and hallucinations 230
mental spaces 75–6
Menuhin, Yehudi 63
Mermin, David 151
Metamorphosis (Kafka) 50
metaphysical enquiry, retreat from 146–7
metaphysical hypothesis 123–4
mice 91
"Michael: A Pastoral Poem" (Wordsworth) 196
migraine 232–3
Mill, John Stuart 269–70
m'illumino d'immenso 26, 28
mind-blindness 66–7
mirror images 117–18, 119
mirroring 107–8
misdiagnosis, assisted dying 258

monism 100–101
Monsieur Teste 280
mosquito analogy 167
Mrs A 183–4, 190, 196–9, 200–201
lessons of 201–4
mulberry leaves 137
music
appreciation of 51–2
as biological phenomenon 53–6
biological purpose 54
developing understanding of 64–5
and emotions 62–3
form 63
importance of 50–51
and neuro-aesthetics 51–3
unbiological meaning 58–64
musical brain 49–50
musical sounds, perception of 51–2
Musser, George 160
mutual dependency 215–16

Nagel, Thomas 96, 121
naive realism 236
National Health Service (NHS)
see also professional care
business ethos 208–9
quality of care 207–8
valuing of care 210
natural philosophy 144–6
nature, place of consciousness 98–102
Nausea (Sartre) 277–8
"The Need to Sleep" (Hamilton) 276
Neighbour, Roger 47–8
Netherlands
assisted dying 253
dementia care 223–5, 226, 262
non-voluntary euthanasia 255–6
neural activity
and consciousness 38
correlation 103–4
neural correlates, of consciousness 103–4
neural networks, memory 85
neural structure, and functions 92
neural theory of memory 87–8
neuro-aesthetics 50, 51–3
neurobiology, of creativity 56–8
neurological damage 215
Neurophilosophy (Churchland) 147

neutrality, assisted dying 266–7
newspaper 19–20
NHS Ombudsman reports 207–10
Nietzsche, Friedrich 1, 50, 74, 164, 167, 277
Nightingale, Florence 218–19
Nixon, Richard 244
non-voluntary euthanasia 255–6
nonreductive representationalism 119–20
normative sense 77
North Korea 178
North Pole 172–3
novelty 57
now 153
nurses 210–13
  assisted dying 266–7
nutrition and hydration, and medical ethics 189–91
Nutt, David 246

object perception 34–5
objective knowledge, and subjective reality 168
objective reality 152
obligation, and choice 6
observation, and physics 155–8
observers 156–7
"The Old Fools" (Larkin) 223
On Dreams (Aristotle) 279
onlooker 9–10
orchestration 177–8
order, and disorder 17
Oregon, assisted dying 252–3, 255, 257

pain 98
painting 22–3, 59
palliative care 250–51, 252–3
Palliative Medicine 256
panniers 141–2
panpsychism 98–9, 101, 124
pansimulationism 124
paradoxes, physics 157–8
Parmenides 145
Pascal, Blaise 165–6, 168
past 24–5, 41–2
Patel, Aniruddh 52
paternalism 266
Paterson, Ian 220

patient's wishes 192–9
pelican crossings 5, 6
Penfield, Wilder 31–2
perception 39–40
  and deception 124
  of material objects 34–5
  of musical sounds 51–2
perceptions 121
perceptual loss, and hallucinations 231–2
person-specific memory 85
personality disorders 70
personhood
  see also consciousness
  as brain activity 29–34
  existential reality 39–41
  temporal depth 41–2
phenomenal appearances 33, 36–8
phenomenal consciousness 121–2
phenomenal unity 105
philosophers, retreat before physics 146–8
philosophy
  as ally of physics 161
  need for 160–62
  as science 146
philosophy, as servant of science 147
philosophy of mind 147
physics 13
  as ally of philosophy 161
  attitudes to philosophy 149–50
  and consciousness 151–2
  denigrating humanity 164
  and matter 154–5
  need for philosophy 160
  and observation 155–8
  philosophical questions 158–9
  and philosophy 144
  something not nothing 158–60
  and time 152–4
Pinker, Steven 54
Plato 144–5
points of view 122–3
poplars 3–4
Popper, Karl 166
portraits 22–3
Portugal, drug policy 245
possibility 109–12
potty training 127–8

INDEX

pragmatic self-refutation 165–6
presentations 107, 118
presuppositions, in humour 74–6
primary qualities 152
principle of autonomy 250
The Principles of Psychology (James) 229
print 19
private care 208
pro-life campaigns 263–4
problems of experience 96
professional care 206–7
 as business 216
 demands on 227–8
 dementia 222–5
 dependency 213–16
 inquiries 209
 neurological damage 215
 NHS Ombudsman reports 206–7
 nurses 210–13
 outsourcing compassion 226
 private 208
 regulation 227
 in societal context 210
 soul searching 209–10
 surgeons 219–22
 whistleblowing 221
 see also medical ethics; National Health Service (NHS)
prognosis, assisted dying 258
propositional awareness 121
protophenomenal property 101–2
Putnam, Hilary 123, 147

qualia 96, 120
quality of life 194–6
quantum field 159
quantum mechanics 148, 157–8
quantum vacuum 159–60, 171
Quimby, Isaac 199
Quine, W. V. 60

Ramachandran, V. S. 64
rationalization, of dreams 280
reading 19
reality, shared 167
red hat 40
reductive materialism 99
regulation 6–7

Reid, Melanie 214–15
relationships, mediation through authority 7–8
relativity, paradoxes 157–8
representational content 121
representationalism 107–8, 117–20
return 27
reward pathways 52–3, 54
Richardson, Baroness Kathleen 249
rigour 146
Rilke, Rainer Maria 11
Robins, Joyce 267
Rosenberg, Alex 36
Rosenthal, David 106
roundabout 4–5
Rousseau, Jean-Jacques 1–2
Rovelli, Carlo 160
Royal College of Nursing, assisted dying 266–7
RTr 82, 84, 85–9, 90
Russell, Bertrand 101, 167, 257
Ryle, Gilbert 124, 236

Sacks, Oliver 229, 230, 231, 232–3
sanctity of life 250, 259–62
Sartre, Jean-Paul 277–8
Satel, Sally 239
Saunders, John 186
Saunders, Peter 263
Schopenhauer, Arthur 195–6
Schubert, Franz
 biography 46–7
 cultural environment 49
 as musical brain 49–50
 psychoanalytic viewpoints 47–9
science
 and other ways of understanding 50
 progress 148
science cringe 147
scientific revolution 163–4
scientists, and philosophy 145
"The Sea and the Mirror" (Auden) 229
Searle, John 33, 44, 78, 93, 94, 101
"The Second Coming" (Yeats) 205
second law of thermodynamics 17
seeing, as means to thought 21–2
Self Comes to Mind: Constructing the Conscious Brain (Damasio) 128–9
Sellars, Wilfrid 148, 150, 161

semantic memory   85
semiosphere   128
sensory experience, coherence of   236–7
sentience   128–9
sericulture   137, 139
setting out   3–4
Seung, Sebastian   82
sex differences   67
Shanahan, Murray   89–90, 91
shared experiences   230
shared reality   167
sharing, of consciousness   142–3
Sheldrake, Rupert   35
Sibelius   26–7
Sickert, Walter   22–3
silk
  discovery of   139
  human achievements   140–42
  journeys   140–42
  preparation of   137, 139
  properties of   133–4
Silk Road   138–42
silk trade   137–9
silk-weaving   135, 136
silkworms   132–3, 137
Simpson, William   144, 161
simulation   124
simultaneity   41, 173
situation dependence   69
sleep
  dreams   279–81
  as extraordinary state   276–7
  philosophers on   277–9
  philosophy-induced   278
  purpose   277
sleep paralysis   234–5
Smolin, Lee   160
social brain   70–71
something, not nothing   158–60
space, division of   4
speciesism   130–31
Spinal Column (Reid)   214–15
Stalnaker, Robert   110
Stecker, M.   90
Straw Dogs (Gray)   164
strolling   2
Stroud, Barry   35
study   20–21

subject unity   105
subjective reality, and objective knowledge   168
subjectivity   152
subsumptive unity   106
suffering   131
sun   25
sunlight   19–20
superposition   154–5, 158
supervenience   43–4
surgeons   219–22
survival   181
suspicion, of authority   182
synchronous activity   41
systems   43–4, 103

tables   36–7
Tallis, Raymond   60, 79, 111, 272
  consciousness   81–3
  and RTr   82–3, 84, 86–9, 90, 92
Teahan, M.   263
team-based decision-making   199
temporal depth   41, 91
temporality, of memory   87–8
tensed time   153
theory   22
theory of everything   150–1, 153, 156, 161
thinking   2–3
  vs. looking   21–4
thinking by transferred epithets   42–3
thought
  aim of   22
  visible as print   19
time   42
  beginning   169–70
  dating beginning   172
  human relationship with   176–7
  and physics   152–4
  simultaneity with beginning of universe   173
  time zero   171–3
timing   175–6
  benefits and costs of   176–9
  and coordination   177–8
  locating ourselves   176
  and possibility   179
Tyndall, John   33–4
toilet training   127–8

INDEX

Tolstoy, Leo 68–9
tools 135
total institutions 224
Tractatus Logico-Philosophicus (Wittgenstein) 196
trade 137
train journey 26
training, nurses 211–13
trauma, and genius 47–9
Travels in Four Dimensions (Le Poidevin) 169
Trilling, Lionel 146
The Trouble with Physics (Smolin) 160
The Truman Show 224
trust 6–7
  assisted dying 253
  medical decision-making 203–4
  in surgeons 219
truth 110, 167–8
Twilight of the Idols (Nietzsche) 1
type-F monism 100–102

uncertainty 157
understanding, ways of 50
Ungaretti, Giuseppe 26
United Kingdom, drug policy 245–6
unity of consciousness 104–8
unity of elements 105
universe from nothing 159
up and down 10
urination 126–7
Uruguay, drug policy 245
utilitarianism 131, 271

Valéry, Paul 21–2, 60, 168, 280–81
value, and price 216
valuing life 261–2
valuing, of care 210
Van der Heide, A. 256
"Veterinarian, Heal Thy Profession!" (Marks) 128–9
viewpoint 39
viewpoints
  awakening of 13–14
  changing 11
vision 8–12, 23, 27–8, 166
visual art 59
vivisection 129–30
Voltaire 163, 164

walking 1–3
  crossing the road 4–8
  looking 8–12
  setting out 3–4
Wallace, David 155, 156
war on drugs 243–6
warfare, and timing 178
Warnock, Mary 249–50, 255, 260
water 110–12
way out, and way back 10–11
ways of understanding 50
weaving 135–7
Weinberg, Steven 149
Wheeler, John 157
Whewell, William 145
whistleblowing 221
White, Thomas 131
Whitehead, A. N. 146
"Why Not Nothing?" (Kuhn) 160
Williams, Rowan 260, 261, 270
Winehouse, Amy 238, 240
Winterbourne View 208, 211, 225
Withholding and Withdrawing Life-Prolonging Treatments (GMC) 188
Wittgenstein, Ludwig 21, 23, 146, 196
wood pigeon 11–12
Woods, Tiger 240–43
words 20, 60
Wordsworth, William 196
working together 161
world
  beginning in time 169–70
  coherence of 12–14
  images of 161
writing 60

Xi Lingshi 139, 143

Yeats, W. B. 176, 205

Zatorre, Robert 52, 54
zebra crossings 5–6
Zero Degrees of Empathy: A New Theory of Human Cruelty (Baron-Cohen) 67–8
Zola, Émile 238–9
zombies 108–12